ECONOMIC IDEAS OF THE HINDUS

ECONOMIC IDEAS OF THE HINDUS

R. Kumar
S. Ram

CRESCENT
PUBLISHING CORPORATION

Economic Ideas of the Hindus

First Published 2008

ISBN 978-81-8342-086-0

Published by :
Crescent Publishing Corporation
4831/24, Prahlad Street,
Ansari Road, Darya Ganj,
New Delhi - 110002
Phones : 23272541, 23257835
Fax : 91-011-23257835
e-mail-campusbooks@hotmail.com

Typesetting by :
Stylish Laser Typesetter
Delhi - 110053

Printed at :
Roshan Offset Printers
Delhi

Preface

The Hindus fully recognised the importance of economic science. This is evident from the fact that even before the days of Kautilya learning was divided into four branches i.e., Philosophy, religion, economics and polity. The economic stability was considered as important as the vedas for the spiritual well being.

Aim of this volume is to make available to our readers material on our basic ideas of the Hindus on the economic science, from different literary sources. In selecting the sources effort has been made to provide to our readers a cross section of essays from progressive scholars as well as from the original texts. This will enable them to formulate their own final judgement on the subject.

We take this opportunity to gratefully acknowledge the authorities on the subject.

We have received co-operation and all possible help from the librarian and their staff members. We thank them.

Our publisher and of course, a good friend, his able and hard-working sons Ajay and Amit and their staff members have given me all possible assistance, love and regard which has facilitated publication of this otherwise, difficult assignment. They deserve my readers care and patronage.

Authors

CONTENTS

1 Economic Ideas of the Hindus

Economic ideas and practices as reflected principally in the literature on law and polity as well as Epics and Puranas.

Varta and Artha Sastra

Ancient Indians, even before the days of Kautilya, divided knowledge or learning (*sastra* or *vidya*) into four branches.[1] *viz.*, *(i) anviksiki, (ii) trayi, (iii) varta,* and *(iv) dandaniti,* which in the light of traditional interpretation, may be broadly interpreted respectively as *(i)* philosophy, *(ii)* three Vedas or religion, *(iii)* economics, and *(iv)* polity. The word *varta* primarily or etymologically represents *vrtti* or means of livelihood, but was particularly employed to denote the *vrtti* allotted to the Vaisyas; secondarily *varta* meant the science that had *varta* as its subject of study.

Varta, according to Kautilya and others, dealt with agriculture, cattle breeding, and trade.[2] Later on, money-lending or usury was included under *varta* by the *Bhagavata Purana, Sukra-Nitisara,* etc., and the *Mahabhhararta* included *'vividhani silpani'* (arts and crafts), referred to by the *Devi Purana* as *karmanta* (manufacture).[3] Thus, in modern nomenclature, *varta* dealt with the economics of agriculture, trade, banking, and industry, which shows that consumption, distribution, and taxation, forming part of modern economics, were left out of the scope of *varta.* These latter topics were included in the works on Artha-sastra and Dharma-sastra.

Artha-sastra, in its technical sense, covers a wider field than *varta* and *dandaniti*, and may be said to include the subjects of jurisprudence, politics, and economics. It has been called *'Arthaveda'* and classed as an Upaveda, either of the *Rg-Veda* or of the *Atharva-Veda*.[4] The *Arthasastra* makes it clear that *varta* and Artha-sastra were quite distinct. The latter never dealt with *artha* in the sense of wealth, which was the subject-matter of *varta*.[5]

That the ancient Indians fully recognized the importance of economic science would be evident not only from its inclusion among the fourfold division of *vidyas*[6] and from its forming an important part of the regal curriculum, but also from the passages expressly stressing its necessity for the economic stability of a country and so on. These passages indicate that *varta* was considered as essential for the material interests of the people as were the Vedas for their spiritual well-being; we may take it to have been regarded as not less important than the Vedas.

Equally interesting as the conception of economics are the ideas constituting the Indian conception of wealth. Analysing the several meanings of *dhana* and *artha*, which stand for wealth, K.V. Rangaswami Aiyangar states the root ideas of the ancient Indian conception of wealth to be 'its material quality, its appropriability, its being the result of acquisition, its not being quite identical with gold, its consumability, and its attractiveness due to scarcity'.[7] The Artha-sastra, the Epics, the Smrtis and other works on ancient Indian economics knew the importance of wealth in the scheme of life for gaining the *purusarthas* (ends of human life), and were fully conscious of the depressing influence of poverty. Wealth, however, was never regarded as an end in itself, but as a means to an end. Contrary to common notions, they condemned asceticism and held those seeking to embrace the ascetic order without discharging their duties liable to punishment.

Rural Economics

Agriculture : Indian economists, both ancient and modern, give predominance to rural economics because agriculture has been the occupation of the population throughout the ages. Along with cattle breeding and dairy farming, agriculture constituted the most important part of *varta*, which a king was enjoined to study.[8] Though agriculture was prescribed as a profession mainly for the Vaisyas, and as a secondary occupation for the Sudras, the Brahmanas and Ksatriyas were permitted to follow it under certain restrictive regulations.[9]

Land : Land, without which agriculture would not be possible, labour, capital, and organization appear to have been the four agents of production according to ancient Indian economists.

According to Sukra, land is the source of all wealth.[10] The creation of proprietary interests in land and the laying down of elaborate rules for the survey and demarcation of individual holdings, since the days of Kautilya, probably indicate the recognition by ancient Indian economists of 'the magic of property' in dealing with agriculture. Development of land was the principal factor in the success of agriculture. The State and the community were enjoined to strive for the prosperity of agriculture. The creation of a beneficial interest by law in favour of the person who first cleared the forest or reclaimed waste land facilitated the clearing of jungles and bringing of waste land under cultivation, which were laid down as duties.[11] For ensuring the productivity of uncultivable or waste land fertilizers were to be used.[12] That our ancient economists knew the law of Diminishing Return would appear from their rules reserving certain types of land for particular crops or for pasture alone, and from their plea for extending the area under cultivation.[13] In the interest of agriculture the non-cultivating proprietors were to be discouraged.[14]

The great advance in agriculture in ancient India and the thorough knowledge of the minute details of agricultural pursuits possessed by Indian economists are seen not only in the treatises of Kautilya followed by Sukra but also in the Smrti literature. The fact that following principles and practices, along with several others, were clearly understood by them speaks volumes about their sharp perception : the interdependence of agriculture and cattle farming; the use of fertilizers; the rotation of crops; the relative advantages of extensive and intensive cultivation; the evils of fragmentation of holdings; the relative advantages of large-and small-scale farming according to the crops cultivated; the adjustment of crops to soils and *vice versa*; the wisdom of carefully selecting seed grains; the value of forest conservation and game preservation to the agriculturist; the use of fallow; the value of even inferior land in the vicinity of centres of population; irrigation by rain, rivers, tanks, reservoirs, and mechanical agencies; agricultural drainage; prevention, correction, and eradication of numerous risks or blights, such as rain, drought, hail, ravages of locusts, pests, mice, birds, and wild pigs; the beneficial uses of opening up communications.[15]

Highly beneficent agricultural administration and a good knowledge of rural economics are seen from Kautilya's precepts regarding irrigation, fixing of prices, etc. The members of a village were held jointly and severally liable for keeping their roads, water channels, and tanks in efficient repair, which ensured perfect maintenance of irrigational works. Any damage to such works of public utility was to be urgently rectified even from the resources of temples. Special facilities were to be given to those who constructed tanks, dams, and roads out of piety, so that the State might receive co-operation from individuals in providing irrigation works. Fixing fair prices for agricultural products at frequent intervals not only served the interest of the people as producers and consumers, but of the State as well, since a large part of its revenue was collected in kind. In order to meet the menace of famine, different parts of the kingdom were to be provided with granaries capable of holding grain sufficient to meet the normal requirements of three years, which were always to be kept full.[16]

The interests of the cultivators were guarded against distraction or nuisance by banning the intrusion of actors, dancers, singers, drummers, buffoons, and wandering minstrels into villages.[17] Officers and servants of the king were to live outside the limits of the village, apparently to save the villagers from oppression. Soldiers also were prohibited from entering villages except on the king's business, and even then they were not to oppress cultivators or have any dealings with them. It was laid down that the army was to be used for no other purpose than fighting.[18] Our ancient economists advocated an uninterrupted pursuit of agriculture even in times of war, and the accounts of foreign travellers confirm that agriculturists were unaffected by the march of armies and the clash of arms. The economic interests of cultivators were safeguarded by fixing fair prices and by providing against combines and cornering by traders with a view to lowering agricultural prices. [19]

Labour: Labour was the second important factor of production and our economists fully appreciated its value for efficient production. Kautilya and Sukra not merely permit the employment of women in State factories and agricultural operations but prescribe it. Though on the basis of the evidence of the Jatakas, other Buddhist works and the Smrtis a dismal picture has been painted concerning the social and economic position of a labourer, which is stated to have been worse than that of a slave, the labour regulations in Sukra and other works indicate a different state of affairs.[20] According to Sukra, the remuneration of a labourer should be proportionate to his productivity and qualification and the wages should be sufficient to maintain the labourer and his family in tolerable comfort. It is not clear whether Sukra's rules,[21] which provide leisure hours, leave, and bonus for domestic servants, and workmen's insurance in sickness, old age, or accident, show the actual practice or are merely his own views in the matter. The labourer or servant, on the other hand, had to pay penalties for breach of contract in addition to being liable for damages caused by his neglect. Further, strikes of workmen to raise wages were declared illegal.

The influence of sacred literature on the economists is seen from their making a distinction between 'pure' and 'impure' types of labour, the test of purity lying in the nature of the occupation and the material employed.[22] This distinction perhaps resulted in the segregation of the two higher castes from the manual labourers.

These are some of the concepts of the old writers on economics—Kautilya, Kamandaka, Sukra and others—regarding labour : hired labour cannot be abolished; efficient labour results from training; workmen are incapable of conducting industry; competent supervisory authority is necessary for getting work done; a proper output can be ensured only through payment by results.

Capital: Our economists visualized the importance of capital to industry and other productive undertakings. Several factors conspired to bring about scarcity of loan capital, of which we get indication from the very high maximum interest mentioned in the Smrtis and the reference to fifteen percent as the just rate of interest both in the *Arthasastra* and in the Smrtis.[23] The lack of capital was due to extravagance and hoarding. The State consumed a large slice in the form of taxes, rents, cesses, fines, etc. The normal aim of our ancient financiers to budget for heavy and recurring surpluses resulted in swelling the State hoard. The danger of prodigal kings wasting the accumulations of their predecessors on their personal gratifications was always there. Another factor contributing to liquidate State hoards was the presence of a large number of parasitical subcastes or professions, who mostly depended on State patronage.

The inference about the scarcity of private capital or about its falling far short of the demands for it, is also implied by the evidence in the *Mahabharata,* which advocates that the State should advance cash grants and seed grain to agriculturists and run a large number of industrial concerns.[24]

Organization: Of the two types of organizations or corporations, *viz.,* the capitalistic and the guild, the latter deserves some mention here; it will be exhaustively dealt with in the next chapter; while the capitalistic organizations are considered in the next section of this chapter.

The movement for the organization of guilds started towards the end of the Vedic period and Panini refers to the *gana, puga, vrata,* and *sangha.*[23] It appears that the words *gana* and *sangha* were used to denote any corporation or union for political or other purposes, while *puga* and *sreni* signified corporations of merchants, artisans or others whose principal object was to gain wealth by trade or industry. The Dharma-Sutras indicate that the chief industries were all organized in guilds. *Sreni, naigama* (or *nigama*), *pasanda, samuha,* etc. find mention in later literature.[26] Worker's or craftsmen's guilds correspond to the modern labour organizations, while Merchants' guilds approximate to the Guild Merchant of mediaeval Europe.

Early literature provides very little information about the constitution and organization of these guilds. The Dharma-Sutras recognized the validity of the laws and customs established by the guilds of cultivators, traders, usurers, herdsmen, artisans, craftsmen, etc., whose headmen occupied a high place in the royal tribunal. Manu and Yajnavalkya invest the customs of the *srenis* and analogous bodies with legal authority.[27] The Dharma-Sutras and Smrtis recognize the binding force of the agreements with the *sanghas,* breaches of which were dealt with severely, the punishments ranging from heavy fine or imprisonment to confiscation and banishment.[28]

Kautilya's elaborate treatment of this subject demonstrates the important role played by the guilds in the economic system of the Mauryan and post-Mauryan epochs. They effectively controlled local sources of production, arts and crafts, and trades and industries and served as an important link between the central authority and the several economic units in the country.

Trade and Industry

Trade as an important form of economic activity appears to have existed from the Vedic or even protohistoric times in India and its indispensable accessories—money, currency, credit, exchange and banking—were freely used and understood not only by the trading community and the administrative staff but by the mass of people as well.

Kautilya advocates considerable State control both in trade and industry. It was obligatory on traders to get a licence, while foreign traders required a passport in addition. In connection with prices, which were controlled by the State, it is interesting to observe that ancient Indian economists had a fairly correct conception of the fundamental causes of value. According to both Kautilya and Sukra, the two factors to be considered in fixing value or price are *(i)* the cost of production as determining the supply, and *(ii)* the demand for the article as determined by its utility.[29] Even writers of the smrtis correctly understood the causes of value, as seen from Manu's precepts for the guidance of the king in fixing the rates of duty.[30] References to absolute and relative prices are found in Sukra and in Buddhist works.

Wholesale prices for goods were fixed by the Superintendent of Commerce, as they passed the Customs House. A margin of profit was allowed to retailers. The public, consumers and customers were protected by the State, which employed an army of spies and market inspectors against unauthorized prices and fraudulent transactions. Goods had to be sold at fixed market-places and the dealer had to specify particulars as to quality, quantity and price, which were scrutinized and recorded in official books. The duties of the Superintendent of Commerce thus included not only the prevention or minimization of the chances of deceit or of undue advantage being taken by seller over the buyer, but also ensuring that the prices were not exorbitant or unconscionable and that the material, its style, quantity or measure precisely corresponded to the terms of the bargain.[31]

To encourage, promote and facilitate trade, both inland and foreign, states were enjoined to improve and increase means of communication and transport. They had also to secure new markets for the surplus products of the country. Rest-houses and store-houses were to be provided for traders, for whose protection proper police escorts were also recommended. River boats and ocean-going ships were to be pressed into service.[32] As a compensation for the taxes paid by the trade, the government granted it security against thieves, forest tribes, wild forest folk, etc., and undertook to make goods losses in transit.[33] To encourage imports, suitable rebates were granted to foreign traders, if current rates did not leave a proper margin of profit for them.[34]

Several facilities were afforded to encourage foreign trade. Foreign merchants could sue in Indian courts, and were protected from being harassed by suits against them in local courts.[35] This wise fostering of foreign trade enabled India to have a permanent excess of exports over imports, resulting in India becoming a veritable sink of precious metals.

Localization of industry and creation of local markets for the sale of products resulted from the caste and guild organizations. Elaborate rules were framed for the organization, establishment and management of markets. To ensure the freedom of the market, the king was prohibited from going to the market with his retinue. Cornering, speculation, smuggling, adulteration, cheating and dishonesty were punishable, according to the gravity of the offence, with fines, or imprisonment or even mutilation.

Kautilya advocates State monopoly of industries on the basis of risk, cost or rarity. The State was advised to become both the manufacturer and trader and to sell articles through departmental agency. Mines, comprising those of gold, silver, diamonds, gems, precious stones, copper, lead, tin, iron and bitumen, which provided the main source of State revenue, were nationalized. Pearl, mother-of-pearl, conch shell, coral, etc. were explored from ocean mines, and it was a State concern. Ores provided minerals, while *rasas* like mercury came from oil fields. Salt manufacture was a State monopoly, for which licences were granted to private lessees of salt fields. There was also State monopoly of armament industry, coinage and ship-building; further, the State controlled the manufacture and sale of wines and liquors. Cotton, oil and sugar factories were also state concerns.[36]

Prison factories, worked through penal labour, added to the State produce. Yarns of cotton, wool, silk and jute came from the State spinning factory, which manufactured clothing of all types, coat-of-mail, blankets, curtains and ropes.[37] For spinning yarn, helpless and *purdah* women were employed under women supervisors.

Just as rent or profit was a compensation, interest constituted a just return to the capitalist, *Kusida* is the term used for the lending of money on interest and early Dharma-Sutras display a strong prejudice against usury. Later, however, money-lending or usury (*kusida*) came to be recognized as one of the four divisions of *varta*, as already stated, and interest came to be regarded as a normal share of the national dividend. That our ancient economists knew the difference between gross interest and net interest, and held sound views about the nature and necessity of interest, may be inferred from the references in the *Arthasastra*, Smrtis, and *Agni Purana*.[38]

There are different rates of interest for loans with or without pledge. According to the Dharma-sastras, the rates of interest varied with the caste of the borrower,[39] presumably on the assumption that his credit-worthiness varied directly with his caste. Fifteen per cent per annum was the normal rate of interest, but it could be higher according to the security given, the nature of the risk involved, and other factors. The welfare of the debtor was safeguarded by forbidding compound interest, interest above the normal customary rate, accumulation of interest exceeding the amount of the principal, or personal service in lieu of interest. Further, no interest was to accumulate on debts due from minors, from those engaged in long-drawn sacrifices, and from those who were diseased, or in their teacher's homes as students. Interest in excess of the legal rate was permissible under certain circumstances, Yajnavalkya allowing a higher rate by agreement. In the case of certain select articles the rule about *damdupat* was waived.

Banking : Some kind of banking may be inferred from the elaborate Dharma-sastra rules regarding loans, deposits, interest, etc. Guilds, partnerships, and joint-stock organizations must have helped the evolution of the system of group credit. The Jatakas and the *Arthasastra* testify to the existence of instruments of credit, promissory notes, or debt sheets, and banking pledges, and book credits.[40]

Coinage: Though the bulk of retail transactions was conducted by barter on account of the scarcity of currency and the low prices of products, the use of coins was also in evidence. Barter, however, commended itself to the higher castes in early times when the sale of , or trade in, articles of production by the higher castes was looked down upon. Further, the prohibition of the use of gold and silver by many classes worked in favour of barter. Money was more common in urban areas.

It seems that coins originated and developed in India before foreign contact. Indian coinage, comprising punch-marked silver and copper coins, goes back to about 600 B.C The earliest coins were based on the weight system given in the *Manu Smrti*, of which the unit was *raktika* (*rati* or *gunja* berry, *i.e.*, 15/16 grain troy). *Suvarna* was the standard gold coin of eighty *ratis*, while the copper coin of the same weight was called *karsapana*, though a copper *pana* of a hundred *ratis* was also known. *Purana* or *dharana* was silver coin of thirty-two *ratis.* Actual specimens show that rulers, guilds, and even merchants issued these coins duly stamped with their symbol, signifying correctness of weight and purity of the metal. Under the *Arthasastra* scheme, coinage was a State monopoly, and officials under the Mint Master (*laksanadhyaksa*) received bullion from the public to be struck into coins on payment of seigniorage charges.

Commercial (Capitalists') organizations : Of the different kinds of corporate organizations mentioned earlier, *puga* alone according to Katyayana, corresponds to a merchants' guild. Partnerships, (*sambhuya-samutthana*) or combines, which constituted another type of industrial and commercial organization, are included among the eighteen titles of law by the Smrtis. The profit and loss in partnership was to be imposed in accordance with the share of each partner.

The guilds were autonomous; they taxed themselves; and

they were competent to proceed with any lawful undertaking and to do everything not prejudicial to State interests. The king was enjoined to restrain the illegal, immoral, indecent, or seditious activities of the corporations. Dissension or dissidence was not tolerated, and offenders received severe punishments.

By the time of Kautilya, the *sanghas* and *srenis* had become very rich and powerful, and some of them maintained troops of their own. The *Arthasastra* refers to the danger of provoking these corporations, and advocates several methods of exploiting them in the king's name.[41] The potential danger to the State from the unrestrained power of these organizations seems to underlie the severe regulations restricting their activities. The Smrtis, however, generally favour the growth of *samuhas* (industrial and commercial guilds).

Revenue and Expenditure

That ancient Indian writers on policy recognized the importance of the State treasury would be evident from their placing *kosa* (treasury) as one of the seven constituent elements of the State and holding it as of supreme importance, along with army. The prime necessity of a competent army and a rich treasury for subduing the subversive element on the king's side as well as those in the opposite camp for the well-being of the State was constantly emphasized. Gautama[42] goes to the length of declaring the treasury to be the basis of the other six basic elements of the State. The *Arthasastra*,[43] the *Mahabharata*,[44] *Kamandakiya Nitisara*,[45] *Visnudharmottara Purana*,[46] and other works hold that the king depends on the treasury, or that the treasury is the root of the State. Revenue and the army, as stated earlier, were the two great pillars of the State in ancient India.

The head of the treasury department was called *Kosadhyaksa*, under whom was the superintendent of granary (Kosthagaradhyaksa). A large portion of the State revenue was collected in kind; and the proper keeping and periodical renewal of the collected stock rendered the task of the treasury department in ancient India arduous. The works cited in the previous paragraph stress that a full treasury and ample reserve funds should be included among the essential constituents of the State; they also regard their deterioration as a very serious national calamity. They insist on a full and flowing treasury for the State by appropriating a large portion of the State revenue for the creation of a reserve fund or treasury, which is not to be touched except on occasions of grave a calamity. This policy of the *Arthasastra* and later works on economics is quite understandable when on considers the unstable political conditions of the time demanding constant preparedness for war because of the constant danger from a neighbouring State. Further, provision had to be made against famines—not a phenomenon of rare occurrence even then—which necessitated the maintenance of the treasury and gold hoards. In ancient times, when State loans were unknown, the only means available for a State to tide over a crisis was the possession of a well-stocked treasury and granary. Richness of the treasury depended on the surplus of revenue over expenditure; and therefore elaborate rules were laid down for the efficient accounting of public receipts and expenditure and their auditing. Sukra emphasizes the keeping of daily, monthly, and annual accounts, and the entering of the several items of income on the left side of the accounts and those of the expenditure on the right.[47] Somadeva recommends the appointment of auditors when there is discrepancy in the items of income and expenditure.[48]

Revenue, in several forms, constituted the chief factor of the State income. Kautilaya[49] classifies the sources or items of revenue differently at different places. Two important classifications are *ayasarira* (body of income) and *ayamukha* (source of income), each being subdivided under seven heads. *Ayasarira*, which refers to the convenient centres of collection, comprises *durga* (fortified cities), *rastra* (rural areas), *khani* (mines), *setu* (irrigation works), *vana* (forests), *uraja* (herds), and *varipatha* (river-borne trade routes), *Bhaga* (royal share), *vyaji* (compensation), *parigha* (gate duty), *klpta* (fixed tax), *rupika* (premia on coins), and *atyaya* (money fine) are the subdivisions of *ayamukha*. Another classification is *anyajata* (accidental revenue), *Vartamana* (current revenue), and *paryusita* (outstanding revenue).[50] Kamandaka enumerates eight principal categories (*astvarga*) of filling the treasury through the heads of departments, *viz*., agriculture, trade routes (both land and water), the capital, water embankments, catching of elephants, working mines and collecting gold etc., levying wealth (from the rich), and founding towns and villages in uninhabited tracts.[51] It will be seen that these classifications do not differentiate between direct and indirect taxes, rent, fees, royalties and non-tax receipts.

In connection with revenue administration, besides the several superintendents dealing with different branches of revenue, such as taxation, finance, state dues, fees, tolls, and mines, mentioned in the section entitled Adhyaksapracara, Kautilya refers to two important officials, *samaharta* and *sannidhata*. It is interesting to note that the duties of the *samaharta* (Collector General)[52] embrace all the components of *ayasarira*. He supervised the collection of revenue in the whole State. All the *adhyaksas* (Superintendents), whose duties covered the entire range of the civic and economic life of the people, were subordinate to the *samaharta*. His functions included the maintenance of census and survey, recording the enumeration of the people, their houses and cattle as also the measurement of their pastures, gardens, arable lands, etc. Cola records confirm the existence of such surveys. The *samaharta* controlled expenditure also and was advised to exert himself for the increase in revenue and decrease in expenditure. The *sannidhata*[53] appears to have been a chamberlain and a treasurer, a custodian of all revenues realized in cash and kind, and was in charge of stores of all kinds, construction of treasuries, warehouses, armouries, and the like, as also of royal trading houses, courts of justice, etc.

The principal source of revenue in ancient India was taxation. In the financial theories of the *Arthasastra* and allied works, the ruler's right to levy taxes and contributions and the people's obligation to pay them arise from an implied contract between the State and its subjects. The imposition of taxes depends solely on the protection afforded by the State. The principles that guided the State in matters of taxation show the solicitude of the economists for the welfare of the community. Taxation was to be reasonable and equitable; the criterion of judging its equitableness consisted in the feeling of the State on the one hand and that of the agriculturists and the traders on the other, that they have received adequate and reasonable return for their mutual services. The first principle was that in matters of taxation the State was to be guided by the rules in the Smrtis. The tax was to be collected at a specified time and place and at a definite proportion or percentage. Any increase in taxation, if unavoidable, was to be gradual. Additional taxation was an exceptional measure to be resorted to only under grave national emergency in the absence of any other alternative. An article was to be taxed only once. Net profit, and not gross earning, was the basis for taxation of trade and industry.

In the context of the canons of taxation it is worthwhile to note whether there were any limits to the king's levying exorbitant taxes. Kautilya[54] has considered the point, and according to him, the threat of disaffection among his subjects and their possible migration to another country appears to have worked as a deterrent on kings taxing their subjects beyond their means. In a similar vein the *Mahabharata*[55] states that the Vaisyas, if neglected, would disappear from the kingdom and would reside in the forest, Yajnavalkya[56] points out that the king who extracts taxes by unjust means not only loses his wealth but also goes to destruction along with his relatives.

On a careful examination of the grounds of partial or total remission of taxation, it is found that religious beliefs as well as humanitarian ideas of the age were responsible for exempting from taxation certain classes of people like learned Brahmanas and Bhiksus. The dumb, the deaf, the blind, students studying in a Gurukula, and hermits were also not taxable; infants, those far advanced in age, women newly confined or destitute, poor widows, and people otherwise helpless were also tax-free. In view of the fact that certain villages supplied recruits to the State army, those military villages were exempted from taxation. Untaxable property included articles required for sacrifice, earnings of craftsmanship, receipts from alms, and articles worth less than a copper coin. Only a nominal tax was to be collected for the first four or five years from those agriculturalists who newly brought land under cultivation and made it more fertile and productive; but the tax in their case also gradually rose to the normal rate in subsequent years.

Kautilya advises the tapping of every available source for securing revenue, and recommends emergency measures under special circumstances. Later authorities have supplemented these different items by suggesting fresh avenues. Some important sources of taxation are listed below illustratively :

(i) Land revenue formed the mainstay of the State finances. The rate of land tax, which was fixed at one-sixth in theory, varied from one-twelfth, one-tenth, one-eighth, or one-sixth in normal times to one-fourth or even one-third in times of emergency. Besides general land revenue, there were other cesses and charges on land, which included water cess, periodical levy on agricultural live-stock of the cultivators, taxes on agricultural and industrial products, and tax in cash on certain special crops. Under this heading also comes income from State properties, *viz.*, crown land, waste land, forests, and natural tanks and reservoirs.

(ii) Revenue from cities, trade, and industry, falling broadly under 'fortified city' (*durga*) and 'country part' (*rastra*), constituted another important item, including house tax. There were also profession tax; property tax; income from slaughter houses, liquor, and gambling; licence fees on weights and measures; tolls,

customs, octroi, port dues, and transit duties; fee from passports; contributions from artisans in cash or service; dues collected from Bahirikas; charge of one-fiftieth of the interest earned by money-lenders,[57] analogous to modern income-tax; and shop tax, not mentioned in the Smrtis but referred to in the inscriptions.[58]

(iii) Income from State monopolies, state establishments, etc. provided another source, and these comprised mines and minerals, salt, saffron, mint, workshops, State manufactories, jail industries, and elephants.

(iv) Under miscellaneous and special taxes and revenues came fins from law courts; forced labour; income from unclaimed, lost, or ownerless property; escheat; treasure trove; occasional taxes such as those paid on the birth of a prince; and irregular receipts from plunder, tributes from feudatories, etc. Taxes which pilgrims had to pay, such as, those levied by Caulukya Siddharaja (A.D. 1094-*c.* 1143) of Gujarat from visitors to Somanatha, those collected at Gaya from Kashmirians performing *sraddha* (offerings to the dead) there,[59] or the pilgrim taxes collected from the Jains which Kumarapala (*c.* A.D. 1145-71) of Gujarat is stated to have abolished, come under special taxes; those levied at the time of the *upanayana* (sacred thread ceremony), marriage, Vedic sacrifices, and the like also fall under the same category.[60] Another variety of tax levied is the *Turuska-danda* and the *Malla-danda,* which were raised to meet the expenses necessitated by the invasions of the Turks and the Mallas respectively. The Cola king Virarajendra (A.D. 1063-70) supplied a later instance of levying a special tax to finance his war against the Calukyas of Vengi.[62]

(v) Emergency revenue formed yet another source. Sources of raising emergency revenue were to be tapped only under exceptional circumstances when the treasury was empty, and there was the threat of

an impending danger. Besides benevolences, forcible loans and donations, emergency taxes, arbitrary enhancement of normal rates, and fraudulent and forcible collections under several pretexts, which are exhaustively dealt with by Kautilya and others,[63] reference may also be made to the sale of divine images by the Mauryas, recorded by Patanjali,[64] and the scheme of debased coinage resorted to by the Mauryas[65] and the Guptas,[66] which must have been instrumental in filling the State treasury to a great extent. It may, however, be observed that Kautilya prescribes that some of these taxing devices should be levied on the seditious and irreligious only, and not on all.[67]

Compared with the minute treatment of the several sources of revenue by the cited authorities, expenditure does not seem to have received its due share of attention. However, before coming to the different items of expenditure, let it be seen what the economists have to say regarding the proportion of revenue to expenditure. According to Sukra,[68] one-sixth of the income should go to saving; one-half should be spent on the army; and one-twelfth each on charity, ministers, inferior officials, and the privy purse. The *Manasollasa*[69] recommends that ordinarily three-fourths of the revenue should be spent, and one-fourth should be saved.

First and foremost among the sources of expenditure was the maintenance of the security of the realm, which involved not only the maintenance of a well-equipped armed force in the four branches and the navy, capable of both offence and defence, but also of the storehouses, armouries, and, above all the entire organization of the secret service. The observations of Megasthenes along with Kautilya's regulations indicate that this head of national defence absorbed a considerable portion of the revenue. The other items on the expenditure side answered the several obligations of a welfare State, which included the king's privy purse; civil list for the king and court—his ministers and officers; police and other protective establishments for citizens, merchants, and travellers; legal, judicial, and punitive departments; granaries and *gosalas* (cow infirmaries) as insurance against famine; grants to local governments; roads and other equipment with bridges, rest-houses, trees, and watering places; ships and ferries; irrigation works; maintenance of mines, forests, forts, public factories, mints, store-houses, and palaces; religious and charitable endowments like temples, hospitals, schools, an universities; maintenance of windows and orphans, the indigent and the unemployed, and the families of soldiers and civil servants dying in State service.

REFERENCES

1. Cf. *Kaut.*, I. 2, p. 6.
2. *Kaut.*, I. 4, p. 8; *Kam.*, II. 14; *Visnu P.*, V. 10. 28.
3. *Bhag. P.*, X. 24. 21; *Sukra*, I. 156; *Mbh.*, XII. 167. 11-12; *Davi P.*, 67. 13.
4. *Caranavyuha*, ascribed to Saunaka, tags Arthasastra as an *Upaveda* to *R.V.*, while *Caranavyuha* of *A.V.*, *Parisista* (49.3), links it to *A.V.*, *Vayu P.* (61-79), *Visnu P.* (III. 6. 28), etc. mention Arthasastra as an *Upaveda.*
5. Cf. *Kaut.*, I. 4, p. 8 (about *varta*) and XV. I, p. 427 (About *Arthasastra*).
6. *Mbh.*, II. 5. 79, III. 150, 30, XII. 68, 35, XII. 263, 3, etc.; *Ram.*, II. 100. 47; *Kam.*, I. 12; *Sukra*, I. 156; *Nitiv.*, p. 93.
7. *Ancient Indian Economic Thought*, p. 22.
8. *Kaut.*, I. 5, p. 10.
9. They were not to engage themselves personally in agriculture, but through the agency of others. There is a conflict of opinion among the writers of Dharma-sastras about allowing the Brahmanas to follow the profession of agriculture. *Vide* Kane, *H.Dh.*, II. pp. 124-126.
10. Cf. *Sukra*, I. 179 f.
11. *Kaut.*, II. I, p. 47; *Manu*, IX. 44.
12. *Ibid.*, II. 24, p. 117.

13. *Ibid.*, II. 24, p. 117.
14. *Ibid.*, II. I, p. 47.
15. Cf. *Kaut.*, II. I (p. 47), II. 2 (p. 49), II. 24 (pp. 115-8), VII. II (p. 297), VIII. 4 (p. 334), etc.
16. *Sukra,* IV. 2. 25.
17. *Kaut.*, II. I. p. 48.
18. Cf. *Sukra,* V. 90-93.
19. *Kaut.*, IV. 2, p. 205.
20. A.N. Bose, *Social and Rural Economy of Northern India,* II. pp. 424-35; *contra,* K.V.R. Aiyangar, *op. cit.*, pp. 110-11; K.T. Shah, *Ancient Foundations of Economic in India,* pp. 54, 94.
21. *Sukra,* II. 480-18.
22. For *Subha* (pure) and *asubha* (impure) work and different kinds of servers or labourers to do them, cf. Kane, *H.Dh.*, III. pp. 482-6.
23. *Kaut.*, III. II, p. 174. *Narada* (IV. 105-6), allows even 8% per month, while 2% is not improper according to him.
24. *Mbh.*, II. 5. 77-78.
25. *Pan.*, V. 2. 21 (*vrata*), V. 2. 52 (*puga, gana, sangha*). Katyayana includes *gana, pasanda, puga, vrata,* and *sreni* under *samuha* or *varga.*
26. For explanations of the different terms denoting group organizations, employed in the above paragraph, refer to Kane, *H.Dh.*, II. pp. 66-69, III. 486-489; Majumdar, *Corporate Life in Ancient India,* Ch. I; K.V. Rangaswami Aiyangar, op. cit, pp. 58, 184 ff; Mookerji, *Local Government in Ancient India,* pp 29-34, 39.
27. *Manu,* VIII. 41; *Yaj.*, I. 361.
28. *Visnu Dh.* S., V. 167; *Manu.*, VIII. 219-20; *Yaj.*, II. 187.
29. *Kaut.*, I. 16, pp. 97-98; *Sukra,* II. 358 ff.
30. *Manu,* VII. 127.
31. *Kaut.*, II. 16 (pp. 98-9). II. 21 (pp. 110-11), IV. 2 (p. 205); *Manu,* IX. 286-91; *Yaj.*, II. 245-6; 296.

32. *Kaut.*, II. 34 (p. 141), II. 22 (p. 113), II. 28 (pp. 126-8).
33. *Kaut.*, II. 21 (p. 111), IV. 13 (p. 234).
34. *Kaut.*, II. 16, p. 98.
35. *Ibid.*, II. 16, p. 98.
36. It is interesting to note that according to Medhatithi (on *Manu*, VIII. 400) royal monopolies extended to elephants, as they were most useful to kings, as also to saffron, silks, and woollens in Kashmir, horses in the West, and precious stones and pearls in the South, private trading in them being punishable with confiscation of all property. Saffron is still a monopoly of Kashmir.
37. *Kaut.*, II. 23.
38. *Agni. P.*, 253. 63-66; also *Kaut.*, and the Smrtis on *Rnadana* (recovery of debts).
39. *Visnu Dh. S.*, VI. 2; *Manu*, VIII. 142; *Yaj.*, II. 37.
40. *Jat.*, I. 121, 230; IV 256; etc; *Kaut.*, II. 7.
41. *Kaut.*, XI. I. (pp. 378 ff).
42. Cf. *Sarasvati vilasa*, p. 46; *Kosas tu sarvatha abhisamraksya ityaha Gautamah; tanmulatvat prakrtinam iti.*
43. II. 8, p. 65 : *Kosapurvah sarvarambhah.*
44. XII. 119. 16.
45. XIII. 33.
46. II. 61. 17.
47. II. 319-21, 370.
48. *Nitiv.*, p. 189.
49. II. 6, p. 60.
50. II. 6, p. 61 : *Vartamanah paryusto nyajatasca ayah.*
51. *Kam.*, V. 78-79.
52. II. 6, 35; pp. 59-62, 141-143.
53. *Kaut.*, II. 5.
54. VII. 5, pp. 276-7; also . . . *paratra gacchamah* . . . (p. 394).

55. XII. 87. 36.
56. I. 340-I.
57. Cf. *Manu,* VII. 130; *Gautama,* X. 25; etc.; *Sukra* (IV. 2. 128), makes the tax to be a thirty-second fraction.
58. Cf. Altekar, *State and Government in Ancient India,* 1st Ed., p. 204.
59. *Raj.,* VII. 1008.
60. *EI,* XX. p. 64 (Vikramaditya V).
61. Cf. Ghoshal, *Hindu Revenue System,* pp. 232 f, 262 f.
62. *Annual Report on South Indian Epigraphy,* No. 520 of 1920.
63. *Kaut.,* V. 2, pp. 242-246; *Manu,* X. 118-120; *Nitiv.,* p. 82; *Sukra,* IV. 2. 9; etc.
64. On *Pan.,* IV 3. 99 : *Mauryair hiranyarthibhir arcyah prakalpitah.*
65. Cf. Jayaswal, *Hindu Polity,* p. 333.
66. Cf. Ghoshal, *op. cit.,* p. 193.
67. V. 2, p. 246 : *Evam dusyesu adharmikesu varteta, netaresu.*
68. I. 315-7.
69. II. 4. 439-40.

2 Socio-Economic Conditions—I

Family Life

The foundation of social life was the patriarchal family. In *Rigveda* (I. 24. 12-15 and V. 2. 7), where we find the rudiments of the Sunahsepa story, a kind of absolute control by parents over children is suggested. That family discipline was strict is illustrated by the case of *Rijrasva* who was deprived of his sight as a punishment by his father (I. 116. 16). Similarly in *RV*, X. 34. 4 we are told how the insolvent gambler is disowned by his parents and brothers, in front of his creditor. This does not mean that the relation between the parents and children was not generally one of warm affection; for a father is looked upon as the type of all that is good and kind. The weeding hymn (X. 35) indicates that the newly—married wife rules over (or wins by her love?) her brothers-in-law and even over her husband's parents although she herself entertains a feeling of respect for them. This is clear evidence of joint family life. That under certain circumstances this joint family included the wife's mother is suggested by X. 34. 3 where the gambler complains that "his mother-in-law hates him." After the death of the father, the eldest son took charge of the family.

A notable feature of the etiquette of the Rigvedic age was the great store set on hospitality. The frequent epithet of Agni, *viz., Atithi*, the beloved guest in human abodes, takes for granted the affection and respect generally shown to a guest. No wonder that in later literature detailed descriptions of the merits of hospitality should occur, and that hospitality to a guest should be elevated to the rank of a religious duty, as one of the five great daily sacrifices (*pancha-mahayajnas*).

The Caste System

The elaborate institution known as the Caste System among the Hindus in India may almost be said to be without a parallel in the world, although there is hardly a country where classes or orders of society or grades of social distinction of some kind or other are not met with. A common origin, name, tutelary deity, occupation, and ceremonies generally distinguish one homogeneous caste-group from another, but today caste is rigidly fixed by birth, and exclusive *commensality* and *connubium* between the members of a caste-group to the exclusion of all others are its fundamental and outstanding characteristics. Further, the conception of impurity communicable to a higher caste by contact with a lower one underlies this fissiparous tendency, and has resulted in the untouchability of the so-called Sudra, who by popular error is almost identified with the *panchama,* or one outside the framework of the *Chaturvarnya.* Again, in place of the four original *varnas* or class-groups, there are today thousands of caste divisions and sub-divisions and the number is still growing. This unique development of an ordinary social phenomenon naturally invests its history with a special importance.

The extent to which caste had been developed in the age of the *Rigveda Samhita* has formed a subject of keen controversy among scholars.[1] The uncertainty regarding the exact interpretation of the basic words and phrases in the *Rigveda,* and the relative chronology of the various relevant passages scattered throughout that Veda, make it difficult to arrive at any conclusion that is likely to meet with general acceptance. We shall, therefore, state first of all in detail the most widely accepted version—in a sense, almost, the recognized version—of the development of caste in the *Rigveda,* contenting ourselves with only a brief statement of divergent views. Much confusion will be avoided, if we keep in view the fact, generally agreed to, that the development of caste has been a progressive one, and that we should not expect in the *Rigveda*

Samhita the picture of the Casts System which is presented even in the *Yajurveda Samhitas.*

There are various speculations in later Brahmanical literature regarding the origin of castes. The most common is that which represents the Brahmans, Kshatriyas, Vaisyas, and Sudras to have been created respectively from the head, breast or arms, the things, and the feet of the Creator. An echo of this is found in a hymn of the *RV* (X. 90), the famous Purusha-sukta, which describes the mythical legend of the sacrifice of a primeval giant called Purusha, the ideal "Man" or World-Spirit. The relevant passage has been translated thus :[2]

"When (the gods) divided Purusha, into how many parts did they cut him up? What was his mouth? What arms (had he)? What (two objects) are said (to have been) his thighs and feet? The Brahmana was his mouth; the Rajanya was made his arms; the being (called) the Vaisya, he was his thighs; the Sudra sprang from his feet."

This passage refers to the first three Castes not as sprung from, but as identical with, the mouth, arms and the thighs of the Creator. But in spite of this difference many regard this hymn of the *RV* as the earliest exposition of the later Brahmanical view, and regard the essential features of the Caste System as existing even in the earliest Aryan society in India.

This theory has been challenged by many scholars whose views may be briefly started as follows :

The evidence of the Purusha-sukta, an admittedly late hymn, is not valid for the bulk of the *Rigveda,* which was produced by the as yet un-Brahmanized tribes of Vedic Indians living in the Indus region and the Punjab. The Caste System was developed only later, when a section of these Vedic tribes migrated farther east. The term *Varna* (*lit.,* Aryan colour) is used in the *Rigveda* of all three highest castes of later times, being contrasted only with Dasa (the *dasyu-varna* or "aboriginal colour"). The terms "Rajanya," "Vaisya" and "Sudra" occur only in the Purusha-sukta, the term "Brahmana," also, being rare in the *Rigveda*. The term "Kshatriya," of which "Rajanya" is an earliest variant, occurs but seldom in the *Rigveda*. The term "Brahman" denotes "a priest by profession" only in some passage, while in others it denotes any person who was distinguished by genius or one who, for some reason, was deemed specially receptive of the divine inspiration.

The transition from the casteless, though classified, society of the bulk of the *Rigveda* to the elaborate Caste System of the *Yajurveda* is to be traced to the complication of life resulting from the further migration of the Vedic Aryans from the Punjab to the east. The necessity of carrying on a ceaseless fight with and the conquest of, the aborigines called for an organization of the conquering people by the merger or fusion of petty tribes into centralized kingdoms. Thus emerged the powerful monarch, while the lesser tribal princes, deprived of their royal rank, sank to the position of nobles. The monarchy, moreover, needed now a standing armed force, prepared to meet all eventualities, such as resisting the sudden incursions of native or other Aryan tribes and quelling revolts on the part of the subdued aborigines. This standing army was naturally recruited from the ranks of the nobility of tribal princes and the chief armed retainers of the king. This is the genesis of the warrior class. At the same time, the "people" of the Aryan masses, secure in the protection afforded by the warrior class, ceased to take interest in military matters and settled down to a peaceful life devoted to agriculture, pastoral pursuits, trade and industry. They constituted the third class, the *Vis*, later called "Vaisyas".

Side by side also grew a distinct community of priests. In the earlier period, not only the householder but even the petty prince could offer sacrifice to the gods for himself and his people, the ritual being very simple. But when the size of the kingdom grew and military and administrative affairs kept the hands not only of the king but also of the warrior class full, while, at the same time, the ritual tended to become more complicated and elaborate, the need was keenly felt of a hieratic order, composed of the more intellectual elements among the non-fighters who could dedicate themselves, undisturbed by the distractions of war or peace, to the faithful and exact performance of the highly developed ritual and to the preservation (by word of mouth) of the traditional formulae and sacred hymnology of the Aryans, a heritage in part at least from almost prehistoric times.

As regards the fourth class, the Sudra is mentioned for the first and only time in the "Purusha-sukta". But *dasyu* and *dasa* are known to the *Rigveda,* both as aborigines independent of Aryan control and as conquered slaves. The latter may reasonably be supposed to represent the Sudras of the later texts. But not all the defeated aborigines could be absorbed as slaves in the royal household or in the houses of individual owners. There must have been whole villages of the aborigines, though under Aryan control. The term "Sudra" was evidently applied to the inhabitants of these villages as well as to the wild hill tribes which lived by hunting neighbours. In course of time it included even *dasyu-varna* (or dark-skinned) people who remained beyond the pale of the Aryan state and who were virtually excluded from the religious and ritual cult of the Aryans. The development of the Caste System in a rigid form, with strictly hereditary and mutually exclusive caste groups, did not take place till the time when the Vedic Aryans had settled down in the Middle Country and were already Brahmanized enough to look upon the inhabitants of the North-west—the home of the *Rigveda*—as uncivilized Vratyas because they did not follow the strict Caste System.

The view summed up above may be regarded as the one now generally accepted by scholars. According to this recognized version, in the earliest society represented by the bulk of the *Rigveda,* there were probably different classes and professions, but none, not even the priestly and the warrior classes, were hereditary; the warriors were drawn from the people at large, and any person with the requisite qualifications could officiate as a priest.

This view is not, however, accepted by some whose arguments may be briefly stated thus : (1) The main, if not the earliest part of the *Rigveda* was, in all probability, composed not in the Punjab but in the east, in the country later known as the Madhyadesa or Brahmavarta. So the argument based on the non-Brahmanical character of the Vratyas of the Indus and the Punjab becomes pointless. (2) The term Brahmana, "son of a Brahman or priest," suggests that the priesthood was normally hereditary. There is no definite instance of a person other than priest exercising priestly functions. Nor was this feasible, as the priesthood, even in the *Rigveda*, distinguishes within its fold a vast number of sub-groups of specialists and experts. (3) The power of the Purohita over the king in the *Rigveda*, derivable from the fact that the correct performance of the sacrifice demanded the services of a hereditary priest, is nearly as great as in the post-Rigvedic age. (4) The *Rigveda* knows of a ruling class – the Kshatriya – who, as a class of nobles, are appropriately named in the Purusha-sukta as "Rajanya" or "men of kingly family". As kingship was normally hereditary, the Kshatriyas were also in all probability a hereditary body. The Sudras were admittedly a separate group; so all the elements of the Caste System were in existence of in the age of the *Rigveda*. (5) There are glimpses in the *Rigveda* of a threefold (VIII. 35. 16-18) or fourfold (I. 113. 6) division of the people, corresponding to the well-known three upper or all the four divisions of the Caste System. (6) The existence of similar classes among the Iranians, namely priests, warriors, agriculturists and artisans, makes it very probable that by the time of the *Rigveda* the four classed had developed into hereditary caste-groups, owing to the contact of the *Arya-varna* Aryans with the dark-skinned aborigines and the necessity this imposed on Aryan society of reorganizing its whole structure.

Although there is great force in some of these objections, it must be conceded that they are not strong enough to upset the recognized version. The existence of the four classes in Avestan literature certainly argues for the existence of somewhat similar classes in Rigvedic society but much stronger positive evidence is necessary to establish that these classes were hereditary.

Further, the term Brahmana, son of a priest, occurs very rarely and the word Brahmaputra, in the same sense is found only once. This, when contrasted with the numerous references to Brahman, seems to indicate that there was no idea of a hereditary priesthood in the earlier Vedic period.

On the whole, it is difficult not to agree with the views, propounded long ago by Muir, that the Brahmanas (far less the Kshatriyas or Vaisyas) did not constitute an exclusive caste or race and that the prerogatives of composing hymns and officiating at the services of the gods were not regarded, in the age of the *Rigveda*, as entirely confined to men of priestly families.[3] The same thing was equally or perhaps more, true of the minor professions, as the hymn, quoted above on p. 350, refers to the father, mother and the son following three different vocations in life, *viz.*, those of a poet, a grinder of corn and a physician. The heredity of occupation was, therefore, not yet a recognized principle, far less an established fact. The utmost that can be said is that there were recognized professions like priesthood or distinctions of nobility and these had in many cases a tendency to become hereditary but as in other countries or societies, their ranks might have been recruited from all sections of the community. Of the other essential features of the Caste System *viz.*, prohibition of interdining and intermarriage, no such restriction is even remotely hinted at in the hymns of the *Rigveda*.

Marriage and the Position of Women

The frequent mention of unmarried girls like Ghosha, who grew up in the houses of their parents (I. 117. 7; X. 39. 3; 40. 5), the references to the ornaments worn by maidens at festival occasions in order to win lovers (I. 123. 11; VII. 2. 5), to a youth's courtship of the maiden he loves (I. 115. 2), to the lover's gifts. (I. 117. 18), to their mutual love (I. 167. 3; IX. 32. 5, etc.) and to the spell (VII, 55. 5. 8.) by which a lover hopes to lull the whole household to sleep while he visits his beloved—all this evidence speaks in favour of the custom of girls normally marrying long after they had reached puberty. Some of the passages mentioned above, but not all, may refer to the *hetaera* class as existing in vedic society. The marriage ceremony also supports this view, as it is presumed to be immediately followed by consummation (X. 85. 29 ff.).

The restrictions on the field of choice in marriage were few. Marriage connections with the *dasyu-varna* people, with whom the Aryans came into conflict in India, were probably prohibited. Among Aryans only the marriages of brother and sister (X. 10), and of father and daughter were banned.

There seems to have been considerable freedom on the part of young persons concerned in the selection of a wife or husband, as they generally married at a mature age. There is no clear evidence that the consent of the parent or brother was essential. The later appeared on the scene after the parties concerned had come to an understanding, and their participation as well as that of the "wooer" (*vara*) in the formal "wooing" was a mere formality, though it was an essential preliminary to the marriage ceremony.

The uncomplimentary references to some sons-in-law (VIII. 2. 20; I. 109. 2) suggest that in some cases a bride-price was paid by a not very desirable son-in-law. Similarly when girls had some physical defect, dowries, it seems, had to be given (VI. 28. 5; X. 27. 12). When Vimada carried off Purumitra's daughter against his will, but probably with the consent of the daughter (I. 112. 19; 116. 1, etc.), we have an admixture of those elements which led to the formulation, later, of the Gandharva and Rakshasa forms of marriage.

A hymn in *RV* (X. 85)—which may be called the wedding hymn- gives us some idea of the oldest marriage ritual. The bridegroom and party proceed to the bride's house (X. 17. 1), where the well-adorned bride remains ready (IV. 58. 9) to join the marriage-feast. The guests are entertained with the flesh of cows killed on the occasion (X. 85. 13). The ceremony proper now commences. The bridegroom grasps the hand of the bride and leads her round the fire (X. 85. 36, 38). These two acts constitute the essence of the marriage and the bridegroom is now the husband who takes her by the hand (*hasta-grabha*: X. 18. 8). The bridegroom next takes the bride home in a car, in a wedding procession (X. 85. 7, 8, 10. 24-27, 42). Then follows the consummation which is signified chiefly by the purification of the bride's garment (X. 85. 28-30, 35).

Perfect harmony and happiness are praved for in conjugal life, which (it is hoped) will be long enough to bless the couple with sons and grandsons (VIII. 31. 5-9 : X. 34. 11; 85. 18, 19, 42 ff.). X. 85. 46 describes the newly married wife as taking up a most respected position as the mistress of her new household, wielding authority over the husband's father, brother and unmarried sisters. This verse envisages the case (very probably) of the marriage of the eldest son in the family, when the old father has retired from active life. The authority exercised must have been more or less the rule of love. The wife participated regularly in the sacrificial offerings of her husband.

The fulfilment of the desire for offspring, and male offspring in particular, was the chief aim of marriage. Abundance of sons is constantly prayed for along with cattle and land , but no desire for daughters is expressed. This desire for a son is natural in a patriarchal organization of society. The son alone could perform the funeral rites for the father and continue the line. Sonlessness was as much deplored as poverty (III. 16. 5). The adoption of sons was recognized, though not favoured (VII. 4. 7. 8).

There is very little evidence of the prevalence of the custom of *Sati* or widow-burning in the *Rigveda,* though we may detect a semblance or reminiscence of this ancient custom in X. 18. 8, where the widow is asked to descend from the funeral pyre of her dead husband on which she was first made to lie. The only safe conclusion would be that the practice, even if known, was not widely prevalent, or at best was confined to the Rajanya class, if Indo–Germanic parallels are a correct guide. *Rigveda,* X. 40. 2 and X. 18. 7, 8 point to the practice of requiring a childless widow to cohabit with her brother-in-law until the birth of a son. This *niyoga* is a kind of short–term levirate. These passages (and I. 124. 7 also which mentions a *garta-ruh*) are clear evidence that the remarriage of widows was permitted in certain circumstances, though there is no clear or definite reference to it in *RV.*

The *Rigveda* certainly permits polygamy (I. 62. 11; 71. 1; 104. 3; 105. 8; 112. 19; 186. 7; VI. 53. 4; VII. 18. 2; 26. 3; X. 43. 1 101. 11, etc.), though monogamy may have been the rule (I. 124. 7; IV. 3. 2; X. 71. 4). Whether monogamy developed from polygamy in the Rigvedic age as Zimmer[4] thinks, or whether polygamy is secondary as Weber[5] believes, cannot be decided. Probably polygamy, though allowed, was practically confined to the Rajanya class. Polyandry is not referred to anywhere in the *Rigveda*. The few passages in the wedding hymn (X. 85. 37, 38) in which "husbands" (plural) are spoken of in connection with a single wife can be explained on a mythological basis. Female morality maintained a high standard, the same degree of fidelity not being expected from the husbands.

There are few doubtful references to lovers and love-making (I. 134. 3; VIII. 17. 7). A *raha-suh,* "bearing in secret" is mentioned in II. 29. 1. A protege of Indra is referred to as the "castaway" (*paravrji or paravrikta*), presumably as the offspring of illegitimate love. It is difficult to accept the view of Pischel and Geldner[6] that Ushas is the characteristic hetaera , nor are hetaerae referred to when women are described as going to the *samana,* though the dancer (*nritu*) may have belonged to that class. The so-called incestuous intercourse between father and daughter in the story of Prajapati (X. 61. 5-7), and between brother and sister in the dialogue between Yama and Yami (X. 10) can be satisfactorily explained (in the opinion of the present writer) on a mythological or astronomical basis.

Women had to be under the protection of some guardian or other; for example, in the care of their fathers until marriage, of their husbands after marriage, and of their brothers if not married; still they enjoyed much freedom. They did not always remain indoors, but moved about freely; they publicily attended feasts and dances, and there are references to "fair ladies flocking to festive gatherings."

Education

In the *Rigveda,* there is no explicit reference to the ceremony of *Upanayana* or Initiation (*lit.,* the drawing near or leading forth of a boy for study under the teacher) which is regarded as of such great importance in later ages. But all primitive people have some kind of ceremony, signifying the formal admission of an adult youth to membership of tribe, and we may infer from the closely parallel Indo-Iranian ceremony of Navjot that the elements of this ceremony probably existed in the Rigvedic age and even earlier.

The Frog-hymn (VII. 103) quoted above, on p. 349 gives us a glimpse of the educational system (if system it can be called) of the Rigvedic age. The fifth verse gives a picture of the earliest Vedic school by the comparison of the croaking of the frogs to the chorus of voice heard when a teacher recites Veda, section by section *(parvan)*, and the pupils repeat his words after him. The first verse of the hymn suggest through a simile that this concerted school-recitation sprang into life suddenly, at a stated time (the opening of the monsoon?), because frogs raising their (rain -inspired) voice at the opening of the monsoon of the after lying low for (the rest of) the year are compared to Brahmanas, conforming to their fixed annul routine *(vrata)*. Evidently the entire instruction was orally given. Debates are also referred to (X. 71). The word "*Brahmacharin*" in the technical sense of a "religious student" is found in X. 109. 5. The father was not rarely also a teacher, his son taking lessons from him along with few neighbouring students. That the sharpening of the intellect, as well as the development of character, in the *Brahmacharin* was aimed at, is seen from the celebrated Gayatri verse (III. 62. 10) which prays is Savitri for a stimulation (a whetting) of the intellect.

While there is no doubt that the instruction was orally imparted, it is a very debatable point whether the art of writing was known at all in this age. It is a well-known fact that no actual specimens of alphabets have been discovered in India which can be definitely dated before the fourth century B.C. Consequently most of the scholars are of opinion that the art of writing was unknown in ancient India. Buhler sought to prove that the Indian merchants learnt this art in Western Asia and introduced it in their country some time about the eighth century B.C. This view, which regards the most ancient alphabet of India (the Brahmi alphabet of Asoka's inscriptions) as derived from the North Semitic types of the ninth century B.C., now holds the field. But the discovery of the numerous seals at Mohenjo-daro, with pictographic writing (Ch. IX, p. 195) has put an altogether new complexion on the whole question. It is now believed by many that the Indus script formed the parent-source from which the oldest Brahmi alphabets have been derived. Some are even of opinion that when the *Rigveda* was finally arranged in its present form it was written in a script which formed an intermediate stage between the Indus script and the Asokan alphabet. If we accept the old theory of Buhler, we have to presume that the vast Vedic literature was composed and preserved by oral transmission alone—a stupendous feat of memory which appears to be almost miraculous. On the other hand, if we believe that these voluminous texts were committed in those old days to writing, we are faced with the problem of writing materials, of which we definitely know nothing. The whole thing is shrouded in mystery which cannot be solved until more definite facts come to light.

Amusements and Entertainments

Music, both vocal and instrumental, was well known. The Frog-hymn (VII. 103. 7-8) refers to the musical chanting of Brahmanas engaged in the extraction of the Soma juice. Different vocal sounds are carefully analysed in that hymn and elsewhere. Singing is often mentioned as adapted to different ends, such as "chanting," "reciting," "hymning," etc.

Among instruments we find reference to the *vina* (lute or string-instrument), *vana* (flute or wind-instrument), and the drum. The dancing of maidens is mentioned. Probably, men also danced, as is implied in a simile in X. 76. 6. The dialogue-hymns of the *Rigveda* have been the fruitful source of many theories regarding the earliest form of the drama (*ante*,p. 349). One theory is that they are relics of old mysteries from Indo-European times. Dr. Keith[7] holds that dramatic spectacles, religious in character, were known in the Rigvedic age. The chariot-race was a favourite sport and source of entertainment, and the race in general is the source of numerous similes and metaphors in the *Rigveda*. The fascination exercised by gambling and the ruin caused by addiction to it, is often referred to and is actually the subject-matter of a hymn (X. 34).

Food and Drink

Milk and its products, chiefly *ghrita* (*ghi* or clarified butter), formed the principal ingredient of food. Grain (*yava*) was parched or ground into flour with a mill-stone and then mixed with milk or butter, and finally made into cakes. Vegetables and fruits were eaten in large quantities.

Meat also formed a part of the dietary. The flesh of the ox, the sheep and the goat was normally eaten, after being roasted on spits or cooked in earthenware or metal pots. Probably meat was eaten, as a rule, only on occasions of sacrifice, though such occasions were by no means rare, the domestic and the grand sacrifices being the order of the day. This explains why horse-flesh was eaten only at the horse-sacrifice to gain the strength and swiftness of the horse. The cow receives the epithet *aghnya* (not to be killed) in the *Rigveda* and is otherwise a very valued possession. It is difficult to reconcile this with the eating of beef, but we may get some explanation if we remember the following : *(i)* Firstly, it was the flesh of the ox rather than of the cow that was eaten; a distinction definitely made. *(ii)* The flesh of the cow was (if at all) eaten at the sacrifices only and it is well known that one sacrifices one's dearest possession to please the gods. *(iii)* Even in the *Rigveda,* only *Vasas* (barren cows) were sacrificed. For example, Agni is called in VIII. 43. 11 as *vasanna.* The expression "*atithinir gah*' (cows fit for guests) in X. 68. 3 implies the same distinction.

Milk, drunk warm as it came from the cow, was a favourite drink. Though the Soma juice, in *Rigveda,* appears exclusively as a sacrificial drink (as "Haoma," it was prepared and similarly celebrated in the Indo-Iranian period), it must have been a very popular inebriating drink in the original home of the Aryans. It had three kinds of admixture, with milk, sour milk, and *yava.* In the Rigvedic period, *sura* was the popular drink, extremely intoxicating as compared to the Soma which, though mildly inebriating, was an invigorating beverage. *Sura* was probably distilled from grain. It is condemned as "leading people to crime and godlessness." *Madhu,* though often used to denote "Soma" or milk or any sweet food or drink, has also the sense of "honey" in the *Rigveda.*

Dress and Decoration

The dress (*vāsana* or *vastra*) consisted of two garments according to the strictly Rigvedic evidence, namely the *vasas* (or "lower garment" in a narrow sense) and the *adhivasa* (an "over-garment" or an "upper garment"), though in the days of the later *Samhitas,* the *nivi* (or under-garment) came to be used in addition. The Maruts wear deer-skins, and a *muni* (X. 136. 2) is clad in skins or soiled garments.

The *atka* (a "garment") appears to be described as woven and well-fitting, though the real meaning is doubtful. Woollen clothing was in vogue. A sort of mantle or cloak (*drapi*) is often mentioned. A kind of embroidered garment (*pesas*) seems to have been used by female dancers (I. 92. 4, II. 3. 6, etc.). A special garment was worn by the bride at the marriage ceremony; it was later given to a Brahmana and is called *Vadhuya.* The Maruts are described as wearing mantles adorned with gold. There was a general fashion for dressing well as may be inferred from words like *suvasas* (well-clad) and *suvasana,* and there were garments of different colours too. There is no clear evidence of any differentiation between male and female dress.

Several ornaments are mentioned in *Rigveda*. The *Karnasobhana* was "an ornament for the ear," apparently for the use of men (VIII. 78. 3) and that it may have been a gold ornament is suggested by I. 122. 14 which refers to a deity as gold-eared (*hiranya-karna*). The *Kurira* (X. 85. 8) was some kind of head-ornament worn by females, specially brides. The same may be said of *nyochani* (X. 85. 6), a bride's ornament. *Khadi* was a kind of ring, worn as an armlet or an anklet (I. 166. 9; VII. 56. 13). *Nishka* was a gold ornament worn on the neck and we shall presently see that it must have been of a size suitable for its use also as a sort of currency. *Mani* was some kind of jewel (whether "pearl" or "diamond" is not certain) worn round the neck (I. 122. 14). *Rukma* was an ornament worn on the breast (II. 34. 2, 8). Garlands were often worn by men desiring to appear to advantage (IV. 38. 6 : V. 53. 4. etc.). One hymn (X. 184. 3) refers to the Asvins as "lotus-wreathed."

The hair were kept combed and oiled. The use of the word "*opasa*" indicates that plaits were worn by women in dressing the hair. There are undoubted references to the custom of wearing the hair in braids or plaits. A maiden had her hair made in four plaits (X. 114. 3). It seems from the descriptions of Rudra and Pushan that men also wore their hair plaited or braided, and the Vasishthas were noted for wearing their hair in a plait or coil on the right (VII. 33. 1). The beard and moustache are mentioned, but shaving is referred to (X. 142. 4). Most probably *Kshura* means "razor" in the *Rigveda*.

Knowledge of Medicine and Sanitation

The physician is often mentioned with respect for his skill. Miraculous cures are ascribed to the twin-gods, the Asvins, who are the great healers of diseases and experts in the surgical art. Among diseases *Yakshma* is frequently mentioned (I. 122. 9; X. 85. 31; 97. 11, 12; 137. 4; 163. 1-6). It denotes "illness" in general, and probably "consumption" in particular, rendering the body emaciated. IX. 112. 1 speaks of a physician wanting to cure a fracture in a way which seems to indicate that the practice of medicine was already a profession. The entire hymn X. 97 is addressed to the *Oshadhis* (the plants) with special reference to their curative powers. So herbs and plants figured prominently in the materia medica of this period. Prayers for long life are pretty frequent. The legends illustrating the reputed healing powers of the Asvins give us an idea of the general ailments and bodily mishaps. They are divine physicians who restore eye-sight and cure the blind, sick and maimed (VIII. 18. 8; 22. 10; I. 116; X. 39. 3). They rejuvenate the sage Chyavana (I. 116. 10) and revive the sage Rebha when drowned and given up as dead. They give a cooling and refreshing draught to Atri Saptavadhri when suffering from suffocation. They cure Paravrij of blindness and lameness, and when the leg of Vispala is cut off in battle, they replace it with an iron one. The last instance proves that a kind of primitive surgery was practiced.

ECONOMIC CONDITION

Agriculture and Cattle

Agriculture made real headway during the Rigvedic age, although the practice of ploughing can be traced to Indo-Iranian times. The operation of tilling the soil meant (as now) the cutting of furrows in the field with the wooden ploughshare drawn by bulls, the sowing of seeds in the furrows thus made, the cutting of the corn with the sickle, the laying of the bundles of corn on the threshing-floor, threshing, and finally sifting the winnowing. Irrigation was known, and helped cultivation. The exact nature of the grain which was thus grown cannot be ascertained. It was called *Yava* and may have been "barley" as it was understood to be in the later Samhitas. Rice was not cultivated until a later period.

The Rigvedic Aryans were primarily a pastoral people and naturally cows and bullocks were their most valued possession. These constituted the chief form of wealth and the only original *dakshina* (sacrificial fee). The word "*dakshina*" in fact is an adjective meaning "right," or "valuable," with an ellipse of go (cow), because the sacrificial fee was a cow placed "on the right side" of the singer to be rewarded. Similarly one of the words for "fight" was *gavishti* "a search for cows." The name of *Aghnya* ("not to be killed"), applied several times to the cow, shows that the cow was coming to be regarded as a sacred animal. This feeling of sanctity of the cow can be traced even to Indo-Iranian times. Cows were kept in stalls during the night and in the heat of the day. They were allowed to roam freely in the pastures at other times, and were milked three times every day. The cow returning from the pasture-land in the evening and licking her calf fastened by a rope was one of the most gladdening sights, and the lowing of the milch-kine the most musical sound to the Rigvedic Aryans. There are even special terms like "*sva-sara*" for the time of the grazing of the cows in the morning, and *sam-gava*, for the time when the grazing cows are driven home together for the milking. The *Rigveda* is aware of the dangers to which the grazing cows were liable, such as being lost, falling into pits, breaking limbs, and being stolen. The ears of cattle were marked, probably to indicate ownership. Bulls and oxen were regularly used for ploughing and drawing carts. That the cow should give warm or cooked milk was a standing wonder. That the dark or red cow could give shining milk was little short of a miracle. (VIII. 93. 13).

Trade and Commerce

There are clear references in the hymns (I. 56. 2) to trading in distant lands for profit. The prayers and oblations offered for "gaining a hundred treasures" (III. 18. 3) are also probably those of merchants seeking divine aid for success in trade. Apart from trade with foreign countries, or alien tribes, there must have been quite an extensive inland trade, but no definite details are available. Haggling in the market was, well-known.

The exchange of commodities on the principle of barter seems to have been in vogue, but cow had already come to be regarded as a unit of value (IV. 24. 10). There might have been other recognized units of value. Great importance attaches to one such unit called *nishka*. It meant originally a gold ornament of the shape of a necklace or a necklet (V. 19. 3). When, however, in I. 126. 2 the poet celebrates the receipt of a hundred *nishkas* with a hundred horses, as a gift, he could hardly be referring to a hundred necklets. So it probably came to be used as a sort of currency even during the Rigvedic Age.

Booty in battle was one of the sources of wealth to the State, and consisted chiefly of flocks and herds. In individual economy, dowry and bride-price played no small part. Movable property could change hands by gift or sale which amounted to barter. Land was not an article of commerce , and does not seem to have presented any problems in connection with the transfer of immovable property in the case of the family or of the individual. The population being scanty and scattered over wide areas, fresh land could be easily obtained, if needed by a family which had grown to a very large size with several sons. The rivers of the North-West are referred to as yielding gold.

Whether any sea-borne trade was carried on during this age is a much disputed question, as already noted above (p. 248). The view that the Rigvedic Indians took part in ocean-shipping is opposed on the following grounds : (1) The *nau* (boat or ship) was, in the majority of cases, merely a boat or "dug-out" for crossing rivers, and there may have been large boats in use for crossing the broad rivers of the Punjab. These boats were so simple in their construction that only the paddle or oar (*aritra*) needed for propelling them is mentioned. There is no mention of masts or sails, of rudder or anchor. Thus the Vedic Indian was not much of a navigator. (2) Metaphors used by a people familiar with the ocean are lacking in the *Rigveda*. (3) The numerous mouths of the Indus are ignored, although that river was the convenient natural outlet to the sea. Against these arguments must be set down the following facts : (1) The *Rigveda* mentions men who go to the ocean (*samudra*) eager for gain (I. 56. 2; IV. 55. 6) and *samudra* cannot be explained away in these passages as standing for the very broad and wide stream of the lower Indus. (2) There are some allusions to a trade more extensive than that implied by boats for crossing rivers. (3) Verses I. 116. 3 ff. tell us that the Asvins rescued Bhujyu in the ocean with a ship of a hundred oars (*sataritra*). A ship of this type could be needed only for a sea-voyage. (4) X. 136. 5 refers to "eastern and western oceans." These passages, in the opinion of the present writer, clearly indicate that sea-trade was carried on during this age.

Occupations and Industries

Some of the important professions and vocations of this period have been incidentally referred to above. The Brahmanas or the priestly class dedicated themselves to the highly specialized occupation or profession of officiating at the sacrifices and preserving the sacred hymnology of the Aryans by conducting Vedic classes. The Kshatriya or Rajanya class had taken to the fighting profession. Members of the third – the Vaisya – class naturally took to agriculture, cattle-breeding and other pastoral pursuits, and the various arts, crafts, and industries. The lowest, the Sudra class, was engaged in service of all kinds. But, as noted above, the classes were not irrevocably bound up with specific occupations. Many Rajanyas are found among the poets of the *Rigveda,* and members of the three higher classes were not rarely promiscuously engaged in cattle-breeding, during times of peace, and in fighting, during times of war. Money-lending was practiced chiefly by the Vaisyas, but also occasionally by Brahmanas.

It appears from the large number of the similes and metaphors drawn from the art of fashioning chariots for war and race, and carts for agriculture and transport, that carpentry was an honoured profession, the carpenter being also a wheelwright and joiner. He did all sorts of work in wood, and even carved work of a finer type was not beyond his skill

(X. 86. 5; I. 161. 9; III. 60. 2). The worker in metal smelted ore in the furnace using the wing of a bird as a bellows to fan the flames. Household utensils like kettles were made of metal (*ayas*). What metal the *ayas* was in uncertain. It may have been either copper, bronze, or iron, if we suppose that the word is consistently used in the same sense; but it is also possible that it is used in more senses than one. Its colour is to be inferred from the epithets used with it, such as : reddish." As the use of copper precedes that of iron in the development of civilization, *ayas* may have indicated "copper" or its alloy "bronze"; but this is by no means certain, and iron may have been known. Earthenware and wooden vessels were used for purposes of eating and drinking, along with those of metal. The art of the tanner (*charmamna* in VIII. 5. 38) and the use of hide are well known. Earthenware and wooden vessels were used for purposes of eating and drinking, along with those of metal. The art of the tanner (*charmamna* in VIII. 5. 38) and the use of hide are well known. Ox-hide was used to manufacture bowstrings, thongs (to fasten parts of the chariots), reins and the lash of the whip (VI. 75. 11; I. 121. 9; VI. 47. 26; 46. 14; 53. 9, etc.). It was also placed above the boards on which the Soma was pressed with the stones. It is not unlikely that skin bags were also made with it (X. 106. 10). Among the home and cottage industries may be mentioned sewing, the plaiting of mats from grass or reeds, and the spinning and weaving of cloth, chiefly done by women. Among the other professions may be mentioned those of the dancer, both male and female, barber (*Vaptri*) and vintner. It is noteworthy that those who practised these professions were not looked upon as inferiors in the age of the *Rigveda.*

Hunting as a sport and profession was known and must have been practised by the Rajanya class, chiefly with the aid of practised professionals. Nets and pitfalls were the normal instruments of capture, and the bow and arrow was also employed. Birds were caught in nets, and antelopes (*risya*) in pits. There are some obscure references to the capture of boars and buffaloes (*gaura*). The lion was caught in traps. The *Rigveda* is an important source of our knowledge of hunting in early times. The butcher's profession was also probably known, as the services of a Samitri (in the sense of "one who cuts up") were probably needed at animal sacrifices (I. 162. 9; II. 3. 10; III. 4. 10, etc.).

There is no distinct reference to the specific occupation of slaves. They probably assisted their Aryan masters who did not think it beneath their dignity to practise all the arts and crafts needed by society.

House-Building and Means of Transport

Although it is suggested that some kind of a distinction between villages and towns is indicated in I. 44. 10 and 114. 1, city-life is not much in evidence. The village was a group of houses, built near each other for purposes of safety, and was surrounded by some kind of a hedge as a protective barrier against enemies and wild beasts. It is difficult to determine the exact sense in the *Rigveda* of *pur* which later meant a town. It seems to have been an earthwork fortification, protected by a palisade or stone wall. The frequent mention of the capture or destruction of such strongholds indicates that they were numerous and scattered all over the country, and that they could be easily erected like the stockades made by primitive tribes all over the world. The *pur* or earth-work fortification may either have been part of the village or just outside it, to be resorted to in times of emergency. It was called autumnal, probably because the emergency arose generally in autumn, when raids from neighbouring tribes became possible at the end of the monsoon, or the emergency was in the shape of a flooding of the plains owing to the rising of rivers in autumn.

Houses were made of wood, the beams (*vamsa*) being made of bamboo (also *vamsa*). The so-called strongholds or forts probably had a series of concentric walls.

The conception of Pushan as the guardian of the pathways gives occasion for the numerous references of all kinds of transport and means of communication such as carts (*anas*) and chariots (*ratha*) on land and ships on the sea. The Asvins are credited with ships (or conveyances) moving through the air (*antariksha*), which come uncannily near the modern conception of airships.

The chariots and carts were drawn by oxen, mules, or horses. The chariots of the rich were drawn by two and sometimes even four horses. Riding on horseback was also much in vogue. Names of various parts of chariots occur very frequently in the *RV* hymns, and indicate a considerable improvement in their construction over the primitive types. Travelling was fairly common. Prayers are offered to the gods (VII. 35. 15) to "give broad paths to travel," – paths that should be straight in direction and thornless (X. 85. 23). A solemn prayer to Indra for the safety of the journey (III. 53. 17-20) gives many interesting details of a cart driven by oxen in which the journey was made.

The references to artificial waterways such as *kulya* in III. 45. 3 and "*khanitrima apah*" in VII. 49. 2 make it certain that some kind of an irrigation system was known. Wells artificially made are contrasted with springs. Such wells were covered, and are described as unfailing and full of water. The water was raised by a wheel to which a strap with a pail attached to it was fastened. These wells could be used for irrigation purposes, when the water was led off into broad channels (*RV*, I. 55. 8; X. 101. 6, 7; 102. 11; VIII. 69. 12; 72. 10).

REFERENCES

1. There is a voluminous literature on the origin and antiquity of the Caste System in India, to some of which reference will be made in the bibliography. For the views mentioned in this section see *CHI*, I pp. 92 ff.; Muir, *Original Sanskrit Texts*, Vol. I; N.K. Dutt, *Origin and Growth of Caste in India*. In an article entitled : "Were Castes formulated in the Age of the Rigveda" in *BDCRI*, II, 34 ff., the present writer has sought to prove that the formulation of castes, if not the Caste System, was already a *fait accompli* in the age of the *Rigveda*.

2. *Muir, op. cit.*, p. 10.
3. *Op. cit.*, pp. 263-4, 280.
4. *AL*, p. 323.
5. *Ind. Stud.*, V, p. 222.
6. *Ved. Stud.*, I, pp. xxv, 196, 275, 299, 309; II, pp. 120, 154, 179, etc.
7. *SD*, p. 16.

3 Socio-Economic Conditions—II

Family Life

The very use of the term *kula,* which does not occur as an uncompounded word before the period of the Brahmanas, suggests a system of individual families, each consisting of several members, under the headship of the father or eldest brother to whom belongs the *kula* (originally "home or house of the family," then by metonymy "the family" itself). As distinguished from *gotra* it seems to mean the undivided family living under one roof.

The case of the sale Sunahsepa in the *Aitareya Brahmana* (VII. 12-18) suggests that the son was under the absolute control of the father, but the story may only reflect the horror evoked by the father's heartless treatment of his son. The father as a rule did not arrange the marriage of his son or daughter (*Jaiminiya Upanishad-Brahmana,* III.12. 2). The relationship between father and son was one of great affection. The kissing of a grown-up son on the head on important occasions as a token of love is a custom found in *Sankhayana Aranyaka.* Adoption was resorted to, not only in the absence of natural children, but also to secure the addition of a specially qualified member to the family, as in Visvamitra's adoption of Sunahsepa.

Certain special terms show that it was considered improper for younger brothers and sisters to marry before their elders. The brother and his wife played the part of guardians of the sister in the absence of the father. Quarrels between brothers are mentioned. The family was sometimes large enough to include the great-grandfather as well as the great-grandsons. Among relations are mentioned the wife's brother, the sister's son, the cousin (*bhratrivya*), the maternal uncle, etc.

An entire hymn in the *Atharvaveda* is devoted to the praise of hospitality (IX. 6), and the *Aitareya Aranyaka* also lays stress on it. The guest-offering is an integral part of the daily ritual of the household.

The Caste-System

The term *varna* is used definitely in the sense of "caste," without reference to colour, in this age. The system of Caste, whose beginnings may be traced in the broad fourfold classification of society in the Rigvedic Age (*ante*, pp. 387 ff), developed during this period in various directions. Many causes contributed to the rise of sub-castes and other caste-divisions. Guilds of workers tended to crystallize into castes, as occupations became more or less hereditary; as examples we may cite the chariot-makers, the smiths, the leather-workers, and the carpenters. The peculiar family constitution or the *gotra* tradition, whereby exogamy as well as endogamy regulated marriage connections, and whereby a man should normally marry a woman of equal birth, *i.e.,* within his caste, but not of the same *gens* or within the *gotra,* was another factor in the development of complications and distinctions in the Caste-System. The original race-feeling or the contrast which the *Arya-varna* (Vedic Aryans) felt between themselves and the *Dasyu-varna* (aborigines), and which was sought to be mitigated by the incorporation of the conquered population into the framework of Aryan society by admitting them into the fourth class or caste, left its mark in the shape of the rule of hypergamy, whereby an Aryan could marry a Sudra wife but the Sudra never an Aryan wife. The same rule was also gradually applied in marriages between the three Aryan classes, and while a Brahmana would normally marry a Kshatriya or a Vaisya girl, and the Kshatriya, a Vaisya girl, the male of a lower class could not ordinarily marry a girl of a higher class. This peculiar feeling as to mixed marriages is fundamental to all caste-divisions, and may be looked upon as the third factor in caste elaboration during this age.

As has been noted in chapter XIX (p. 400), it was the third caste-group, that of the Vaisyas (called also *vis* or *visya),* which by virtue of its occupations came into the closest touch with the fourth caste-group, that of the Sudras. The latter was continually receiving accretions from the conquered aboriginal population and could not therefore keep up its cultural purity to the Aryan level. There arose, therefore, the necessity of clearly distinguishing the Aryan Vaisya from the Sudra who was a doubtful Aryan. An evidence of this precaution is seen in the variants of caste-names for the last two groups, namely as *Arya* and *Sudra,* found in some passages in the *Taittiriya, Kathaka, Vajasaneyi,* and *Atharvaveda Samhitas.*

Along with their functions and duties, the privileges and status of the four castes were being differentiated minutely in the religious and social spheres. The *Satapatha Brahmana* prescribes varying sizes of funeral mounds for the four castes. The deities to whom victims of the different castes are offered in the Purushamedha are different. Different degrees of politeness are noticed in the modes of address prescribed for the four castes.

The Sudra class was naturally the hardest hit in these invidious distinctions, but the texts are not consistent in the position they assign to it. If, for example, the Satapatha (III. 1. 1. 10) says that a Sudra is not worthy of being addressed by a consecrated person the stories of Satyakama Jabala and Janasruti in the Upanishads show that the teaching of philosophy was not without from him. The Sudra cannot milk the cow for the Agnihotra-milk according to the *Kathaka Samhita* (XXXI. 2), but the *Satapatha Brahmana* (V. 5. 4. 9) gives the Sudra a place in the Soma sacrifice, and the *Taittiriya Brahmana* prescribes formulae for establishing the sacrificial fire for the *rathakara* also who was counted a Sudra. The *Aitareya Brahmana,* however, lays down the most reactionary doctrine. It describes the Sudra as *yatha-kama-vadhya* (fit to be beaten with impunity), who could be expelled at will and who is always the servant of another. It is also declared that the Sudra has no rights of property as against the *rajanya,* especially the king. How far these extreme views were actually followed in practice it is difficult to say.

The Vaisya class (*Vis*) was engaged in agriculture, pastoral pursuits, industry, and trade, and paid tribute to the king and the nobles, in return for the protection given to them. A late passage (VII. 29. 3) in the *Aitareya Brahmana* gives rather a low estimate of him with reference to the Kshatriya, when it says that "he is to be lived on by another and to be oppressed at will." Although things might not have been really so bad as this, there is no doubt that the position of the Vaisya was steadily deteriorating in this age.

The Kshatriya class was composed of the king's relations, his nobility, his retainers and other chiefs of petty states. They fought for the protection of the country and maintained peace. They received revenue in kind from the people or masses (Vaisyas mainly) during war. For their normal or peace-time subsistence some of them were probably granted villages, because the Gramani seems to have been more often nominee of the king rather than a popularly elected officer, and probably the post was hereditary in such cases. Others had their lands cultivated by tenants. In war, they were helped by the people, who fought alongside them.

While it is generally recognized that the Brahmana and the Kshatriya have undoubted precedence over the Vaisya and Sudra, there is not the same unanimity in respect of the relative position of the first two.[1] The more common view is that the Brahmana is superior to the king, as recorded in the *Vajasaneyi Samhita* (XXI. 21) and the *Satapatha, Aitareya* and *Panchavimsa Brahmanas.* The Brahmana is dependent on the king *(Satapatha Br.* 1. 2. 3. 3) and takes a lower seat by his side, but is superior to the king. A Kshatriya can never get along without a Brahmana while a Brahmana can; may, the power of the Kshatriya is derived from the Brahmana (*Satapatha Br. IV.* 1. 4, 6; XII. 7. 3. 12). On the other hand, the *Kathaka Samhita*

(XXVIII. 5) says that the Kshatriya is superior to the Brahmana, while the *Aitareya Br.* (VII. 29) rates the Brahmana rather low, describing him as a receiver (of gifts), a drinker (of Soma) and as liable to be removed at will (by the king). Though this is not the common view of this age it explains some facts very satisfactorily; the fact, for example, that many kings were seers of hymns and sacrificers, and some of them were even instructors of Brahmanas in the Brahmanical lore.

Brahmanas are contrasted with the members of the three other castes as the privileged eaters of the oblation. According to some scholars the Brahmanas were divided into two classes—the Purohitas of the kings, who guided their employers by their counsel, and the ordinary village priests, who led quiet lives.[2] In the view of the present writer these were not separate classes as such. Any one of the ordinary priests could come into contact with the king when they were engaged in some great festival and could be selected for the post of Purohita, if found pre-eminent and distinguished for his learning. The post remained hereditary, only if the son was as well qualified as the father. Imprecations against royal oppressors of Brahmanas in the *Atharvaveda* and the statement therein that kings that persecute the Brahmanas do not prosper, suggest on the one hand that the persecution of Brahmanas was not unknown, and on the other, the gradual consolidation of the prestige of the priesthood. Even though a passage in the *Aitareya Br.* (VII. 29. 4) exalts the Rajanya above the Brahmana whom (it says) the former can control, the references to the *visah* only, as the subjects of the king *(Tandya Brahmana)*, suggest that Brahmana class received preferential treatment and enjoyed certain privileges and exemptions denied to the other caste-groups. The greed and cunning of the Brahmanas and many prerogatives claimed by them are reflected in the *Atharvaveda* and other text (ante, pp. 412, 422), but they may not be a true picture of the class as a whole. There can be hardly any doubt that many of them deserved the highest position in society by their character and intellect.

The most glaring evil of the caste-system, namely the doctrine of the impurity communicated by the touch or contact of lower castes (known as "untouchability" today), had not yet reared its ugly head. Restrictions on inter-dining are known, but not on the basis of caste. Great importance is attached to purity of descent in the Samhitas and Brahmanas, but there are instances of Brahmanas of impure descent such as Kavasha, Vatsa, and Satyakama Jabala. On the whole it is quite clear that caste had not yet become a rigid system, and none of the three factors which definitely characterize it today, *viz.*, prohibition of inter-dining and inter-marriage, and determination by hereditary descent, was yet established on a secure basis.

Marriage and the Position of Women

There are evidences that marriage did not normally take place before puberty. As regards restrictions on marriage. It was banned within the circle of agnates and cognates, but the *Satapatha Brahmana* (I. 8. 3. 6) allows marriages within the third or fourth degree on either side. Though marriage within the *gotra* was not explicitly prohibited, marriage outside the *gotra* must have been more frequent. Brothers and sisters were not to marry before their elders; so the order of birth was generally respected. The re-marriage of a widow was allowed, as seen from the *Atharvaveda* IX. 5, 27, 28. Polygamy undoubtedly prevailed. The *Maitrayani Samhita* mentions the ten wives of Manu. The king has four wives, the *mahishi* (the official or chief wife), the favourite one (*vavata*) the *parivrkti* or the neglected one (owing to the absence of a son?), and the *palagali* (daughter of a court official?). The instances of Kavasha and Vatsa, as well as that of Janasruti in the *Chhandogya Upanishad*, who offers his daughter in marriage to a Brahamana, indicate that hypergamy was permitted during this period. The wife wedded first must necessarily have claimed all the privileges of a wife in the religious and social life of the couple, but the two wives of Yajnavalkya were apparently on a footing of equality. The verses from the *Atharvaveda* quoted above (p. 412) indicate the prevalence of polyandry. Conjugal morality generally stood on a high level, but the infidelity of the wife was certainly not unknown. The ritual of the Varunapraghasa (in the *Maitrayani Samhita* and the *Satapatha* and the *Taittiriya Brahmanas)*, in which the wife of the sacrificer is questioned as regards her lovers, is evidently a rite to expiate unchastity (even platonic or purely mental) on the part of the wife. The son of a *Kumariputra* (son of a maiden) is mentioned in the *Vajasaneyi Samhita* which refers also to illicit unions of Sudars and Aryas, both male and female. But all these may be looked upon rather as exceptions that prove the rule of a high standard of ordinary sexual morality. The metronymics in the lists of teachers in the *Brihadaranyaka Upanishad* may be explained as the relic of an ancient sociological feature rather than as evidence of recognized immorality. After all the society is human, and while we should not entertain highly exaggerated notions of unfailing chastity during the age, disproportionate importance need not be attached to isolated cases, or peculiar and exceptional customs and institutions.

The sale of a daughter was known, but viewed with disfavour. Dowries were generally given. The various types of marriage detailed in the later law books had not been formulated as yet. The story of Chyavana in the *Jaiminiya Brahmana* is an instance of the gift of a maiden for services rendered. The elements of the marriage ceremony described in the marriage-hymn of the *Rigveda* are reproduced without much change in the corresponding *Atharvaveda*-hymn, which adds only one important feature, which later became essential, namely the bridegroom causing the bride to mount a stone before grasping her hand. The poetic picture of an ideal family life in which the newly-wedded wife becomes the mistress of her husband's home, as depicted in the *Rigveda,* holds true for the texts of this period also, and this ideal was possibly often realized. The term *patni* regularly applied to wife in the Brahmanas is indicative of her equal share in social and religious side of the husband's life, while the term *jaya* refers only to her conjugal position. Gradually, however, she lost this important position, as a priest was more and more employed to offer the oblations in certain ceremonies instead of the wife. This deterioration of her status and dignity went so far as to result in woman being classed with dice and wine, as one of the three chief evils (*Maitrayani Samhita,* III. 6. 3). On the whole, judging from references in the *Taittiriya* (VI. 5. 8. 2) and the *Kathaka Samhita,* it appears clearly that woman, who held a high position in the age of the *Rigveda Samhita,* had fallen on evil days in this age (*ante,* Ch. XX, p. 424).

It is true that sometimes high praise is showered on her in the texts of this period. Thus it is said that she is half her husband and completes him (*satapatha Br.* V. 2. 1. 10). But in spite of this praise she is not allowed to take part in political life, by attending the assembly like men. According to the *Aitareya Brahmana* (III. 24. 7), a good woman is one who does not talk back. In the *Satapatha,* there is actually the rule that the wife should dine after her husband. The relative position of the two sexes is reflected in the keen desire for male progeny. This may be regarded as natural in a patriarchal society where relationship was recognized through the father. But this natural predilection exceeds all bounds of propriety or morality when we read in the *Aitareya Brahmana* (VII.15) that a daughter is a source of misery and a son alone can be the saviour of the family. The *Atharvaveda* (VI. 11. 3) also deplores the birth of daughters.

The *Atharvaveda* (XVIII. 3. 1) merely refers to the ancient practice of *sati* (widow-burning) and the *Rigveda* does not countenance it. So it appears that this custom was not very prevalent during the Vedic age. The Vedic texts also tacitly admit the non-existence of the custom, by discussing the question of widow re-marriage, which is permitted by some text and prohibited by others.

Education

With the development and elaboration of the institution of the sacrifice and the growth of a vast literature connected with it, the problem of the preservation of this literature became very acute, particularly because during the age under discussion the whole of it (the *Samhitas* and *Brahmanas,* including the *Aranyakas* and *Upanishads* appended to them) was looked upon as *Sruti* or revealed literature. The Vedic literature must therefore have formed the chief subject of instruction and the vital part of education. Naturally, then, the process of imparting the knowledge of the sacred hymnology and sacrificial ritual must have become more and more systematized during this age. Literary education was transmitted only orally, *i.e.,* by word of mouth from teacher to pupil. We find an echo of this system in the famous frog-hymn of the *Rigveda,* quoted above (*ante,* p. 349). The art of writing was very probably known to the Vedic Indians,[3] but that it played no part in the educational system of ancient Indian is accepted by all.

The *Atharvaveda* (XI. 5) refers to a *brahmacharin* (Vedic student) gathering sacred fuel for fire-worship and bringing alms (begged from door to door) to the teacher. There are also prayers in the *AV* for liturgical employment at the ceremony of Initiation (*Upanyana*). *Svadhyaya* or the daily portion or lesson of Vedic study is referred to in the *Samhitas* of the *Yajurveda.* In the *Kathaka Samhita,* a rite for the benefit of one who, though not a Brahmana, has recited or studied the *vidya,* is mentioned, and the well-known fact that Kshatriya kings like Janaka were not only keen students of the Vedas, but also great philosophers renders it almost certain that members of Kshatriya and Vaisya castes received the sacrament of the *Upanayana* and went through part (at least) of the period of studentship, although normally the Kshatriya would study the art of war.

Vedic study, service to the teacher, and chastity were the principal duties of a *brahmacharin.* The fairly detailed description of the *Upanayana* as a sacrament (*samskara*) in the *Satapatha Br.* (XI. 3. 3. 1-7) includes all the essential features of the same sacrament and life of studentship which are treated at length in the Grihya-sutras, such as : (1) The formal acceptance of the pupil by the teacher at the request of the former; (2) the entrusting of the pupil to the care of certain deities; (3) the vows and duties to be discharged by the pupil while residing at the house of the *guru,* such as: putting fuel on the fire, sipping water, and begging alms; (4) the dress of the pupil consisting of the *ajina,* the girdle, etc. The description of young Angirasa teaching his elders, in the *Tandya Br.* (XIII. 3. 23-4), and the stories of Nabhanedishtha and Bharadvaja in the *Aitareya* and *Taittiriya Brahmanas,* gives us vivid picture of the educational system of those days, with its insistence on truthfulness, observance of duty (dharma), devotion to the *acharya* or *guru* (preceptor) and to one's parents, hospitality, faith, and generosity. The *Taittiriya Aranyaka* even anticipates some minute directions of the type given in the Grihya-sutras, such as: the pupil should not run while it is raining, nor urinate in water, nor bathe naked, etc.

Women probably took part in the intellectual life of the society, but we have no such definite reference in the later *Samhita* and *Brahmana* texts as we get in Upanishads. From the *Taittiriya Sainhita* (VI. 1. 6. 5) the *Maitrayani Samhita* (III. 7. 3) and the *Satapatha Br.,* we know that women were taught to dance and to sing, which appear to be recognized feminine accomplishments.

Among subjects of study figured arithmetic, grammar, and prosody (*Tandya Br.*) Language was obviously an important subject of study, since Northerners are mentioned as experts in language and grammar.

There was then no system of state education. The Brahmana teachers taught students of the three higher castses at their houses, giving them free board and lodging. In return, the pupils served the teacher and gave him fees (*guru-dakshina*). That the education in this Home University was not merely literary, but also included physical and moral training, is seen from the hard daily routine of the pupil and the code of moral conduct prescribed for him, while residing with the teacher.

The existence of Vedic schools in this age, that is, even before the establishment of Sutra-*charanas,* is clear evidence that even in these early times, centres of Vedic learning presided over by a celebrated Vedic teacher were scattered all over the country. The Samaveda Sutras refer to Brahmana-*charanas* (schools) and as many as fifteen *charanas* of the Vajasaneyins are known, including the Kanva and Madhyamdina ones that have survived. The only *Samhita-charanas* known are those of the Bashkalas and Sakalas for the *Rigveda Samhita*. The separate Samhita and Brahamana-*charanas* originated owing to a difference in the texts of the Samhitas and Brahmanas respectively. Whatever we might think of Max Muller's theory of the origin of Samhita and Brahmana-*charanas*, it is important to note that numerous Vedic schools existed all over the country. The example of the assembly of the learned in the court of Janaka shows that debates (philosophical and literary) were often held under royal auspices.

Amusements and Entertainments

Music, both vocal and instrument, and dancing continue to be among the amusements of this age.[4] The *Samaveda* is a standing monument to the wonderful skill and originality of the ancients in the science of vocal music. Several professional musicians are known, and the variety of instrumental music in vogue can be inferred from the types of musicians enumerated, such as lute-players, flute-players, conch-blowers, drummers, etc. Among the musical instruments known are the *aghati* (cymbal) to accompany dancing *(RV* and *AV)*, drums, flutes, and lutes of various types, and the harp or lyre with a hundred strings (*vana*). Many other instruments, of which we cannot form an exact idea, are also named.

The Sailusha, included in the list of victims at the Purushamedha in the *Vajasaneyi Samhita,* probably means an "actor" or "dancer." There is a theory that a precursor of the later classical drama existed in this period, support being lent to this view by the supposed reference to the Nata-sutras in Panini.

How deeply racing (especially chariot-racing) had entered into the popular scheme of entertainment is seen from its ritual transformation into a ceremony which, by sympathetic magic, secures the success of the sacrificer. The essential part of the Vajapeya ceremony is a chariot-race, in which the sacrificer is made victorious. Horse-racing was a favourite amusement. A semi-circular course and prizes for such a race are mentioned in the *Atharvaveda*. A formal race is also a feature of the Rajasuya ritual. Dicing was another popular amusement. The number of dice, the method of dice-playing, and the names of the throws are all described in detail in the various texts of this period. A ritual game of dice is played at the Agnyadheya and the Rajasuya ceremonies. So gambling is probably sought to be restricted by elevating racing and dicing to the rank of religious ceremonies. It is interesting to note that a *vamsa-nartin*, "pole-dancer" or "acrobat," is mentioned in the *Yajurveda*.

Food and Drink

Various eatables are mentioned in the texts of this period. The *apupa* is a cake mixed with *ghi* (clarified butter) or made of rice or barley; odana is a mess, generally of grain cooked with milk. Special varieties are those made with water, milk, curds or *ghi*, and beans, sesame or meat, and named appropriately, such as "*tilaudana*," etc. A porridge made of grain, barley or sesame unhusked, slightly parched and kneaded, is called *Karambha*. Rice cooked with milk and with beans is mentioned in the *Satapatha Brahmana* and the *Vajasaneyi Samhita*. Fried grains of rice were known. Barley-gruel (*yavagu*) and decoctions of other grains are also referred to.

Meat-eating seems to be fairly common, as in the Rigvedic age. The *Satapatha Brahmana* prescribes the killing of a great ox or goat in honour of a guest. Generally meat was eaten on the occasion of some ceremony or other, but such ceremonies were performed almost every day. Its use is forbidden during the observance of a vow. It appears that killing of cows gradually came into disfavour. The normal meat-diet consisted of the flesh of the sheep, the goat and the ox, the usual sacrificial victims. What man ate, he offered to the gods.

Among the chief products of milk may be mentioned

clotted curds (*amiksha*), sour milk (*dadhi*), fresh butter (*nava-nita), payasya* or curds consisting of a mixture of sour milk and hot or cold fresh milk, butter, mixed with sour milk (*prishad-ajya), phanta,* creamy butter or the first clotted lumps produced by churning, and finally *vajina,* a mixture of hot fresh milk with sour milk. This formidable list of milk-products and their mixtures shows the great popularity of milk as a drink.

Sura, an intoxicating spirituous liquor already known in the Rigvedic age, is often mentioned. Though tolerated as an ordinary drink (the drink of the people in the *sabha*), it is often condemned as leading to quarrels and as seducing men from the path of virtue like dicing and meat-eating (*AV,* VI, 70. 1). The Sautramani sacrifice is of the nature of an expiation or penance for an indulgence in *sura.* The method of its preparation cannot be ascertained. Probably it was prepared from fermented grains and plants. It was kept in skins. The *Yajurveda Samhitas* mention a beverage called *masara,* which appears to have been a mixture of rice and *syamaka* with grass and parched barley, etc. *Madhu* primarily means "sweet" as an adjective, and so denotes any sweet food or drink such as the Soma or milk. The sense "honey," though known in the *Rigvedha,* is only now its most definite sense, and there are taboos against its use by students and women under certain circumstances.

Already in the Brahmana period, the real Soma plant was difficult to obtain, and so substitutes were being allowed. For example, the *Panchavimsa Brahmana* (XI, 5. 3) suggests that if *putika,* a substitute for the Soma, cannot be procured, *arjunani* may be used as a substitute for the Soma. In the *Yajurveda,* the plant is ceremoniously purchased before it is pressed. The plant was sometimes subjected to the technical process of *apyayana* (causing to swell) by being steeped in water, thus increasing its yield of juice. These few details, culled from the texts of our period, supplement the almost exhaustive description of the preparation of the Soma which can be gathered from the *Rigveda* (*ante,* p. 378).

Dress and Decoration

Urna-sutra (woollen thread) is repeatedly mentioned in the later Samhitas and Brahmanas, but *urna* denoted not merely sheep's wool but probably goat's hair also. Clothes were generally woven of sheep's wool. The fondness of the Vedic people for ornamental or embroidered garments was as keen as in later periods. The dress in this period seems to have consisted of three garments—an under-garment *(nivi)*, a garment proper *(vasas)*, and an over-garment *(adhi-vasas)*, like a mantle or cloak. The *Satapatha Brahmana* describes the set of sacrificial garments as consisting of a silk under-garment *(tarpya)*, a garment of undyed wool, an over-garment and a turban *(ushnisha)*. The turban was worn by men as well as by women. A royal head-gear or turban is worn at the Rajasuya and Vajapeya ceremonies by the king. The turban of the Vratya is referred to the "sandal" or "shoe" was made of boar-skin (*Satapatha Br.)*. The combination of *dandopanaha* ("staff and sandals") is mentioned in the *Kaushitaki Brahmana*. Skins were used as clothing. The frequent use of the variant terms for "warp" and "woof" shows the great development of the art of weaving garments.

The *pra-ghata* or closely woven ends of a cloth to which is attached the trimming, fringe, or border of a garment *(dasa)* is mentioned. The *Sankhayana Aranyaka* (XI. 4) refers to a garment of (dyed with?) saffron. But uncoloured woollen garments are also mentioned (*Satapatha Br.)*. From the manner of wearing the sacred thread outside, can be inferred the manner of wearing the over-garment which probably passed over the left shoulder and under right arm. The *Satapatha Brahmana* (XI. 5. 1. 1) has an interesting legend to explain why man alone wears clothes. So none but the ascetics could go naked.

The *Taittiriya Brahmana* mentions an article called *Sthagara*, probably an ornament made of a fragrant substance. *Salali*, the quill of the porcupine, is used now for parting the hair and anointing the eyes. The *Sankha* or conch-shell is used as an amulet (AV.). The late *Shadvimsa Brahmana* (V. 6) mentions the pearl *(Vi-mukta)*. A jewel *(mani)* strung on a thread was worn round the neck as an amulet. The *pra-kasa,* an ornament of metal or a metal mirror, is often mentioned in the Brahmanas. The *pra-varta* in the *Atharvaveda* (XV. 2. 5. 9. etc.) probably means an ear-ring. A *nishka* of silver (an ornament worn round the neck) as worn by the Vratayas is mentioned in the *Panchavimsa Brahmana.*

Knowledge of Medicine

The inclusion of a physician in the list of victims at the Purushamedha in the *Vajasaneyi Samhita* (XXX. 10) and *Taittiriya Brahmana* (III. 4. 4. 1) shows that the profession of the physician had already become well established. But where as the profession was held in high esteem in the *Rigveda* – the Asvins being called "physicians – a dislike for it seems to have developed in this age, because in some Samhita and Brahmana texts of the *Yajurveda,* the Asvins are looked down upon because as physician they have to mix too freely with men. From the *Atharvaveda* one can say that although their treatment of diseases is somewhat primitive, consisting as it does of the uses of herbs in combination with spells and of water – remedies Indo-European in character – their knowledge of pathology is anything but elementary. The *Atharvaveda* enumerates quite a large variety of diseases and the demons supposed to cause them. *Takman* (a kind of fever) is the subject of five hymns of the *Atharvaveda* and is also often mentioned elsewhere. But it is in the *Atharvaveda* that its symptoms are described in detail *(ante,* p. 418). Consumption, scrofula, dysentery, boils, swellings, convulsions, ulcers, rheumatism, headache, jaundice, cramps, eye-disease, senility, fractures and wounds, bites of snakes and other harmful insects, poison in general, lunacy, leprosy are the diseases mentioned in the *Atharvaveda.* The use of sandbags to stop bleeding is interesting. The practice of dissecting animals at the sacrifice was a great help to the knowledge of anatomy which was developed to an appreciable extent. Finally may be noted an interesting remark in the *Sankhayana Brahmana* (V. I) that "sickness is particularly prevalent at the junction of the seasons" – a very accurate observation indeed.

ECONOMIC CONDITION

Agriculture and Cattle

According to various texts, such as the *Atharvaveda, Vajasaneyi, Maithrayani, Taittiriya,* and *Kathaka Samhitas,* and the *Taittiriya* and the *Satapatha Brahmanas,* six eight, twelve, and even twenty-four oxen were used to drag the plough which must have been large and heavy. The oxen were yoked and harnessed with traces and guided by the goad of the ploughman. The furrow *(sita),* is often mentioned. The value of the natural manure of animal in the fields was very much appreciated *(AV).* Dung *(sakrit)* and dry cow-dung *(karisha)* are often mentioned. The plough is described as having a smooth handle, well-lying and lance-pointed *(paviravat).* There is a special name *kinasa* for the ploughman or cultivator of the soil. The *Atharvaveda* gives the credit of introducing the art of ploughing to Prithi Vainya, but ploughing is constantly referred to in the texts of this period as practised by the Vedic Aryans, the Vratyas who were outside the pale of the Vedic religion being described as not cultivating the soil. The *Satapatha Br.* enumerates the various operations of agriculture, as "ploughing, sowing, reaping, and threshing." The ripe grain was cut with a sickle. From the *Taittiriya Samhita* and other texts we gather that *Yava* (meaning "barley" now) sown in winter was harvested in summer, that rice sown in the rains ripened in autumn, and that beans and sesamum planted at the time of the summer rains ripended in winter. Wheat was known and is distinguished from rice *(vrihi)* and barley. Groats *(saktavah)* made of wheat-grain are mentioned.

Cultivation suffered from the usual pests – the moles that destroyed the seed and the other creatures that harmed the tender shoots. Evidently to prevent these and similar evils the cultivators used charms at the time of both sowing seed and gathering corn (*ante, p. 416*). Similar other spells in the *Atharvaveda* to avert drought and excess of rains show that these inevitable mishaps threatened agriculture then (as now) in spite some sort of a system of irrigation that sought to minimize its evil effects.

Draft-oxen were generally castrated. Female draft-cattle also were used. A four-year old ox or cow *(turyavah)* is mentioned in the *Taittiriya, Maitrayani,* and *Vajasaneyi, Samhitas.* The milch-cow (*dhenu*) is contrasted with the bull, and there are special terms for cows, oxen, and calves of different ages, for cows barren or otherwise and in various stages of growth and motherhood, as well as for a cow with a calf substituted for one of her own which had died.

A fairly long human in the *Atharvaveda* shows the reverence inspired by the cow, and the death penalty prescribed for cow-killing outside the sacrificial enclosure tells the same tale. Pasture-lands were carefully looked after, and large sheds or stalls were erected for accommodating cattle. On the whole, the cows were taken extremely good care of. The origin of the sanctity of the cow lay in the inestimable value of the cow for purposes other than eating, and the occasional mythological identification of the cow with the earth or Aditi helped process which culminated in the full-fledged deification of the cow in later times.

Trade and Commerce

Rich Vaisyas *(sreshthins)*, who had acquired wealth in trade or agriculture, and who were probably the headmen of guilds, are often referred to. That money-lending was a flourishing business is indicated in various ways. *Kusidin* is a designation of the usurer in the *Satapatha Br.*, and *Kusida* has the sense of a "loan" in the *Taittiriya Samhita.* The rate of interest is not specified. No regular system of currency or coinage appears to have been introduce yet, as no coins definitely belonging to this period have been unearthed and no specific and undoubted reference to coins occurs in the literature of the period. The *mana* is a measure of weight equivalent to the *Krishnala* (*i.e.*, the berry of the *gunja*) which was a unit of weight. The *satamana,* a piece of gold equivalent in weight to a hundred *Krishnala,* must have been in use as currency among the merchants. The *nishka* also had become by now a unit of value in addition to the old-time unit, the cow. The profession of the merchant was often hereditary, as the term *vanija* ("son of a *vanij*") in the sense of a merchant shows. The haggling of the market, already known in the Rigvedic age, had now become such a pronounced feature of commerce that a whole hymn of the *Atharvaveda* (111. 15) aims at procuring success in trade through clever bargaining. Garments, coverlets, and goat-skins are among the articles of commerce and market commodities (*AV*).

The sea was undoubtedly known and there was probably some amount of sea-born trade. In the texts of this period, *samudra* is frequently used in the definite sense of the "sea." The *Aitareya Brahmana* speaks of the "inexhaustible sea." (V. 16. 7) and "the sea as encircling the earth." The eastern and western oceans (mentioned in the *Satapatha Brahmana*) are probably references to the Indian Ocean and the Arabian Sea.

Occupations and Industries

The principal occupations and professions and the various arts and crafts were distributed among, and assigned to, the various groups of people in accordance with the scheme of the caste-system, which had by now taken root in Vedic society and was being elaborated and complicated by the rise of mixed castes. For example, agricultural and pastoral pursuits were mainly in the hands of the Vaisyas. The professions of teaching and officiating as priests at the sacrifices (Srauta or Grihya) were confined to the Brahmanas. The fighting profession was mainly the monopoly of the Rajanya or Kshatriya class. Service of all kinds – menial or otherwise – felt to the lot of one fourth class – that of the Sudras. This is but a rough distribution, and the division was not rigidly adhered to, member of one caste not rarely following the occupation of another.

Although hunting did not form the chief source of livelihood of any particular class, it was practised for procuring sustenance and for the protection of herds and flocks from wild beasts; and it was also occasionally indulged in as a pastime and sport, chiefly by members of the Rajanya class, as in the Rigvedic age (*ante*, p. 401). Among the victims at the Purusha-medha are found many curious technical names of persons maintaining themselves on hunting and fishing. Birds were caught in nets (*jala*) and the net was fastened on pegs (*AV*, X. 1. 30; VIII. 8. 5.).

Fortunately a very comprehensive list of the professions, occupations, arts, crafts, and industries of this period is to be found in the list of victims at the Purusha-medha as given in the *Vajasaneyi Samhita* (XXX) and the *Taittiriya Brahmana* (III. 4). The *anu-Kshattri*, a special type of attendant on the doorkeeper or on the charioteer, the *anu-chara*, an attendant in general, a drummer, a worker in thorns cut up and used to plait mats, a smith, a plough-man, an astrologer, a cow-killer (or butcher?), a herdsman, a maker of bow-strings, a carpenter, a gatherer of wood, a fire-watcher (*dava-pa)*, a hand-clapper, who presumably scared away birds from the field by making a noise, a female embroiderer or a basket maker, a jeweller, the yoker and unyoker of horses, the maker of *sura*, an elephant-keeper and a worker in gold – all these figure in the list of victims in the Purushamedha. In the other texts of this age are mentioned a few additional callings, *viz.*, a ferryman or poleman, a washerman (*mala-ga*), a menial *(purusha)*, a potter, a usurer or money-lender, a blower, a barber, a boat-propeller, a cook, a messenger, and a footman running by the side of a chariot. To this multiplicity of occupations must be added the arts and crafts as there was no appreciable break in the economic life of the Vedic Aryans from the age of the *Rigveda Samhita* down to the age of the *Brahmanas*, save that there was a more extensive knowledge and use of different kinds of metals.

House-Building and Means of Transport

The "House" (*harmya*) was large enough to contain not only a large family, but also pens for cattle and sheep, and evidently had many rooms with a special place for the Garhapatya fire which was kept continuously burning. The door with a fastener is often mentioned. House apparently were generally built of wood as in the Rigvedic period. The method of constructing them is not definitely known. Probably four pillars were erected, propped up by beams leaning against them at an angle, Ribs of bamboo-cane *(vamsa)*, a ridge, and a net or thatched covering over the bamboo ribs probably made up the roof. Grass in bundles was used to fill in the walls which were finished with reed work. The *dhana-dhani* ("treasure-house") mentioned in the *Taittiriya Aranyaka* (X. 67) probably indicates a special type of room or house. The *Atharavaveda* mentions *patninam sadana* or a part of the house called women's quarters. A seat with a pillow or cushion or coverlet, a bed, and a couch are among the articles of furniture mentioned.

As regards means of transport, the draft wagon (*anas*) is distinguished from the chariot *(ratha)* used for war and sport. The axle-box of a conveyance is mentioned. Since the *Atharavaveda* (XV. 2. 1) mentions *vi-patha,* a rough vehicle used for bad tracks, it can be inferred that there were some well-made roads. The wagon was drawn by oxen generally, but riding of horses and elephants was in use. Ships and boats plying on rivers and seas were a popular mode of transport.

REFERENCES

1. For a detailed discussion on the relation between the Brahmanas and Kshatriyas in this age, cf. Ghoshal, *History, of Hindu Political Theories,* pp. 44-52.
2. *Ved. Ind., II,* p. 255; *CHI,* I, pp. 127-8.
3. Cf. the author's paper "The spoken words in Sanskrit Literature" (*BDCRI, IV*). Cf. also Dr. S. K. Chatterji's view *(ante,* p. 157). There is, however, a sharp difference of opinion on the antiquity of the art of writing in ancient India (*ante,* p. 395).
4. These three are referred to as the threefold *Silpa* in the *Kaushitaki Brahmana.*

4 Socio-Economic Conditions—III

Family Life

The family life was the framework on which society rested, and the Grihya-sutras that deal with the domestic sacrifices and other duties performed by the householders supply valuable information regarding it.

As in the age of the Later Samhitas and Brahmanas, the family was normally a joint one with the most senior married member or householder as the head. But partitions often took place as the rules in the Grihya-sutras regarding the kindling of the domestic fire show. Among the occasions mentioned there for fresh formal kindling are the division of the inheritance or the death of the head of the family, in which case the eldest son kindled it. Seniority in age constituted an important claim for respect in the family. The directions about the *Vaisvadeva-bali*—one of the daily domestic sacrifices—that it need not be repeated every time the food was cooked, and that it may be offered from the kitchen of the chief householder or from that of the member whose food was ready first, show that the joint family was big enough to necessitate cooking at different kitchens. The fact that a rite is prescribed for one desirous of a large family shows that the people liked to have many children. Male additions to the family were preferred to female ones. An interesting formality in the family life of these days is the manner in which the father greeted the children in the house after his return from a journey, the mode of greeting being different for male and female children. The high sense of responsibility and duty expected to be shown by the head of the family towards the other members is seen in the Grihaya-sutra rule that he was to take his food only after feeding all the children and old persons, as well as any female residing under his protection, and any pregnant lady in the house. The respect and authority that the father commanded is shown by the fact that the Dharma-sutras, describing in detail the acts of courtesy which a son owed to his father, mention that he is allowed to eat the remnants of his father's food. The father on his part is expected to kind. The heartless conduct of the father in the story of Sunahsepa is condemned in the *Sankhayana Shauta-sutra*. The spiritual succession from father to son is almost taken for granted by the Upanishads. The gradation of the relations in family is given, as it were, in the *Chhandogya Upanishad* (VII. 15. 2), where father, mother, brother, and sister are mentioned in succession.

The Caste-System

The period of the Sutras witnessed the gradual hardening of the caste-system in general and the deterioration of the position of the Vaisyas and Sudras in particular. We can trace this process step by step if we follow the evidence of the three broadly distinguishable chronological strata, namely (1) the Srauta-sutras with which may be conveniently considered the evidence of the Sutras of Panini also; (2) the Grihya-sutras; and (3) the Dharma-sutras.

From the evidence of the *Sankhayana Srauta-sutra* which records that the Vajapeya sacrifice – a sacrifice of which the chariot face forms an integral part – was at one time a sacrifice for a Vaisya as well as a priest or king, it is clear that the position of the Vaisya is deteriorating now and Caste distinctions are hardening. The power of the Brahmanas is growing. They are exempt from taxes and could, on occasions, be kings, but Kshatriyas could hardly become priests. The prestige and influence of the Purohita in the state are considerable. Panini's division of the Sudras into *nirvasita* and *aniravasita* shows that certain degraded Sudras with unclean habits like the Nishadas were forced to reside outside the limits of the village or town. The Sudra was denied the privilege of *samnyasa* ("renunciation"). The *rashtra* or nation consisted only of the three higher Castes, the Sudras being excluded from it. Although some Caste-sections were degraded, it is quite certain if the Mixed Castes had arisen in this period.

The Grihya-sutras clearly differentiate the status, occupations, obligations, duties, and privileges of the four principal Castes in matter both spiritual and secular. A different age is prescribed for each of the three higher castes for the various sacraments, such as the *Chudakarana* (the tonsure ceremony of the child) and the *Upanayana* ("initiation") ceremonies. One is not sure whether these different prescriptions were adjustments necessitated originally by the differences of mental calibre and moral fibre in the various caste-groups (for the *Upanayana* ceremony, for example). Different seasons are also prescribed for the different castes. The differentiation extends to such minor thing as the girdle, the staff, the skin, and the garment to be used by the student, and the *Upanayana mantra* to be recited by him. The story is the same with regard to most of the sacraments such as the naming of the child, the building of a house, marriage, and even such unessential matters as *anulepana* or salving which is part of the *snana* ceremony signifying the completion of the period of studentship. Even in the giving of gifts, the Caste determined the nature of the gift as much as the financial condition of the giver.

The Brahmanas in particular have now become a well-organized priesthood. Among their special duties and privileges are the study and the teaching of the Veda, sacrificing for themselves and others, and the receiving of gifts. The feasting of learned Brahmanas to invoke their blessing is, without exception, laid down as the concluding feature of every sacrament. That this feasting was originally more a disinterested homage to the noble qualities of the spiritually-minded Brahmanas, than a sop to a worldly-minded priesthood, is clear from the rules that the invitee must not be a relative and that the invitations must not be arranged in a bargaining spirit. The general trend of the Grihya-sutra prescriptions is that if the privileges of a Brahmana were many, he deserved them, and inspired respect and confidence as much by his high ethical standard as by the responsibilities and duties he owed to the other classes.

The Rajanya or Kshatriya class, among the rest, came closest to the Brahmana class in power and prestige, the two together being as it were the moral and material props of society. It was but natural that the cultural and social status of the Vaisyas should gradually deteriorate, because by virtue of their occupations, namely agriculture, cattle-breeding and commerce, they came into close contact with the Sudras. But the popular notion that the Vaisya class had very little in common with the two higher classes in religious and sacramental matters is erroneous, though it has crystallized in the *Bhagavadgita* verse (IX. 32) which puts women, Vaisyas, and Sudras in one and the same category of people to whom eligibility to absolution through *Bhakti* (devotion) is conceded by the Lord. According to the Grihya-sutras, when the domestic fire is to be kindled for the first time, it may be borrowed from the house of a Vaisya rich in cattle, or from the house of one who performs many sacrifices, be he a Brahmana, a Kshatriya or a Vaisya.

When we come to the Sudras, however, we find that a wide gulf separates them from the three higher classes. The mixture of non-Aryan elements was probably responsible for this as the word Arya has a racial as well as moral connotation in this period and meant practically "reborn," that is, a member of the three higher castes. The privilege of performing the sanctifying sacraments (excepting that of marriage which took place in his case without the recitation of *mantras*) is denied to a Sudra, and this was at once the cause and effect of his low position. But the Sudra was certainly not a *pariah.* He enjoyed the status of a regular member of the household, and as a servant he was employed in all departments of the household not excluding the kitchen.

If the *Upanayana* ceremony was neglected for three generations in a family – whether Brahmana, Kshatriya or

Vaisya — the members became outcastes whose very sight was inauspicious and who probably lived outside the village or town. But the *Vratya-stoma* ceremony of expiation and penance could secure for the outcastes readmission into the Aryan fold. Thus the horrors of an age-long and irremediable outcasting were unknown in the days of the Grihya- sutras.

The Dharma-sutras show that caste distinction has outstripped its proper limits and has even invaded the field of civil and criminal law (*ante,* pp. 495 ff.). The legal rate of interest and fines were graded according to the castes and a Sudra received capital punishment for a crime like homicide for which lighter punishments were awarded to members of the higher castes. The contact of the three Aryan castes with the Sudras through inter-marriage was bound to lead to the rise of mixed castes, and the difference of occupations must have resulted sooner or later in an increase in the number of such mixed castes. Whether the mixed castes had arisen as early as the period of the later Samhitas is not certain. The enumeration of different classes or categories of victims in the Purushamedha chapters of the *White Yajurveda,* for example, may refer to different professions rather than castes. Similarly, for the period of the Srauta- sutras and Panini, all that can be said is that certain caste-sections were degraded, but for the period of the Grihya- and Dharma-sutras the existence of Mixed Castes cannot be doubted. The *anuloma* type of marriage, sanctioned by the Sutras, whereby a member of higher caste could take unto himself a wife or wives of the lower castes, in addition to one of his own caste, must necessarily lead to new caste-divisions, although in the beginning, for some time, the rule that the progeny of such *anuloma* unions belonged to the *varna* or caste of the father arrested such a tendency. The Dharma-sutras give the names of the mixed castes that arose not only as a result of the permitted *anuloma* marriages, but also as a result of the prohibited *pratiloma* marriages (where the husband's caste was lower than that of the wife) which apparently took place not rarely. The *Vasishtha Dharma-sutra* (XVIII. 1) for example, tells us that the offspring of a Sudra male and a Brahmana female becomes a *Chandala* who was to be treated as an out caste. The sacramental direction of the Grihya-sutras raise an interesting problems in this connections by mentioning rarely, if ever, the mixed castes. The rules seem to be framed only for the Brahmana, the Kshatriya, and the Vaisya. One can understand that the progeny of *pratiloma* marriages should be excluded from the sacraments, but if *anuloma* progeny was also excluded, then a very large number of people would be denied the spiritual benefit of the sacraments. Apparenly the *Apastamba Grihya-sutra* is of this view when it omits all reference to the *rathakara* (the offspring of an *anuloma* marriage) in its Upanayana rules. The *Baudhayana Grihya-sutra,* which includes the *rathakara* in the initiation rules, seems to reflect the earlier view. The following stages may, therefore be distinguished in the treatment of the mixed castes in the Sutra period from the sacramental point of view. In the earliest, perhaps the progeny of *anuloma* marriages was absorbed in the father's *varna* and thus became eligible for the sacraments as a Brahmana, Kshatriya, or Vaisya. The next stage was probably reached when some important intermediate castes, like that of the *rathakara,* received a separate treatment in the sacramental rules. The third stage is reflected in the exclusion of the *rathakara* and other mixed castes from the sacraments.

It has to be recognized, however, that the caste-system even in this period had not become as wooden and exclusive as it is now. Inter-dining and inter-marriage (in the *anuloma* form) were not prohibited, though it is difficult to decide whether and how far change of caste was permissible. Even outcastes who had performed the prescribed penances could be readmitted to the Aryan fold. Nor were the caste so strictly separated or ramified into so many caste-divisions as obtain today. We see in the Dharma-sutras the beginning of the formal theory of defilement resulting in the taboo of all contact on the part of a pure man of the upper castes with an impure man, namely, a member of the lowest caste. For example, we see in the Dharma-sutras of Vasishtha, Gautama, and Apastamba the idea of impurity communicated by the touch or contact of inferior castes, which is reflected in the purification rendered necessary in the case of contact with a Sudra and implied in the prohibition of eating in company with man of lower castes.

Marriage and the Position of Women

As already mentioned above, the *anuloma* system of marriage (*i.e.*, between a male of a higher and a female of a lower caste) prevailed in this period. The low status of the Sudra wife is reflected in the directions given in the Srauta-sutras that a sacrificer is allowed to cohabit with a *savarna* wife (of the same caste as his own) but not with the Sudra one. The rules of Panini regarding *Abhivadana* (salutation as a mark of respect to elderly persons in the house) show that the presence of wives of the lower castes (especially the Sudra one) in a family and the consequent inevitable association of the higher caste ladies with them in the house has brought down the general level of womanly culture and led to a deterioration in their social status.

Among the Grihya-sutras, only the *Asvalayana Grihya-sutra,* and most of the Dharma-sutras, mention eight forms of marriage. Of these, two call for an explanation, *viz.*, the *paisacha,* in which a girl is carried off while her relatives are sleeping or are indifferent and the *rakshasa* in which the girl is abducted after a fight with her relatives. Probably the names of these marriage forms all derived from the names of the tribes among whom those peculiar marriage customs prevailed. That such immoral practices should be dignified as "forms" of marriage may be due to the desire not to deny some kind of a social status to the unfortunate girl-victim and her progeny, once the regrettable occurrence had taken place and was beyond recall. The Grihya-sutras give detailed rules regarding the proper seasons for marriage, the qualifications of the bride and the bridegroom, and the various stages of the marriage ceremony. The bride should not be a *sapinda* relation of the bridegroom's mother nor belong to the same *gotra* as his own. The bridegroom should be a young man with intelligence, character and good health, and should, above all, come from a good family.

The various stages of the marriage ceremony are as follows : (1) the wooers formally go to the girl's house; (2) when the bride father has given his formal consent, the bridegroom performs sacrifice; (3) early in the morning of the first day of the marriage celebrations the bride is bathed; (4) a sacrifice is offered then by the high priest of the bride's family and dance of four or eight women (not widows) takes place as part of the *Indrani karman;* (5) the bridegroom then goes to the girl's house and makes the gift of garment, unguent, and mirror to the bride who has been bathed a mentioned already; (6) the *Kanya-pradana* or the formal given away of the bride now takes place, followed (7) by the *Pani-grahana* the clasping of the bride's right hand by the bridegroom with his own right hand; (8) the treading on stone; (9) the leading of the bride round the fire by the bridegroom; (10) the sacrifice of fried grains; and the most important ceremony of all, (11) the *saptapad* (the couple walking seven steps together as symbolic of their lifelong concord) follow in due order. Finally the bride is taken in a ceremony to her new house. It must be taken for granted that the offering of oblations to the fire and the feasting of Brahmanas take place at every important stage in this as in other ceremonies.

As regards the age of the bride, the prescriptions of the Grihya-sutras differ. The older texts which describe the consummation of marriage as the *Chaturthi-karman,* or the ceremony of the fourth (night immediately after the marriage), evidently imply that the bride is of mature age. The more modern Grihya-sutras and the Dharma-sutras, however, lay down the rule that the bride should be *nagnika (lit.,* naked), *i.e.* one who has not yet had her monthly period or one whose breasts are not yet developed. Evidently they only reasonable explanation of the incongruity is that the earliest practice is reflected in the older texts.

The prevalence of polygamy is implied in the *anuloma* system of marriage. The elements of bride-price (*sulka*) are discernible in the Asura form of marriage, where the father of the bride is gladdened with money, and there are hints of a dowry in the Brahma and Daiva forms of marriage where the father gives away the daughter after decking her with ornaments.

The prayers and rites of the ceremony clearly indicate that matrimony was a holy bond, and not a contract, and that progeny (especially male progeny) was the goal of marriage. As in the preceding age, the birth of a daughter was not welcome, and this fact in a way reflects the comparatively inferior position of women in society. All the sacraments, except that of marriage, are performed in the case of women without the recitation of Vedic *mantras,* and the *Upanayana* is not performed for them.

The woman, however, held an honoured position in the house-hold. That a life of merriment, song, and dance was not denied to her is seen from certain sacraments in which women are asked to dance and sing. The presence of women who are not widows is particularly desired in marriage and other sacraments. The *Gobhila Grihya-sutra* allows the option that the wife may offer the morning and evening oblations in place of the husband, because "the wife is as it were the house." That there were wives who desired to keep their husbands under control is clear from a rite prescribed for the purpose.

Since the Dharma-sutras treat of the widow's right in the property of her husband, the possibility of the general prevalence of *sati* is ruled out. The *Vasishtha Dharma-sutra* speaks of the marriage of widows under certain circumstances, and the son of a remarried woman is one of the twelve sons enumerated in the Dharma-sutras. So the remarriage of widows was not as strictly prohibited as it appears to have been in later days. In the marriage rules of the Dharma-sutras local customs were recognized. The *Baudhayana Dharma-sutra,* for example, states that marrying the daughter of a maternal uncle is a southern custom. The custom of *niyoga* (levirate) or appointment of widows is recognized by the Dharma-sutras which give detailed rules laying down the circumstances under which it is permissible. Some of the later Dharma-sutras, however, condemn it.

On the whole the Dharma-sutras take a more lenient attitude towards women than the Smritis of a later age or the customs and practices of the present day. Baudhayana (II. 2. 4. 6.) quotes the injunction, which also occurs in the *Manu-smriti* (IX. 81), that "a barren wife should be abandoned in the tenth year, one who bears daughters (only) in the twelfth, one whose children (all) die in the fifteenth, but she who is quarrelsome without delay." But Apastamba (II. 5. 12-14) forbids the husband to take a second wife unless the first wife has no male child or neglected her religious duties. According to Vasishtha (XXVIII. 2-3) a wife shall not be abandoned "even though she be quarrelsome or tainted by sin or have left the house, or have suffered criminal force, or have fallen into the hands of thieves." Even a wife, who has committed adultery, becomes pure and is taken back by her husband after she has done proper penances (*Vas. Dh. S. XXI.* 8-10). As noted above (Ch. XXV, p. 495), Apastamba (I. 10. 28. 19) imposes severe penalties on a husband "who unjustly forsakes his wife." On the other hand "a wife who forsakes her husband has only to perform a penance" (*Ap. Dh. S.I.* 10. 28. 20). This is a singular instance where the law or custom accords more favourable treatment to the wife than to the husband. Again, "a father who has committed a crime causing loss of caste mut be cast off, but a mother does not become an outcast for her son." Similarly, the male offspring of outcasts are (also) outcasts, but not the females, who may be married, even without a dowry, by a twice-born (*Vas. Dh. S.* XIII 47. 51-53). It is interesting to note that according to Baudhayana (V. 1. 15-16) "if a damsel has been abducted by force and has not been wedded with sacred texts, she is to be treated like a maiden and may be lawfully married to another man." Lastly, there is a general agreement among the Dharma-sutras that a grown-up maiden, if not given in marriage in proper time by her father, may choose her own husband after waiting for three years (or months). At the same time the general principle is already enumerated in the later texts that "the males are the masters of women." "Their father protects them in childhood, their husbands protect them in youth, and their sons protect them in age; a woman is never fit for independence" (*Vas. Dh. S.* V. 1-2. *Bau. Dh. S.* II. 2. 3. 44-45).

Education

The Upanishads are a living testimony to the high intellectual attainments of the age. The stories of Svetaketu Aruneya and Satyakama Jabala in the *Chhandogya Upanishad* and the well known passage in the *Taittiriya Upanishad* (I. 11) containing instruction (*anusasana*) given to the student at the end of his studies show that the educational system maintained the high standard and lofty ideals of the preceding age (*ante,* p. 474). Some special features of the educational system are prominently brought out in the Upanishads. We find, for instance, that the highest position in society is willingly yielded to the intellectual aristocracy. Kshatriya kings like Janaka were famous for their learning, and respect was paid to them by all including the Brahmanas. There are many instances on record where even the Brahmanas learned the sacred knowledge, particularly philosophy, from the Kshatriyas. The story of Aruni, in the *Brihadaranyaka Upanishad,* shows that even old men became pupils. But the most pleasing feature is the frequent reference to women teachers, many of whom possessed the highest spiritual knowledge. The famous dialogues between Yajnavalkya and his wife Maitreyi (*Brih.* IV. 5) and Gargi Vachaknavi (*Brih.* III 6. 8) show the height of intellectual and spiritual attainments to which a woman could rise. The stories of these noble and gifted ladies stand in sad contrast to the later age when even the study of Vedic literature was forbidden to women under the most severe penalty.

The Upanishads contain several lists of subjects of study, and these give us a good idea of the wide range of knowledge in those days. One such list[1] mentions not only Veda, Itihasa, Purana, and spiritual knowledge (*Brahma-vidya*), but also grammar, mathematics (*Rasi*), chronology (*Nidhi*), dialectics (*Vakovakya*), ethics (*Ekayana*), astronomy, military science, science of snakes, and knowledge of portents (*Daiva*). There are a few more branches of knowledge mentioned in this list whose exact scope or nature cannot be defined, such as *Pitrya* (science relating to the manes), *Deva-vidya* (etymological interpretation of divine names or knowledge of gods), *Bhuta-vidya* (demonology or science of elements), and *Devajana-vidya* (dancing and music or mythology). It is extremely unfortunate that we have no texts preserved regarding many of the subjects. But the list shows how a very comprehensive view of education was developed at the close of the Vedic Age. It also demonstrates that the six subjects comprised in the Vedangas, to which a detailed reference has been made above (Ch. XXIV, p. 477), formed only a small portion of the curriculum of study, and not the whole of it, as is popularly believed.

The Sutras give us a detailed account of student-life, which commenced with the *upanayana* (initiation). This ceremony, the essential features of which have been described above (Ch. XXIII. P. 459), in all probability originally signified the formal reception of an adult youth as a regular member of the (Aryan) tribe, a custom that prevailed among all primitive people. But, as described in the Grihya-sutras, it is dominated by priestly interest, and this is not unnatural, as in this age, education was entirely under the control of the priestly class, and *upanayana* meant also the formal initiation into an educational career of boys of the three higher castes, at the ages respectively of eight, eleven, and twelve. The youth to be initiated wears a new upper garment or skin (which is to be that of a deer, goat or cow, according to his caste), a lower garment of a suitable colour, a staff of the prescribed length, and a threefold twisted girdle. According to some Grihya-sutras he wears a sacrificial cord also. This equipment constitutes the educational uniform, as it were, of the youth.

Moral training formed the very pivot and the backbone of the educational system, and development of character was the one ideal that dominated it. The numerous vows and observances *oblitory* on the pupil (*Brahmacharin*) after the *upanayana*, which was a kind of initiation by the *Guru* (teacher) into a new spiritual life entailed on him the most rigorous discipline for the prescribed period during which he was to live religiously as a student in the house of his teacher. His daily routine is begging alms, collecting far looking after the sacrificial fires, tending the house (of the teacher learning, and practising austerities. Thus the ancient university were residential, and a more perfect tutorial system was followed than is possible in any modern university, the pupil being under the observation of the *Guru* all the twenty-four hours. The daily begging of alms, on which the student lived, was for the inculcation of "plain living and high thinking," and had probably little or nothing to do with the financial status of the pupil or of the teacher with whom he resided. Attention may be drawn in this connection some interesting practical and thoroughly human aspects of the educational system of this age as reflected in the *Taittiriya Upanishad* (I. 11.). After the admonition "let the *acharya,* the parents etc., be your gods" comes the frank admission that the preceptor as human beings, may have their weaknesses, but it is not these by their good points that have to be copied by the pupils. A very practical streak is revealed in the advice to the pupil to continue the family-line by marrying and begetting children, to attend to *kusal* or well-being (in a wordly sense), to make gifts and practise charity for fear (*bhaya*) of public opinion or out of shame (*hriya*), if not out of the generosity of the heart.

The intellectual side of education was developed through the numerous subjects of study referred to above. Naturally more particulars are given of the study of the Vedic literature. It centred round the preservation by means of recitation, of the Vedas of the particular *Sakha* to which the pupil and the teacher belonged or of as many Vedas as could be mastered by the student. Memory was a specially valued faculty and was most assiduously cultivated. The period of studentship is normally fixed at twelve years or until the pupil has mastered the Veda, though it may extend to much longer periods such as twenty-four or twenty-eight years, nay even for life in exceptional cases. The extent of the daily lesson is described, among others, in the Grihya-sutras of the *Rigveda.* The pupil is to recite either the hymns belonging to each *Rishi* or each Anuvaka of the short hymns (*Kshudra-Suktas*) or an Anuvaka or one verse in the beginning of each hymn. This option was a very useful and practical concession which enabled students, who did not aspire to become Vedic scholars, and (probably and chiefly) students of the Kshatriya and Vaisya castes, to fulfil nominally their duty of learning the Veda. The Grihya-sutras proceed on the assumption that all the three higher castes are to go through a period of studentship, but more often than not, the Kshatriya studied the art of war and the elementary knowledge of administrative functions. There are, however, traditions regarding the Kshatriyas studying philosophy and having taken a prominent part in the evolution of the doctrine of Brahman. As for the Vaisyas it is unlikely that they were engaged in the intellectual life of the day, and at least in their case, this very practical device of a nominal fulfilment of the duty of Vedic study was very useful. A student who knew the first and last hymns of a *Rishi* or of an Anuvaka was by a sort of fiction, considered to have known the whole portion belonging to the *Rishi* or the whole Anuvaka.

The rite prescribed for victory in debates shows that literary debates were very common and were held in special assembly-halls which used to be crowded.

The Vedic term commenced with the *upakarman* (inauguration) ceremony which was performed some time during the bright fortnight of the month of *Sravana* (July-August) when the herbs appear, or during the rainy season. The Vedic study then went on for four months and a half or five months and a half or six months, at the end of which came the *utsarga* (discharge) ceremony which formally closed the first term in the month of Pausha or Magha. After this there is a break of study for five or six months (this appears to be the long vacation of the ancient University), or according to the Dharma-sutras, the Vedas may be studied during the bright fortnight and the Vedangas during the dark one. This almost year-long recitation was subject to numerous interruptions (*anadhyayas*) or "no-lesson" intervals, the special occasions for which were births and deaths, portents, miracles, lightning, thunder, rains or eclipses, and the normal occasions for which were the 14th and 15th days of the two fortnights, the last days of the season, etc. The large number of these interruptions is not surprising, as the ancients held that it was better that there was no recitation at all, rather than that a slight error should creep into it, get repeated in the transmission by word of mouth, and later become an integral part of the Veda itself. The preservation of the Vedic literature by a meticulously correct and scientific method of recitation, down to the minutest part of it, *viz.*, the syllable, was their chief concern, because in the beginning, Vedic texts were not available in a written form and even later were not usually reduced to writing. Impure places were to be avoided for the recitation. Personal purity and good health were also essential conditions for study. After the completion of the whole course came the ceremony of *samavartana* after which the student, now called a *snataka* (*i.e.*, one who has taken a ceremonial *bath* marking the termination of his studentship), can either enter upon the married state and found a household or (in exceptional cases) remain celibate, his principal duty being now the management and support of his family from which he was so long absent.

The *samavartana,* however, does not spell the end either of Vedic study or of moral training. The *snataka* can carry on both either in the role of a teacher or student. The *svadhyaya* or daily recitation of Vedic texts is part of the fivefold daily routine, consisting of the performance of the five *mahayajnas* (Great Sacrifices of the married *snataka* in the capacity of a householder, and comprises portions not only of the Samhitas, Brahmanas, and Kalpa sutras, but also of the Gathas, Narasamsis, Itihasas, and Puranas. In the Dharma-sutras of Vasishtha and Apastamba there is an inhibition against learning a language spoken by barbarians, and the study of *sabda-sastra* (philology) is condemned in the *Vasishtha Dharma-sutra* (X. 20).

The teacher is the central figure, the very pivot of the educational system with which the State had very little to do.

He introduces (*upa-ni*) the boy to studentship, and is in sole charge of his moral, mental, and physical upbringing. The teacher, who was a *snataka,* provided in his own house for the boarding and lodging of a certain number of pupils, and received from them, in return daily service during the period of studentship and, at the end of its gifts voluntarily given by the pupils. Though, thus in a measure the teacher was compensated for his labours, the relationship between the teacher and pupil was in no sense mercenary, but sacred and almost spiritual. Very often the father himself was the teacher, and the student received education at home. The teacher was the friend, philosopher, and guide to the pupil. The initiation of the boy into studentship by the teacher marked, as it were, his second birth (in a spiritual sense), whence the term *dvija* ("twice born") was applied to the three higher castes, who only had the privilege of *upanayana*. The pupil was to show the very greatest respect to the teacher. It was not, however, merely a one-sided discipline. The teacher also observed certain vows and rules while he taught.

That physical training was an integral part of the educational scheme is clear from the unmistakable trend of the numerous prayers for the grant of vigour and strength that form part of the *upanayana* ceremonial. The begging of alms, morning and evening the gathering of fuel-sticks, and the manual labour involved in the worship and tending of the fire made for sufficient hard work or exercise for the student. The recitation of the vedic texts was a strenuous vocal exercise. But the *pranayama* or control of breath, which formed part of the daily *sandhya* (morning, noon, and evening prayers) adoration, was not only an ideal exercise for the lungs, but also one that penetrated to all parts of the body as any careful student of Yogic exercises can testify. Lastly must be noted the fact that the *danda-pradana* (handing the staff to the initiated boy) was a regular ceremony, and the staff was certainly an excellent weapon for self-defence.

Manners and Morals, Habits and Customs

Hospitality not only continues to be recognized as a binding social obligation, but is raised to the status of a religious duty, for an offering of food to the guest attains to the rank of a sacrifice as one of the five daily *mahayajnas*—the *atithi-yajna* or "guest sacrifice"—which the householder must perform. There is a formal definition of an *atithi* or guest, and an authorized list of important guests, which includes a teacher, a *Ritvik* (an officiating priest), a king, a snataka, a father-in-law, and a son-in-law. Though a guest could arrive at any time it was understood that a wedding and a sacrifice were the recognized (or official) occasions for their reception in the grand style. A seat (or a special enclosure, if the guest is *persona grata*), water for washing the feet, *argha* water, water for sipping, and the *madhuparka* (a mixture of curds, honey, and *ghi*) are first offered to him. After this, food containing meat is to be offered to him, and if the occasion is a special one (such as a sacrifice or a wedding), a cow is offered and it is for the guest to have it killed for him or to set it free.

The Grihya-sutras, while prescribing the code of conduct for a *snataka,* give us a fairly detailed account of the manners and etiquette of those days. Only a few rules can be cited here. A scentless wreath is not to be worn. Girls must not be subjected to banter or ridicule. Walking or bathing naked or running without sufficient justification are prohibited. There is a taboo on certain words in the language of a *snataka* ensuring linguistic purity.

Great insistence is laid on moral purity. Self-restraint is the keynote of the ethical code prescribed for the householder. Human nature, of course, is the same in all times and climes, and warnings against the faithlessness of companions, pupils, servants, and wives are conveyed indirectly through rites prescribed for their prevention. Purity of mind is as much inculcated as purity of body. Abstinence of all kinds and respect for elders and for self are valued qualities.

The ancient Indians did not cultivated cleanliness as a mere habit. They had developed a passion for it. The sipping of water (*achamana*) and washing of feet are insisted on everywhere as a preliminary to any, even the most trivial, ritual act. The *pavitrakas* (strainers or purifiers made of grass), the use of which is so marked in the ritual, are symbols of purity and cleanliness. If a bird befouled the person of a *snataka*, or an unknown drop of water fell on him, *mantras* were to be recited by way of expiation. The habit of early rising is also well cultivated.

Life in this age was so thoroughly ritualized that it is difficult to distinguish habits from sacraments. Thus the many rites prescribed for the safety and good health of the mother and child, before and after delivery, may be looked upon as records of remarkable usages also. The rite of *Simantonnayana* or parting of the hair in the middle in the fourth or seventh month of pregnancy is an interesting custom. The child is given two names of which one is to be kept secret. The occasional counting of years, not from birth but from conception, is a practice that has a parallel in the Buddhist ordinances. The Grihya and the Dharma-sutras recognize the force of local custom, and allow it to modify or sometimes even override some of their rules. The father's greeting to the son, when either of the two has returned from a journey, which takes the form of smelling or kissing him on the head, is also a noteworthy custom.

Amusements and Entertainments

As in the preceding age, dancing, and both vocal and instrumental music, were well cultivated. In the *Simantonnayana* ceremony mentioned above, the wife is asked to sing a song merrily, and in the marriage ceremony the bridegroom sings a *gatha* after the treading on the stone by the bride. The vogue of the musical recitations of the *Samaveda* is responsible for the rule in the *Gobhila Grihya-sutra* that the *Vamadevya gana* may be sung, by way of a general expiation, at the end of every ceremony. The lute players are asked to play the lute in the ceremony of "parting the hair," and four or eight women (not widows) perform a dance in the marriage ceremony. The restrictive rule that a *snataka* is not to practice or enjoy a programme of instrumental or vocal music or dance, shows their popularity. It seems that the game of dice was looked upon as a popular entertainment, since a common gaming hall is one of the official public buildings of a town.

The reference in the *Maitrayaniya Upanishad* to a *nata* (actor) changing his dress and painting himself proves the popularity of dramatic shows in this age.

Food and Drink

Rice and barley were evidently the staple articles of diet as they were to be offered into the Grihya fire every morning and evening. Wheat was probably not eaten daily, as it is mentioned but rarely. Beans (*masha*), kidney beans (*mudga*), mustard seed (*sarshapa*), and sesamum were known.

Milk and its products were very liberally used (*ante*, p. 461). The various forms of butter (due to its varying temperature) were distinguished for purposes of the ritual as : clarified (*sarpis*), melted (*ajya*), and solid (*ghrita*) butter. Among other esculent things may be mentioned honey and *kshara-lavana* (saline food), which is supposed to be an irritant and an excitant, and therefore to be eschewed in the interests of celibacy.

The culinary art was fairly well developed. The different processes or operations through which the grains passed before being cooked or eaten are indicated in words like *akshata-dhana* (unbroken grain), *laja* (fried grain), and *saktu* (ground grain). Washing the rice-grains, husking them, baking them, and sprinkling *ajya* over them, and then taking them out of the oven are the different stages mentioned in the preparation of a *sthalipaka*. The preparation of a *Purodasa* (sacrificial cake) implied great skill in baking as it was baked on a pan with varying number of hollows (resembling saucers) which gave a variety of forms to it. An *Apupa* was a cake baked on a flat vessel. Boiled rice (*odana*) eaten with *ghi*, milk-rice (*payasa*) which seems to be a preparation very much akin to *dudha-paka* so popular in Gujarat now, *krisara* (boiled rice mixed with sesamum seeds), *dadhimantha* and *madhu-mantha* (cooked ground grains mixed with curds and honey respectively), and rice and barley gruel are other preparations known. The scum of boiled rice made a very light liquid food. Vegetable food (*saka*) is mentioned as a substitute for flesh-food (*mamsa*).

But people in this age were by no means vegetarians. They ate flesh freely, not excluding even beef which was prohibited later owing to the growing reverence for the cow. Flesh-food must be served to the Brahmanas invited to a *Sraddha* dinner, vegetable food being allowed only in its absence. Similarly in the ceremony of the first feeding of the child with slid food, among the various foods enumerated in order of merit, the flesh of a goat, partridge, or another (specified) bird, and fish come first, boiled rice mixed with *ghi* coming last. Similarly food offered to a guest of consequence *must not be without flesh.* The merit of vegetarian diet is, however, recognized in the rule that a student should abstain from flesh.

In spite of condemnation in the earlier texts (*ante,* p. 462) and severe penalties laid down in the Dharma-sutras, *sura* continued to be a favourite intoxicating drink. The four or eight women who give a dance at the marriage ceremony are to be regaled with food and *sura*. In the *Anvashtakya* ceremony, *sura* is to be offered along with the *pinda* offerings to female ancestors. The *Srauta* ritual is naturally full of references to the Soma drink in the numerous Soma sacrifices, and the *Grihya* ritual in the fitness of things ignores it.

Dress and Decoration

Two pieces of clothing – one the *uttariya* or upper, and the other the *Antariya* or lower – constituted the dress proper (the simple two-piece suit) of males and females; the lower garment being put on first and then the upper one. If one could afford only one garment, then a part of the lower garment may be turned into and worn as an upper garment. In the case of a student, the skin of a deer or goat made a very holy upper garment. The *Aprapa dina pata,* mentioned by Panini, is a garment that reached down to the ankles. A longish piece of cloth wrapped round the head in the fashion prescribed by local custom constituted the ceremonia head-wear or turban. The same piece could be used informally to veil the head. Red turbans and clothes were used for magic rite and silk ones (*kshauma*) for sacrificial purposes.

Woollen blankets were in use. In the list of garments prescribed for the *upanita* (the initiated boy) figure cotton, woollen, linen, and hempen cloth. Silk was also used (as there is a reference to the silk-worm giving silk). Upper garments were dyed with the juice of *lodhra* flowers or with madder or indigo. Black clothes were also worn (as they are forbidden for one practising the *Sakavara vow*). The colour scheme of dyed garments prescribed for the *upanita* is interesting; reddish yellow, light red, and yellow for the Brahmana, the Kshatriya, and Vaisya respectively. The art of washing was, of course, known, though a particular sanctity attaches to a brand new (*ahata*) garment.

A pair of garments, a turban, ear-rings, shoes a bamboo staff and an umbrella, complete the full dress (of a *snataka*, for example) the *danda* (staff) is not only a weapon of defence in the ordinary sense, but also a magic wand for warding off evil. The staff of the *upanita* boy was to be of palasa, bilva, or nyagrodha (or udumbara wood, according to his caste. It had to be of a standard height. In one Grihya-sutra (the *Asvalayana*) there is an invocation to the shoe not to pinch. So shoes have had a tendency to pinch in all times and climes!

Two important sacrament—the *Chuda-karman* or tonsure ceremony for the child, and the *Godana* or the ceremony of hair cutting at the age of sixteen or eighteen—give us a clear idea of development of the tonsorial art as known and practised in those days. Among the details of the *Chuda-karman* are the use of a mixture of hot and cold water to moisten the hair, the tangled locks of which are disentangled with a porcupine's quill—the hair-comb of the ancients—the anointing of the fresh butter, the holding of a mirror before the boy, the use of the razor (with a copped or wooden handle) which makes a sound while it is being plied by the barber on the head, and the leaving of a lock or locks *(Chuda)* according to local custom or family usage. A layer of *Kusa grass* is kept ready to receive the hair that is cut off. In the *Godana* ceremony, the beard and the hair, both on the head and under the arm-pits, are shaved and the nails clipped. Generally a top-lock was kept, as a clean-shaven head was not fashionable. The *Asvalayana* and *Sankhayana Grihya-sutras,* strangely enough, prescribe both these rites for girls. Probably local custom determined what quantity of hair was to be kept and in what fashion in case of both boys and girls. The *Simantonnayana ceremony* (of parting the hair of a pregnant woman mentioned above) clearly shows that the two (shaving) ceremonies did not much affect the growth of hair on a girl's head. Does this ceremonial parting of the hair in pregnancy suggest that unmarried girls and married women who were not mothers did not part their hair but merely brushed it back?

It is noteworthy that the toilet and make-up of the ancient Indians were not as simple as we fondly imagine. Collyrium (*an-jana*), an eye-salve, and other salves for anointing the body before the bath and the nose and mouth after the bath, *sthagara* (a fragrant application) (sea *ante, p. 463*). A bath-powder, and group sandalwood are among the toilet requisites mentioned in connection with the "bath" ceremony which entitles a student who has completed his studies to become a *snataka* (graduate) and settle down as a householder by marrying if he so chooses. Garlands and *kundalas* (an ear ornament) are put on after the *snana* (bath). Three gems strung on a woollen or linen cord make at once an ornament and a charm for a bride when tied round her body. A perforated pellet of sandal or *Badara* wood, overlaid with gold and worn round the neck, and a *Badara-mani* or pellet of *Badra*-wood tied to the left hand, are among the other known ornaments worn by both males and females with distinction.

Health and Hygiene

A keen desire to live a long and healthy life of a hundred years was the natural outcome of the optimistic and robust outlook which the ancient Indians had in life. Their healthy slogan was "prevention is better than cure." Consumption seems to have been a notorious affliction. Epilepsy (*Kumara or Apasmara*), to which children were particularly liable, was very much dreaded and its popular name *Svagraha* indicates that it was supposed to be a seizure or attack by a dog-demon. Among the symptoms are stiffness of the body and much crying aloud. Another peculiar illness, to which again boys were particularly susceptible, was named *Samkha* in which the patient utters tones resembling the sound of a *Samkha* (conch when blown. These diseases were sought to be cured by propitiating the demons by means of rites and ceremonies which afford a *glimpse* into the curious superstitions and magical belief of the period. From the number of rites prescribed during the period of pregnancy, it seems that a safe delivery was a matter of great concern. Headache and poisonous bites are among the minor ailment receiving ritual treatment.

That there were centenarians is seen from the rules in the ceremoney of *Udakadana* or the offering of water librations to the deceased. Fasts are so often recommended in the ritual that the inference their beneficial effects on health.

A knowledge of hygienic principles may be inferred from many a rule in the Grihya-sutras. Cleanliness is most stringently enforced and the free use of water is recommended at every step in the ritual for cleansing purposes. A regular daily bath is insisted on. Floors are to be swept, sprinkled over with water, and smeared with cow-dung. There is a peculiar mixture prescribed for smearing the floor and walls of the lying-in chamber, which must have been an effective disinfectant. A *snataka* is not spit or eject phlegm in the neighbourhood of water. That special places were set apart to receive dirt, accumulated waste, and sweepings is seen from the direction to offer a *bali* on such "heaps of sweeping." Easing was to be done on ground covered with grass and not on the bare ground. That cow stables and cemeteries were located out side the village or town is seen from the rule which enumerated them among landmarks in a journey along with a forest, a boundary-tree, etc.

ECONOMIC CONDITION

Agriculture and Cattle

The fact that there is a domestic rite synchronizing with each stage in the agricultural life of the people, and practically none associated with urban life, shows that the Indians of those days lived mostly in villages, and that the village agriculturist was the true representative of ancient India. There are rites for putting the bulls and oxen to the plough, for sowing, and for honouring *Sita* (*lit.,the* "Furrow") or the Goddess of Agriculture. There is a sacrifice offered to Kshetrapati or the Lord of the Field. The Agrayana sacrifice is the religious ceremony of partaking of the first fruits of the harvest. There are further sacrifices signalizing the other agricultural operations such as threshing, the reaping of the crop, and putting it into the barn.

Rice and barely seem to be the staple crops from the reference to the two harvests – that of barley in the hot season and of rice in autumn. From the direction to the *snataka* to live on the gleanings of uncultivated corn it may be easily inferred that there were extensive stretches of uncultivated land and forest, and wild rice and grains used to grow on untitled tracts. That a cultivated field was measured by the quantity of seeds that could be sown in it is seen from the term *prasthika* in Panini, applied to a field that accommodated a *prastha-full* of seeds.

The cattle were an invaluable possession. "Make us rich in cows" is almost the burden of the *mantras* that accompany the various Grihya rites. All the three higher classes were engaged in cattle-keeping in their own way. There are ceremonies like the *Sulagava* and the *Baudhyavihara* for propitiating Rudra and his hosts, so that they may avert evil from cattle and the fields. Cattle served, in a way, as the standard of value or as a medium of exchange, because kings kept their own herds and gave away thousands of cows as *dakshina* (sacrificial fees). The *Darshadvata* sacrifice, described in the Srauta-sutras, is virtually a description of the tending of the cows of a Brahmana in Kurukshetra for one year. The Grihya-sutras prescribe a number of minor rites on the following occasions :

(1) When the cows are led to the pasture lands;

(2) When they run about;

(3) When they return; and

(4-5) before, and after, their entry into the cow-pen.

The Srauta-sutras prescribe sacrifices for the acquisition and recovery of lost cows. Prayers and rites for prosperity in cattle and their good health abound in the Grihya-sutras. There is ceremony for cattle-breeding called *Vrishotsarga* on the release of a (stud-) bull among the cow. *Yakshma*. A wasting disease affecting cattle, was very much dreaded. It was a custom to brand the cows.

But the cows were not prized merely as property. A feeling of reverence for them is rapidly growing. A suspension of study (*anadhya*) is ordered in the presence of cows that have eaten nothing. Persons riding in a chariot are to do homage to a cow, if met with on the way. Paradoxically enough, in the eyes of the ancient Indians, this veneration of the cow is not only not inconsistent with cow-sacrifice prescribed in funeral ceremonies, on the occasion of a guest-reception, or the *Sulagava* (spitox) sacrifice, but is, in a sense, responsible for it. Nevertheless, the feeling of reverence for the cow went on steadily gathering volume, and the rule for sacrificing a cow was often relaxed by the admissibility of an alternative or substitute ritual whereby the cow was saved.

Trade and Commerce, Arts and Industries

There is a rite called *panyasiddhi* (ensuring success in trade) in which a portion of the particular article of trade is cut off and sacrificed in the fire with the prayer : "If we carry on trade to acquire (new) wealth by means of our (old) wealth, may Soma...prosper that." (*Hiranyakesi G.S.* I. 15. 1). The Vaisya class was engaged in trade and commerce. The Sutras of Panini refer to imports from the north and his *Vamsadi gana* mentions several forest products such as *Vamsa, Kutaja, Ikshu* (sugar-can) and *Mady* (liquor). The Grihya-sutras rule that the relations of a deceased person are not to cook in the house, but to buy food during the period the death-impurity, shows that food could be bought either from public eating houses (?) or private individuals. A system of coinar or currency was probably in vogue, though quite a large volume trade was managed by way of exchanges in kind. Panini mentions coins like *Pana, Karshapana, Pada,* and *Vaha* and measures and weights like *Adhaka, Achita, Patra, Dorna,* and *Prastha*. But, noted above, Panini's date is uncertain, and he probably belonged a period later than 600 B.C.

Implements and vessels of copper, iron, stone, and earthenware are mentioned and must have been locally manufactured. Gold spoons and brass gongs were in use. Silver was also known. Upper and lower millstones, mortar and pestle, cups, ladles, dishes spoons and swords were required for domestic as well as ritual us. Baskets made of leaves are referred to. *Katas* or rush mats man of *Virina* grass were offered as seats for the married couple. The varieties of cloth worn were cotton, linen, woollen, silken, and hempen. That spinning and weaving were daily occupations the people is clear from the rule that the initiated boy is to put a garment spun and woven on the same day, and from the prayer offered to "Goddesses who spun and wove" (*Apastamba G.S.* I. 10. 10). A *Chatra* or spindle is mentioned. A flourishing dyed industry may be inferred from the prescription of garments different colours for the initiated boy.

Many of the occupations, professions, arts, crafts, and industry have been already incidentally referred to in the previous section (also cf. *ante,* Ch. XXIII, pp. 466-7). We may notice here the profession of the butcher, who was so indispensable in the anin sacrifice that there was actually a priest called *Samitri* who did the necessary slaughtering to the accompaniment of sacred verse. Manual labour was so highly prized that it was compulsory for student as a householder (*snataka*).

House-building and Means of Transport

The fact that the Grihya-sutras include the ceremony of house building among sacraments to be performed by the rich and the poor alike, leads to the obvious inference that in those days of vast of spaces and long stretches of jungle, a site for a house and building materials were available to a poor man of three higher classes a nominal cost. The site should be undisputed property. It should be non-saline and with trees, herbs, or at least grass, grow thereon. It should not be hollow or undermined and be of colour prescribed for the particular caste. From the direction given, we gather that a spacious house contained an assembly or drawing room a provision-room, and a resting or a retiring room, with a nursery and privy standing detached from the main building. Measuring the site, digging the pits for the posts, two of which were erected in each of the four directions, setting up the door-jambs and the gable, putting up the beams and the grass or thatch on the roof, are some of the operations detailed. The position of the main door is carefully specified. The setting up of the water-barrel—evidently an arrangement for water supply—is part of the house construction. The repairs and renovation of the house are to be effected every year with ceremony about the same time as the *Divali* holidays of the Hindus. From the directions to erect huts and enclosures in the course of a day, it seems these could be improvised with ease. The consecration ritual for ponds, tanks, wells, covered reservoirs of water, and gardens, shows that these were public works for general use though they seem to have been constructed by individuals rather than by the state; for the ritual is of the domestic type.

Bridges, roads, cross-ways, and spuares where four roads meet are referred to. Among the means of transport may be mentioned the very popular, light two-wheeled wooden carriage (*ratha*). Horses and oxen (even cows occasionally) were the common draught animals, the elephant being employed for a state journey or a procession. Horses, asses, camels, and elephants were ridden for purposes of travel. Rivers were crossed by rafts and boats, and if necessary by ships.

REFERENCE

1. The list is given in *Chhandogya,* 7. 1, 2 and is repeated several times in the following sections. The interpretation of the technical terms denoting different branches of knowledge is not always easy. Max Muller takes *Brahma-vidyaa* as three of the Vedangas (*viz., Siksha, Kalpa, and Chhandas*); *Devajana-vidya* as "the sciences of the genii, such as the making of perfumes, dancing, singing, playing, and other fine arts": *Pitrya* as "the rules for the sacrifices for the ancestors"; and the Veda of the Vedas as grammar (*SBE,* I, pp. 109-10).

5 Literature As Source of Hindu Economic Ideas

According to the established tradition, the whole of the Vedic literature is divided into four groups :

(1) the Samhitas,

(2) the Brahamanas,

(3) the Aranyakas,

(4) the Upanisads.

This division reflects the historical order in which this literature developed : the Samhitas are the most ancient, while the works of the other groups complied in later times are commentaries and additions to the Samhitas. For this reason the Samhitas are referred to as the Vedas proper. In the broad sense, the Vedas comprise all four groups, the entire complex of the Vedic literature.

To have a correct conception of the structure of the Vedas, it is also necessary to take into account that not a single group of the Vedic literature is an integral whole. The Samhitas are four collections—the Rig Veda, the Sama Veda, the Yajur Veda, and the Atharva Veda. Each Brahmana pertains to a certain Samhita : the Rig Veda has Brahamans of its own, and the same is true of the Sama Veda and the other Vedas. The Aranyakas and the Upanisads directly adjoin either the Samhitas or the Brahmanas: any given Samhita or Brahmana has Upanisads and Aranyakas of its own. However, inasmuch as the Brahamanas have the Samhitas for their source, the Aranyakas and the Upanisadas pertaining to them also adjoin the Samhitas. It follows that the whole structure of the Vedas is ultimately determined by the structure of the Samhitas. It is therefore sometimes said that the entire Vedic literature consists of four Vedas (the Rig Veda, the Sama Veda, the Yajur Veda, and the Atharva Veda) and each Veda, of four parts (the Samhitas, the Brahamanas, the Aranyakas, and the Upanisads). Thus the structure of the Vedas reflects both the original division into four Samhitas and the main stages of the historical development of the entire Vedic literature. Of greatest importance, however, is the historical principle.[1]

Let us consider in brief the epoch of the origin and development of the Vedas.

Although many valuable scholarly works have been written by Indologists over a very long period of time (some two and a half thousand year in India and about two centuries in Europe), many problems in the origin and dating of the Vedas remain unsettled. The literature on the Vedas, both old and new, contain widely varying data (from the 5th and even 6th to the middle of the millennium B.C.). Most modern scholars believe, however, that the period of the Vedic literature covers about a thousand years between the middle of the second and the middle of the first millennium B.C.

In the second half of the second millennium B.C., a class society was being formed in the valley of the river Ganges and the areas adjoining it in the south and south-west. The question of what that society was like, concretely, is still open. Although slavery was widespread in India, it did not play a decisive role in the existing mode of production, as was the case in Ancient Greece and in Rome, for instance. The social structure in India at that time cannot therefore be unconditionally described as slave-owning. We know Marx's view of the existence of the Asiatic mode of production. The solution of the question at hand should be sought for in determining the concrete historical meaning of this concept, we believe.

As social inequality and class contradictions in India grew and deepened, and formerly free people with equal rights came to be divided into four groups or *varnas* (Brahmana,

Kshatriya, Vaisya, and Sudra) differing in their social position, rights, and obligations. The brahmana *varna* consisted of priests, kshatriyas were mostly warriors, vaisyas, farmers, artisans, and traders. Sudra was the lowest group in the social organization. The origin of the state in India apparently dates to this time, too.

Thus the thousand years in which the Vedic literature took shape are characterized by essential changes in the structure of the social life of ancient India. The stages of the this development of ancient Indian society reflected in the Vedas.

The earliest and the largest of the Vedas is the Rig Veda ("the Veda of the hymns"; Rig means "laudatory verse", "ode", or "hymn"); it contains 1,028 hymns and more than 10,500 verses, the same as the *Iliad* and the *Odyssey* taken together. It is divided into ten books, or *mandalas* (lit "circle" or "cycle"). The Rig Veda hymns are laudatory verses addressed mostly to the gods personifying the forces or phenomena of nature. In the 11th and 10th centuries B.C. the separate groups of the Indo-Aryan tribes that penetrated India came to form a single community. Modern Vedic scholars believe that the hymns of these tribes took shape as the Rig Veda at the same time.

The Rig Veda hymns took form in the separate clans or tribes and their early redactions were apparently the product of collective creativity. The poets complied the Rigs to praise the gods and the forces of nature. Natural phenomena were regarded as, omnipotent, omniscient, omnipresent, and just divinities. People turned to them with their pleas and requests and offered them sacrifices, a person's life, well-being and happiness were thought to depend on these sacrifices.

Ancient Indians believed that a sacrifice accompanied by the appropriate hymn has magic force and can propitiate the gods. The hymns or the separate acts of sacrifice were distributed throughout the seasons, months, and hours of the day. Nature itself had cult elements ascribed to it: for instance, thunder was thought of as God India throwing his mace.

What was the first sacrifice? Who offered it? These questions are answered in the hymn to the *purusa* (X, 90). *Purusa* is, according to the hymn, the personification of the cosmic principle, the "universal" man. He is the source of all the universe, of the present and future. The gods extracted from him, as it were, the cosmic worlds, the animal world, and men. Of particular interest are verses 11 and 12 of the hymn expounding the myth of the origin of the *varnas* : the Brahmans, or priests, were made of the *purusa's* mouth, the Kshatriya, or warriors, out of his arms, the vaisya, or peasants, shepherds and artisans, out of his thighs, and the sudra (the people without any rights serving the higher varnas), out of his feet.

Many centuries passed before the hymns compiled at different times and in different areas of India were collected in the books of the Samhitas. The compilers of the Rig Veda Samhita had the aim of preserving the hymns from distortion or oblivion; their purpose was in no way liturgical. Indications of this are the sheer volume of the collection and the diversity of the hymns, some of which have no bearing on religious service. In later practices the pronouncement of the holy hymns of the Rig Veda was combined with sacrificial rites (just as the reading of the *yajus* and *samans*[2]) and entrusted to the priest.

The legendary collectors of the hymns and compliers of the Vedas were called the *rishis* (poets or wise men). The *rishis* are not historical personages; they appear now as the authors of the hymns of the Vedic literature.

The Rig Veda hymns contain attempts of the ancient Indians to read the mysteries of being. The first sparks of philosophical thinking emerge in the living fabric of the myths and legends comprising the greater part of the Vedic literature. The authors of the hymns ask these questions: "Why does the sun not fall although it is not supported by anything or fixed to anything?", "Where is the sun by night?", "Where go the stars by day?", "Whence comes the wind, and whither goes it?", "Why does it raise no dust on celestial roads?" etc. Those were the first attempts to find cause-and-effect connections in nature.

The authors of the hymns refer to the existence of matter from which came (or out of which was made) the world surrounding man.[3] What was their conception of this matter?

"What was that tree, and what was that forest, out of which they [the gods] made the earth and the sky?" [x, 37]–there was no single answer given to this by the ancient wise men: the prime substance was believed to be air, or water, or fire, etc. (X, 72; X, 88; X, 121].

Of particular philosophical interest is hymns 129 from the 10th book of the Rig Veda, to which we shall refer as the cosmogonic hymn.[4] Let us quote the text of the hymn in full :

Then even nothingness was not, nor existence.
There was no air, nor the heaven beyond it.
What covered it? Where was it? In whose keeping?
Was there then cosmic water, in depths unfathomed?

Then there was neither death nor immortality,
Nor was there then the torch of night and day.
The One breathed windlessly and self-sustaining.
There was that One then, and there was no other.

At first was only darkness wrapped in darkness.
All there was only unlimited water.
The One who came to be enclosed in nothing,
Arose at last, born of the power of heat (tapas)[5]

In the beginning desire descended on it–
That was the primal seed, born of the mind.
The Sages who have scorched their hearts with wisdom
Know that which is kin to which is not.

And they have stretched their cord across the word,
And know what was above the what below.
Seminal powers made fertile mighty forces.
Below was strength, and over it was impulse.

But, after all, who knows, and who can say,
Whence it all came, and how creation happened?
The gods themselves were later than creation,
So who knows truly whence it has arisen?

Whence all creation had its origin,
He, whether he fashioned it or whether he did not,
He, who surveys it all from highest heaven,
He knows—or may be even he does not know.[6]

Thus the most elementary and primary state of all that is according to the authors of the hymn, something amorphous, undivided, and devoid of concrete content, and in this sense it cannot be said either to exist or not to exist: "There was then neither what is nor what is not." It is noteworthy that there is a tendency towards, or certain beginnings of, a spontaneous materialistic worldview, for the beginning of all beginnings here is matter, some "material" underlying all objects and phenomena of cosmic space. The One (Ekum) existed always, according to the hymns, it was not born of anything; that is the eternally existing of which everything is born—the entire universe, the sun, the earth, heaven, air, water, etc.

But where and what is that motive force through which the "indistinct" became "distinct", taking the definite forms of individual objects and phenomena? The authors of the hymn assert quite positively that the motive force is in the initial matter itself, it is inherent in it ("That One breathed by itself without breath", that is, without an external impetus, without an impact from some outside force). Is this not a profound insight that movement is the property of nature itself?

Neither do the authors of the hymn resort to the concept of outside impetus when they answer the question of the source of self-movement of One ("What did it begin with?"). The first inner impulse which started the formation of the "world of differences" they call "desire" ("love" in the English translation.—*Tr.*) :

"Love overcame it in the beginning, which was the seed sprining from mind.....[7]

In the formation of nature, the original attributes of the One were: that which is and that which is not, top and bottom, night and day, death and immortality, etc. as for gods they appeared later "the gods came later". At best, god "in the highest heaven" "knows whence it [the universe] arose", but that is doubtful too ("does even he not know ?").

Thus the cosmogonic hymn of the Rig Veda is, in our view, fundamentally a realistic work with strong elements of spontaneous materialism and dialectics.

It stands to reason that we speak of the rudiments of materialistic worldview in the first place in the sense that the authors of the hymn view nature and understand it the way it is, without any outside additions. We therefore cannot concur with Prof. Radhakrishan's interpretation of the category of one mentioned in the hymn in the spirit of objective idealism: "The Nasadiya hymn.... makes nature and spirit both aspects of the one Absolute. The Absolute itself is neither the self nor the other, is neither self-consciousness of the type of I, nor unconsciousness of the type of not–I. It is higher than both these. It is a transcending consciousness. The opposition is developed within itself. According to this account the steps of creation, when translated into modern terms, are : (1) the Highest Absolute; (2) the bare self-consciousness, I am I; (3) the limit of self-consciousness in the form of another ...."[8]

The hymn is here obviously modernized in a religious and idealist manner. We come across similar attempts in Max Muller,[9] S. Dasgupta, Aurobindo Ghose, and other bourgeois historians of Indian philosophy.

There are no grounds at all for ascribing such concepts as "the absolute" and "transcending consciousness" to the authors of the cosmogonic hymn. There could be no reference to these concepts in the hymn since divorcing consciousness from matter and raising it to an absolute preceding matter is an epistemological phenomenon characteristic of a later period of the development of philosophical thought. If we turn to similar cosmogonic hymns of other peoples and countries, we shall see that they bear no traces of objective idealism either.

For example, the Babylonian Hymn of Creation (*Enuma Elis*) dating approximately from the middle of the second millennium B.C., says that the original mass of matter contained a contradiction between two irreconcilable hostile forces, the forces of order and chaos. Because of this contradiction all that is divided into earthly and celestial phenomena. The earthly and the celestial, interacting between themselves, in their turn fell into opposites : the animate and the inanimate, the divine and the non-divine, etc. The formation of world order is in this hymn presented in a mythical and concrete shape rather than abstractly or philosophically.

Another example. Let us recall Homer, Hesiod, and other representatives of pre-scientific thinking in Greece. Homer does not consider the origin of the world. In his view, one heaven, visible to us, exists, and one earth. The heaven surrounding earth consists of two parts, the higher (ether) and the lower (air). Lightning proves the existence of fire in heaven. Besides, there also exist earth and water. "We are all water and earth," says Homer, Hesiod (8th 7th cent. B.C.) was the first poet in ancient Greece to contemplate the origin of the universe in his *Works and Days, Theogony* etc., Hesiod says :

.....First Chaos was, next ample-bosom'd Earth,
The seat immovable for evermore
Of those immortals, who the snow-topt heights
Inhabit of Olympus, or the glooms
Tartarean, in the broad-track'd ground's abyss.
Love, then, are most beautiful amongst
The deathless deities; restless he
Of every god and every mortal man
Unnerves the limbs; dissolves the wider breast
By reason steel'd, and quells the very soul.
From Chaos, Erebus and ebon Night :
From Night the Day sprang forth and shining air,
Whom to the love of Erebus she gave.
Earth first produced the Heaven; whose starry cope,
Like to herself immense, might compass her
On every side, and be to blessed gods
A mansion unremoved for eye. She brought

The lofty mountains forth, the pleasant haunts
Of nymphs, who dwell 'midst thickets of the hills.
And next the sea, the swollen and chafing sea,
Apart from love's enchantment. Then, with Heaven
Consorting, Ocean from her bosom burst
With its deep-eddying waters...[10]

In conclusion let us recall a document that only recently became known to the Soviet scholarly circles. In the 16th century, when Spaniards invaded the territory which now forms Mexico and Guatemala, they encountered there a number of Indian tribes at a relatively high cultural stage. The Quiche tribe was discovered to have a book entitled *Popol-Vuh* ("the book of the community") which contained cosmogonic myths showing great resemblance to the Indian, Babylonian, and Greek ones. One of the hymns reads: "At the beginning, everything was in suspension.... Nothing had existence..... There was only the calm sea and the sky in all its extension but empty. Only immobility, obscurity and silence existed. The gods were in water... Creation began. First emptiness filled itself, water retired and earth emerged out of it; mountains and valleys were formed; currents of water divided themselves, streams ran freely between hills, and the waters were separated when high mountains appeared.....[11]

Thus we see that cosmogonic mythical hymns are works of a historical period when philosophical thought made its first steps, and those steps were towards spontaneous materialism and dialectics.

Other Samhitas have a less independent significance than the Rig Veda. Thus, the second Samhita, the Sama Veda (the Veda of Songs), is a collection of melodies composed mostly for the verses of the Rig Veda: 1,474 verses of the 1,594 are already there in the Rig Veda. The third Samhita, the Yajur Veda (the Veda of Sacrifices), duplicates the Rig Veda to a considerable extent, too. The fourth Samhita, the Atharva Veda (the Veda of incantations), differs considerably from the rest. Its hymns are in the nature of incantations. According to the Vedic tradition, the first three Samhitas are regarded as the most "authoritative" and genuine Vedas. As for the Atharva Veda, it was, in the opinion of a number of scholars, composed later and in a different social environment. The Rig Veda speaks of the time of subjugation of non-Aryan tribes by the Aryans, while the Atharva Veda narrates of the time when the Aryan and non-Aryan ideals were confused, that is the views of different peoples were synthesized.[12] The Atharva Veda may serve as the source for the study of the evolution of the philosophical and religious ideas throughout the first period of the Vedic literature.

The Brahmanas, that is, the books written by and for brahmans, are commentaries on the Samhitas. They are collections of instruction, or manuals, for the performance of rites prescribed for the master of a house. The Brahmanas contain a great many legends and historical lays pertaining to the social life of ancient Indian society. The Brahmanas are written in prose. Their emergence is due to the changed social conditions, and in the first place to increased social inequality, to the development of the *Varna* system. Besides, many of the Veda texts became incomprehensible in the course of time, the religious cult changed in many respects, and the ritual became much more complicated. Performing the duties of a priest became a profession. The significance of the sacrifices changed, too. Their purpose was no longer propitiating the gods but affecting humans through the sacrifice to the gods, directing their activities towards the performance of personal and social needs and norms of behaviour. Class differentiation of society gave rise to new social norms. For instance, the Satapatha Brahamana (II 5.2.6) says : "Varuna, doubtless, is the nobility, and the Maruts are the people; he thus makes the nobility superior (uttara) to the people; and hence people here serve the Kshatriya, placed above them.... And the people being the nobleman's food....."

Thus sacrifices and all kinds of rituals were now used to legalise and maintain the new social conditions and in the first place to regulate the relations between individuals belonging to the different *varnas*. Let us consider several fragments as an illustration.

The legend of the origin of the so-called ritual of the water grandson (Aitareya Brahmana II, 19) gives an idea of the social inequality in Indian society of the times. Kavasha was forbidden by the Brahman priests not only to participate in but also to be present at the sacrificial rite for the sole reason that he was the son of a slave woman. Kavasha was banished to the desert with the words: "How should the son of a slave girl, a gamester, who is no Brahman, remain among us and become initiated...? ...he should die of thirst.." True, being persuaded of the great mental and spiritual gifts of Kavasha, later the Brahman priests declared him to be a favourite of the gods and counted him among their own, the fraternity of the wise. Kavasha is believed to be the author of hymns some of which were included in the tenth book of the Rig Veda.

The Aitareya Brahmana (VII. 29) places the accent on the fact that the sudras serve the three upper castes (the kshatriyas, the brahmanas and the vaisyas). The ritual details are now arranged in such a manner as to show, for instance, that a Kshatriya is above the people.

As a servant, a sudra is essentially the master's property; the master's will is his law. A sudra's own property may be taken away from him; he may be severely punished or even killed at the master's whim. (AB VII,29).

The fragment (AB VIII.24) on the *purohita* (family-priest) show the great significance attributed at the time to priests, their authority, and their role in society's spiritual life.

On the historico-philosophical plane, the fragment on "dying round the Brahma" (AB VIII. 28) is worthy of the closest attention. It is very important for reconstructing the history of the formation of the Brahman category. Here Brahman is not yet a substance, as it will become in the Upanisads, but it is no longer a chant or prayer as in the Rig Veda—it is rather the support of nature round which the dying and the birth take place the transition of one natural phenomenon into another (of a lighting into rain, of the moon into the sun, of the sun into fire, etc.).

Some historians of philosophy believe that the Brahmanas, being commendatory literature, have no great value on the philosophical plane. We cannot concur with this view, for the Brahmanas are the connecting link between the Samhitas and the Upanisads, and some important categories of ancient Indian philosophy were developed in them.

The Satapatha Brahmana is, in our view, one of the most interesting collections of Brahmanas in terms of the history of philosophy. What is man? What does man consist of? What is his essence? Which of the senses brings man the most reliable (genuine) information about the surrounding world, vision or hearing? Perhaps, neither the one nor the other but the thought? These are the questions with which the authors of that collection were concerned.

Of great interest are the propositions on the links between thought and the word (1, 4) and between human thought and emotion (X, 3). The sense-process and thought have, according to the authors of the Satapatha Brahmana, a common basis—breath (X, 3). In this connection, reference is made to Atman as the essence ("soul") of man, and not man alone but also of any object or phenomenon in general. Each natural phenomenon that comes into being (is created) "searches for its own Atman", that is, assumes in the course of time definiteness and takes up a suitable place among other natural phenomena; only after that does it "become manifest,—more defined, more substantial". Later, in the Upanisads, Atman is interpreted as an absolute body or absolute soul.

In the fragment "The Thought as the Primary Source" (X, 5), the authors go back to the theme of the Nasadiya hymn (the Rig Veda, X, 129)—the nature of the primary source ("There was then neither what is nor what is not"). However, the Rig Veda declares the undifferentiated original matter to be the beginning of all beginnings, while the Satapatha Brahmana presents thought as that kind of beginning. Thought is here regarded as a kind of potential, a possibility, while the real world and nature are the state in which thought assumes a clear shape or, to put it in modern terms, is realized possibility.

The fragments "Truth and Untruth" (II, 2), "The Genuine and the Non-Genuine" (XI, 5) afford a view of the development of ethic categories. Very characteristic is the tendency of opposing the "genuine" and the "non-genuine", of "good" and evil", etc. The gods are the carriers of the genuine and the Asuras or demons, the carriers of the non-genuine. Noteworthy is idea that men of truth and honesty are, as a rule, more contemptible and poorer than false and dishonest men, though ultimately he "who speaks the truth diligently" triumphs, while he who speaks untruth comes to naught. This ethical principle is later developed in the Upanisads.

The fragments "On the Origin of All from That Which Is Not" (VI, 1), "Water as the First Beginning" (XI, 1), and "Brahman" (XI, 2) confirm that the Brahmanas, being the product of the creativity of different authors, contain the beginnings of two principle philosophical directions, materialist and idealist.

According to one of these texts (VI, 1), the primary principle had no concrete form of existence and was in this sense "the non-existent". But it was not absolute emptiness, for it "breathed" possessing various "desires" and even wisdom ("The Rishis, assuredly, it is they that were the non-existent"). Here too Prajapati is mentioned as the force arising out of the non-existent and becoming the creator (or multiplying in the form) of the concrete kinds of existence. Prajapati created the Brahman, the "foundation" of the universe. According to another fragment (XI, 1), the primary principle of all that is is water. From water an embryo came into being, and from the egg, Prajapati. Prajapati gave birth to the earth, the space, the sky, the seasons, the Asuras, etc. The authors of the third text (XI, 2) believe that "The Brahman (n) is the first-born of this All". The Brahman created the gods, etc. Thus in the fragments quoted here the Brahman is regarded as the original form of organization of all that is (a kind of "universal community") and as a creative force.

Of considerable interest is the Vaisvanara fragment (X, 6). It was apparently compiled at a time when ancient Indians proceeded from the study of natural objects to the study of man himself. The Vaisvanara is everything give to man; everything that forms the basis of man's life; everything by which man exists. Vaisvanara is not only earth, water, space, wind, sun, sky, it is also man's eyes, mouth, breath, etc. The authors of this fragment want to find out what is essential for man to live. They do not yet consider the task of studying man's essence. The ancient Indians endeavoured to solve that task later, in the Upanisads.

The Aranyakas and the Upanisads were compiled later than the other parts of the Vedas.

The Aranyakas (lit, "silvan"; the silvan texts) are usually referred to as the literature of the hermits and for the hermits, that is, those wise men who withdrew to the forest hermitages to contemplate the "essence of all that is and what takes place". Escape from the villages to the forest was due, first of all, to considerations of safety. At a time when social contradictions grew, the priests were afraid to indulge in high contemplation before the eyes of the people, and still more were they afraid of the people beginning to contemplate themselves; they were afraid of the people's free thought. In accordance with the changes in the historical situation, the priests shifted the accents in their interpretations of the Samhitas and Brahmanas. Their goal was justifying and supporting the domination and political activity of the powers that be. There is a distinct tendency in the activities of the priests to monopolise the interpretation of the Vedic texts. He who has no property has no right, and can have no right, to interpret the scriptures. "The wise men of the forest" ascribed great significance to the efficacy of the word and also believed in the magic force of ideas and topics. An incorrectly understood or, still more dangerous, pernicious idea could have a harmful effect on the attitudes and moods of men, of the whole people. The wise men of the forest took great pains to shroud ideological problems in mystery and the super-natural, making them inaccessible to the uninitiated.

The Aranyaka texts contain speculative interpretations of the traditional Vedic themes—the beginning of all beginnings, the *atman*, the *purusa*, man, his essence, predestination, etc. the authors of the Aaitareya Aranyaka, for example, place the main emphasis on the origins of all that is and its links with the concrete phenomena of nature.

The fragment traditionally referred to as Ukta (II, 1) is a hymn to speech. The world surrounding man (the earth, the sky, space) and man himself have their existence in speech, they are expressed in words.

In the third and the fourth parts of the second book of the Aitareya Aranyaka, the *atman* is placed in the centre of everything that is : it is not merely the creator of all (of the worlds, water, light, etc.) but the carrier of the rational principle as well. It is important to note this here, for later, in some of the Upanisads, the *atman* and reason come to be regarded as identical concepts.

The fragments tentatively called "The Atman" and "Man" (II, 3) draw a distinction between man, animal, and plant. Man as a reasoning being is placed above all (he towers above all the worlds). At the same time it is admitted that the *atman* (and, consequently, reason too, to some extent) is inherent implants and animals. Man's superiority to animals lies not only in the fact that he is endowed with reason to a greater degree than others, but also in his reason being continually perfected (the *atman* becomes purer and purer in man). Man never rests content with what he attains (whatever he attains, he tries to surpass). As for animals, they do not know goal-directed activity (their knowledge of other animals derives from hunger and thirst).

The Upanisads is the properly philosophical part of the Vedas. They are not books or philosophical treatises in the proper sense of the word but rather collections of texts compiled by different authors, mostly anonymous ones, at different times and on different subjects. Each texts is a rather short exposition of the philosophical musings of some author speaking on behalf of a legendary or semi-legendary wise man. It is not surprising that the texts contain diverging interpretations of worldview problems: the two tendencies, materialist and idealist, can be discerned here too. The Upanisads, covering a long historical period, are usually divided into "early" and "late" ones. The earliest are Chandogya, Brhadaranyaka, Aitareya, Kausitaki, Taittiriya, and Kena. It should be noted that the Upanisads, as a rule, are unpolished stylistically; they remind one of an uncorrected stenographic script. True, that has some positive aspects as well: we observe the first philosophers in their workroom, as it were.

Let us give a short characteristic and outline the content of some of the Upanisads.

(1) *The Chandogya Upanisad* is part of the Chandogya Brahmana consisting of ten chapters. The first two chapters of this Brahamana are devoted to the sacrificial rituals' the rest comprise the Chandogya Upanisad proper. In the view of some scholars, the Chandogya Upanisad is the most ancient of all the Upanisads. It may be regarded as the first philosophical part of the Vedas.

The Brahmanas attributed prime importance to invoking the forces of nature (the deities) through action (*karmamarga*), that is to say, to the act of sacrifice itself, while the Chandogya Upanisad stresses the internal sacrifice, the one in the mind and the soul, rather than external ritual. The word, speech, and contemplation assume ever greater significance. The authors of the Chandogya Upanisad believe everything to be mortal, including the gods. That which is mortal becomes immortal only when it is expressed in the world, finding asylum in it (I, 4).

The *om* syllable, consisting of three letters (sounds), "a", "u", "m", symbolized the three Vedas – the Rig Veda, the Sama

Veda, the Yajur Veda. In some *slokas* (couplets), the *om* syllable is called the Udgitha, a Sama Veda hymn chanted aloud.

In the subsequent sections the Udgitha is given a broader interpretation (I, 2; 1, 8-9). The Udgitha is regarded as something noncontradictory, homogenous, and eternal. For instance, breathing through the nose cannot be revered as the Udgitha, for it perceives both that which smells good and that which smells evil. Speech is not to be revered as the Udgitha, formen speak both truth and untruth. But breathing through the mouth can be revered as the Udgitha, for it does not perceive that which is contradictory. It is the Udgitha, it is the Atman.

The fragment "The Pranas" (III, 13) gives the first classification of the pranas, or kinds of breathing. The authors of this fragment endeavour to establish a functional connection between the types of breathing, on the one hand, and the mental and sensor processes in the human organism, on the other. A characteristic parallel is drawn between the senses and the human properties and nature; vision is analogous to the sun; hearing, to the moon; speech, to fire; and thought, to rain. The sky is said to be illuminated with the same brightness "as that which shines within mankind".

The following fragments deal mostly with the interpretation of one of the basic concepts of ancient Indian philosophy—the Brahman concept (the substance of primary reality).

The Upanisads contain no precise and clear definition of Brahman. The texts are mostly rough notes comprising a plethora of materials with no direct bearing on the problem of primary reality.

In discussing Brahman, the authors of the Upanishads place considerable emphasis on the "foundation". What is the foundation of man? In other words, what is that property of man without which he cannot exist? Man will continue to live if he is deprived of vision, speech, or hearing, but he cannot live when deprived of breath. It follows that man's foundation is breath.

What is the foundation of all the other objects and phenomena of nature? What becomes of that which is deprived of the foundation (whither go the creations of this world?). Whence returns that which acquires a foundation? The quality of a universal "foundation" is ascribed to Brahman : everything proceeds from it and everything merges in it. Uddalaka, one of the authors and personages of the Chandogya Upanisad, regards any singular thing as closely connected with its substantial basis. Only the substance has genuine existence ("truth in clay", "truth in iron"). As for the singular thing, it is merely a manifestation (of the substance).

Uddalaka and the other authors of the Upanisads link up the concept of Brahman with that of *atman*. *Atman* is regarded as an eternal and invariable essence (*atman* that does not grow old or die) but at the same time an active one: in accordance with its genuine desires and intentions, it is constantly active in this world, particularly in the body of man.

The concept of *atman*, the soul world, which developed from the concept of *purusa* world (in Rig Veda) and the early conception of the personal creator (Prajapati), ultimately grows in the Upanisads into the impersonal cause of all that is, Brahman. Brahman appears as the force, materialized in all the existing objects, which creates, maintains, and returns unto itself all the worlds, the whole nature.

The Chandogya Upanisad contains a number of interesting ideas of epistemological significance. For example, Uddalaka studies the substantial link between thought (or mind) and man's breath as the "foundation" (VI, 8,2). It is necessary to distinguish, says Uddalaka, between the idea of a thing and the thing itself, the "names" of the objects or phenomena of nature from the objects and phenomena themselves. In his view, the knowledge of the name helps to attain a desirable effect within the compass of the name, that is, it helps man to orient himself in the situation surrounding him. In this sense, a name should be appreciated ("revered"). But that is not enough, for there is something greater than the name. What is that which is greater or more important than the name? Speech. But speech is not the most important thing either. Thought is greater than speech, for thought comprises both name and speech. The idea or design is greater than thought, for name, speech, and thought merge in a unity due to design. The next step in the hierarchy, the one that follows thought, is the concept of breath, according to Uddalaka: breath is greater than all the others, for man cannot live without breath.

Of great interest is the fragment on cognition of cognition. It goes without saying that we do not have here a theory of knowledge yet, but the very fact that the problem of the conditions and purpose of human cognition is mooted here is noteworthy. There are also interesting aphorisms here: he triumphs in arguments on whose side is the truth; he attains happiness who acts, etc.

The fragment on "The Five Fires" (V, 10) contains ideas which will later be developed in the doctrine of reincarnation and of requital (*karma*). According to the conceptions of the ancient Indians, a human soul only temporarily leaves this world for the next after a person's death. As it gets back to this world, the soul may find itself in the body of an unworthy person or, which is worse, in the body of an animal (a dog, a pig, etc.), reptile or insect. Everything depends on that person's behaviour during the first sojourn in this world: as you sow, you shall reap.

(2) *The Brhadaranyaka Upanisad* adjoins the Satapatha Brahamana. Just as many other Upanisads, its themes differ but little from the Chandogya Upanisad. Here too, the main thing is establishing the essence of Brahman and Atman.

There are different views of Brahman inherent in the text of this Upanisad. In one of the fragments (I, 6) the concept of Brahman is used to denote the substantial basis of the separate groups of homogenous phenomena : speech is the Brahman of all the names (for "it upholds the names"); eyesight is the

Brahman of all the forms (for "it upholds all forms"); *atman* is the Brahman of all works (for "it upholds all works").

Another fragment (II, 3) ascribes to Brahman two principal forms of existence, *sat* and *tya*. *Sat* is the material or bodily being; it is motionless, inert, transient, and mortal. *Tya* is the immaterial being; it is eternally in motion and immortal.

In the main body of the texts (the teachings of the wise man named Yajnavalkya), Brahman is described as the universal common basis (substance) of all that is. Everything proceeds from Brahman, everything returns to Brahman. Brahman has different properties : it has eyesight, sense of tough, hearing, mind, and knowing. However, when it is in a purely substantial or Brahmanic state (one without another"), it does not and cannot manifest any of these properties, as for any property to manifest itself, it is necessary that "another" should exist, that is, some object relative to which this property may be manifested (IV, 3, 31). Yajnavalkya believes this division of that which is into the "one" and "another" to be only possible in this earthly world.

The Brhadaranyaka Upanisad reflects tendencies both towards objective and subjective idealism and towards materialism. Yajnavalya's teaching contains objective-idealist elements, whereas the fragment "On the Sources of Names, Forms, and Works" (I, 6) shows rudiments of subjective idealism (the individual *atman* as the source of works). The author of the fragment "water as the Primary Source" (v, 5) take a materialist view of the basis of all that is.

Epistemologically, of considerable interest is the fragment "Thought, Speech, Breath" (I, 5, 3). The connection between the senses and reasoning is discussed here. There is no sensation without mind ("a person sees with the mind, hears with the mind").

(3) *The Aitareya Upanisad* adjoins the Rig Veda and consists of three chapters.

This Upanisad apparently gives an explanation of the

meaning of sacrifices, expounding also the author's view of the nature of man, the content and purpose of his life. The fragment "Atman as the Source of Life" is evidence of strong rationalist tendencies in Indian thinking of the times ("The entire universe is based on consciousness").

(4) *The Kausitaki Upanisad,* also called Kausitaki-Brahmana-Upanisad, which adjoins the Rig Veda, consists of four chapters.

The main content of this Upanisad is the doctrine of transmigration of souls, or reincarnation (*samara*). According to this doctrine, the eternal and immortal soul (*atman*) passes after death from one bodily integument into another. Depending on the deeds (*karma*) in the past incarnations, the good and bad deeds, the soul may be reborn in most diverse forms, in the bodily integuments of man, animal, or even insect. The end of reincarnations is believed to be the highest goal of life: it can only be achieved through the merging of the soul with Brahman.

(5) *The Taittiriya Upanisad* adjoins the Yajur Veda and consists of three parts or Vallis. The first or the Shiksha-Valli deals with phonetics, the seconds and third (Brahmananda - Valli and Bhirigu-Valli), with the knowledge of Brahman.

The rationalist tendency in the Upanisads is most strongly manifested in the Taittiriya Upanisad. The principal thesis of this Upanisad is this : everything in human life depends on knowledge. Knowledge directs the acts of men, all gods respect knowledge, and Brahman itself is ultimately knowledge.

As distinct from the pessimists of the Maitri Upanisad, the authors of the Taittiriya Upanisad are full of faith in man, his abilities and creative potential. According to them, man can be happy (attain bliss) on this earth, too. To attain it, however, he must be clever, strong, and adroit (II, 8).

In some texts, *atman* (the spirit, the soul) is regarded as something secondary or derivative.

A different view is adopted in the fragment "On the Ways of Knowing Brahman" (III, 1-9): "from mind, indeed, all living beings are born and having been born, they remain alive by mind and at the end they absorb into mind again"; mind is Brahman.

(6) *The Kenopanisad* adjoins Sama Veda. All of the four parts of which this Upanisad consists are devoted to the interpretation of the essence of Brahman. Brahman is presented as the ultimate cause and purpose of the existence of this world, of nature: everything was born from Brahman and must ultimately return to it. Characteristically, this Upanisad speaks of only one path of man to Brahman– the path through knowledge rather than through abstinence or any other type of asceticism.

(7) *The Isa Upanisad,* also called the Isavasya Upanisad, adjoins the Yajur Veda.

This Upapnisad was apparently compiled in late Vedic times when many concepts had been to some extent worked out and the Upanisad doctrine in certain parts canonised.

In the view of the authors of the Isa Upanisad, there are two objects of knowledge and correspondingly two kinds of knowledge. The first and the primary object of cognition is the substance (*atman-Brahman*). A knowledge of substance is referred to as genuine Knowledge (*vidya*). He who has this knowledge attains "Supreme knowledge". The second object of cognition is the objects and phenomena of nature; he who cognises them, attains only "inferior knowledge", for he knows things, objects, and phenomena, but he does not know their genuine nature; in this sense, this knowledge is absence of knowledge (*avidya*). *Avidya* complements *vidya*.

The division of knowledge into two kinds, *vidya* and *avidya*, and consideration of the conditions of the links between them is evidence of profound penetration by the Isa Upanisad authors into the essence of epistemological problems and of their historical far-sightedness.

This problem would arise before philosophers of various countries, in one form or another, centuries later: knowledge would be divided into speculative philosophical reasoning and concrete scientific knowledge. At present, the difference between speculative philosophical and concrete scientific knowledge has assumed the nature of confrontation and contrariness in bourgeois philosophy, with the two sides considering essentially an identical system of fundamental proposition under opposite axiological signs.

At both of these poles it is actually recognized that scientific methods are inadequate for the solution of the basic problems of human existence.

Marxism-Leninism decidedly rejects the belittling of the role of science. It regards science as a decisive factor of social progress, but it certainly does not deny the essential significance of other forms of culture.

(8) *The Katha Upanisad* adjoins the Yajur Veda and consists of two chapters. It principally contains a legend of the poor pious Brahman who sent his son as a sacrifice to the god of death (Yama). The legend is full of profound philosophical musings.

(9) *The Prasna Upanisad* (prasna means "question") adjoins the Atharva Veda. It consists of six sections containing six questions posed before a wise man by his disciples who are mostly interested in the nature of the original cause of all that is.

(10) *The Mundaka Upanisad* adjoins the Atharva Veda. It consists of three chapters. Mundaka comes from the word mund "to shave", "to plane", "to cleanse": the teaching of the Upanisad must "cleanse" or free man from errors and ignorance.

(11) *The Mandukya Upanisad* adjoins the Atharva Veda. It *contains* 12 stanzas discussing the meaning of the syllable *om.*

(12) *The Svetasvatra Upanisad* adjoins the Yajur Veda. It bears the name of the wise man who taught it. Svetasvatra

regards Brahman not only as the creator of the world but also as the force that rules that world and actively interferes in its affairs.

(13) *The Maitri Upanisad,* adjoining the Yajur Veda, is one of the later Upanisads. It bears a clear imprint of the scepticism and pessimism characteristic of the end of the Vedic period.

The Upanisads, contain an extensive exploration of the philosophical problems. Considerable emphasis is placed on the search for the foundation of being and its nature. Some thoughts on the foundation of being were expressed in the Samhitas, Brahmanas, and the Aranyakas, but these subjects become predominant in the Upanisads. The Vedic literature throws light on the hard and at times painful search for the substantial foundation, the transition from the less complex concepts to the more complex ones, and the formation of philosophical concepts.

Of great importance for the development of the idea of the primary source were the conceptions of Prajapati, Skandhas, and *prana* expounded in the Atharva Veda, the Brahmanas, and the Aranyakas in the form of myths and legends.

As the Satapatha Brahmana (XII. 1.6) tells us, the beginning of all beginnings was water. The waters bore a golden embryo, and out of the egg came Prajapati ("lord of generation"), the ancestor of all living beings. In what way did all living beings emerge? According to the myth, Prajapati had the desire : "May I be reproduced!"[13] He worked himself up through *tapas,* and immersing himself in the *tapas,* he created the worlds : the earth, the aerial space, and the sky. He spread himself over these worlds like a brooding hen and began to hatch them, and out of them three luminaries arose: the Agni (fire) out of the earth, the Vayu (wind) out of air, and the Aditi (infinity) out of the sky. Then he spread himself over these luminaries too (began to hatch them), and three Vedas emerged out of them, the Rig Veda out of the Agni, the Yajur Veda out of the Vayu, and the Sama Veda, out of the Aditi. In some texts Prajapati is regarded as an inner creative force manifesting itself in the crops (the produce) of each season. Human life is maintained thanks to these gifts of nature.

The *skandha* (lit, "support") conception is an attempt to understand and formulate the ultimate or final basis of all things. The authors of this conception proceed from the fact that all the individual foundations taken together have a common foundation (the foundation of foundations) which supports (unifies and expresses) all the other force however great and powerful they might be (*purusa*, Prajapati, etc.). But the *skandha* category was not developed any further either at the time of the formation of the Upanisads or at the time when the Indian philosophical systems were formed.

A few words about the *prana* or breath conception. Already in the Brahmanas, there is a tendency to depart from deifying the forces and phenomena of nature. Gradually that which stands "behind" the natural phenomena, underlying them as a basis or foundation, becomes the object of worship. If man is to be successively deprived of eyesight, hearing, taste, the sense of smell and touch, he will live; but if man is deprived of breath, he will perish. Hence the conclusion was drawn that the foundation of man is breath; the human body is merely the integument concealing something living and breathing—the *prana*. Prana is "the breath of life", life itself, the vital force. In the Upanisads, the *prana* conception is further developed.[14] *Prana* (in the singular) is identified with the concept of soul (*atman*). *Pranas* (in the plural) are regarded as the "organs of the soul" : breath, speech, vision, hearing, and mind. Finally. *Pranas* are types breathing (*prana, apana, vyana, undana, samana*).[15]

The search for the primary principle culminates in the Brahman and Atman categories—the most important, pivotal concepts of ancient Indian philosophy.

The word Brahman has several meanings in Vedic texts : Brahman "member of the priest Varna, the Varna of the Brahmanas"; the Brahmana "part of the Vedas"; Brahma as the name of one of the Vedic gods; finally Brahman[16] as the philosophical concept with in its turn is used in different meanings, which bears testimony to the complexity of the formation of philosophical categories in Vedic literature.

In some texts, the Brahman concept designates the common properties underlying a group of homogeneous objects or phenomena, unifying them and being their cause: speech is the Brahman of all words, for all names came from speech; *atman* (the human soul) is the Brahman of all works, "for it upholds all works" (the Brhadaranyaka Upanisad, 1.6), etc. In others it is asserted that "there are two modes of Brahman, what has form, and what has no form, the one mortal, the other immortal, again finite one, and the other infinite, again the one existing and the other beyond" (The Brhadaranyaka Upanisad, II. 3). In still other texts, Brahman is declared to be truth and rearded as derivative from the material primary principle : "Water was at first this (world). Water created truth. Truth is Brahman..." (The Brhadaranyaka Upanisad, V. 5). Finally, for the authors of the later Upanisads, Brahman is an absolute substance, the ultimate basis and first cause of all that is, the beginning and the end of all things and beings, that is, that "from where all living beings are born, after being born where they live, and where they ultimately dissolve" (see Taittiriya Upanisad, III, 1).

The word *atman* also has several meanings in Vedic texts, and these meanings reflect the history of the formation of this category : *atman* is the body, or breath, or the individual human soul, or finally the universal soul (the primary principle, the absolute substance identical with Brahman).

In the Chandogya Upanisad (VIII, 7-12), two directly opposite views on the nature of *atman* are expounded. According to the first of them, defended by the Asur (demon) Virocana, *atman* and body are one and the same (in the Indian religious tradition, the seed of materialism was sown by the Asuras). According to the second view, defended by the god Indra, *atman* is immaterial, it is the spirit.

In the Upanisads, the second view triumphed, and its

development ultimately led to identifying *atman* as the spiritual self of an individual person with the absolute soul of all that is: "It is thy soul, which is within every (being)" (The Brhadaranyaka Upanisad, III.5) The seed of this idea was sown already in the myths, which drew a parallel between man and the world surrounding him. Surya the Sungod is, according to these myths, the eye of the world; the parts of the world, his ears; the plants, his hair; Vayu (the wind), his breath; the waters, the seed of life, etc. In short, the world is the universal person, *purusa*. If all the universal members are mentally taken away from *purusa* one by one, his foundation turns out to be the universal breath, the universal *atman*, the absolute soul identical with Brahman. "And everything that is, is Brahman. The Self (*atman*) is Brahman" – that is the result of the search for the ultimate reality of being.[17]

Thus, although there are quite a few materialist ideas in the Upanisads, the objective idealist view of the nature of Brahman and *atman* emerges victorious, particularly in the later Upanisads.

The Vedic literature shows the way in which ancient Indians' attention gradually shifted from the phenomena of the external world to man, his psyche and consciousness. Thus the question of the relations between man and the universal substance (*atman*-Brahman) assumes great importance in the Upanisads.

According to the Upanisads, this world, all the objects and phenomena of the world, man included, proceeded from the *atman*-Brahman; a return into the womb of the *atman*-Brahman is in store for everything in this world. This circle of being may be discontinued : man (his soul) may sink into the substance for good, merging with *atman*-Brahman and dissolving in it. That is the purpose of man's existence in general. At the same time, attaining that goal presupposes a certain activity on the part of man. Here the question of the mutual relations between man and substance assumes the nature of an ethical problem that is linked with the doctrine of *karma* and *dharma*.

According to the *karma* doctrine, every person is required according to his or her deeds, good or bad. Only "he who has correct understanding, who is ever, pure and whose mind is well controlled, reaches that goal from where none is again born" (Kathopanisad, Section I, Part III, 8), that is, he who deserved that during his lifetime on earth. Every person has his *dharma,* his law of the mode of life preordained from on high. For instance, the *dharma* of brahmanas performing religious ceremonies and that of kshatriyas consists in ruling society, implementing state power. The duty of the vaisyas is keeping the brahmanas, the kshatriyas, and themselves, they must till the soil, breed cattle, and practice crafts and commerce. The *dharma* of sudras consists in serving the members of the upper three varnas and practicing the handicrafts. Deviation from performance of the *dharma* may result in that person's soul being reborn in the bodily integument of an animal or even an insect. If the *dharma* is followed faithfully, the soul may be reborn in a person of a higher social standing. The social orientation of this doctrine is quite obvious.

In considering the interrelations between man and the substance, and man's activity, the authors of the Upanishads express certain ideas on knowledge. For some authors, the process of cognition, the transition from ignorance to knowledge, signifies the transition from one (lower) state of *atman* to another (higher) state. According to them, there are four states of *atman* all in all: the waking state, the dreaming state, deep dreamless sleep, and Turiya.

The universal *atman's* sojourn on the earth is thought of as sleep. The first or lower kind of sleep (the first state of *atman*) is the action of *atman* in man in his waking hours, that is, when a person is engaged in his daily pursuits, working and accumulating the necessary skills and knowledge; that is the first or lower kind of knowledge. In the waking state, man and his *atman* are the farthest from the truth (the universal *atman*), for all of his attention is directed at the crude and ungenuine matter.

The second kind of sleep, or the second state of *atman*, is the action of *atman* when a man is dreaming. That is the second and higher kind of cognition, for when a person is asleep, his individual *atman* abandons, as it were, the body and the daily cares and impressions, approaching the universal *atman* and true life.

The third kind of sleep (the third state of *atman*) is the action of *atman* in the body of a person in deep dreamless sleep. In this state, constituting the third type of cognition, the individual *atman* is dissolved in the universal *atman* and enjoys bliss.

In the fourth state (Turiya), *atman* has no experience at all, being completely unware of the material world, merging with the universal *atman* and being identical with it.

It is difficult to say anything definite about Turiya as a kind of cognition. Let the Upanisad speak for itself: "Turiya, Lord of the fourth aspect, according to the wise, remains unaware of the external, intermediate, and internal worlds. He lies beyond both consciousness and unconsciousness; where sight cannot penetrate, nor thought, which is indescribable, bearing no relation to anything. Turiya enjoy pure awareness and experiences peace, bliss and nonduality. He is none other than Atman. Realize Him" (Mandukya Upanisad, 7).

The Upanisads also touch on other aspects of the problem of knowledge. Among other things, great attention is paid to the psychological side of knowledge, to the state of man which, in ancient Indians' view, facilitated the attainment of supreme knowledge – the merging of individual *atman* with the universal one. Thus a number of the Upanisads expound the teaching of knowledge through Yoga (the Mundaka Upanisad, III. 2; the Katha Upanisad, II.3, etc.).[18]

Apart from that, one should note the views of the authors of the Upanisads concerning the meaning of words, the formation of speech out of words, the reason directing thought, etc. The Chandogya Upanisad speak of the inalienable links between thought and its material basis (breath); of the need to distinguish the thought about an object from the object itself; and of knowledge of knowledge. The Brhadaranyaka Upanisad (1.5) considers the connection between sensation ("feeling") and thinking ("thought").

The Upanisad texts contain extremely valuable materials for the study of the laws of transition from particular concepts to general ones, from concrete ones to abstract and finally to the categories.

From the historico-philosophical view, the Vedic literature is of the greatest importance for the study and understanding of the history of all subsequent Indian philosophy.

As has been mentioned earlier, there is a long-standing tradition in India of dividing all philosophical systems into two large groups, orthodox (the true ones, recognising the authority of the Vedas) and heterodox. The orthodox ones mainly include six principal schools: Vedanta, Mimamsa, Samkhya, Yoga, Nyaya, and Vaisesika. The heterodox schools comprise three trends: Charvaka Lokayata, Buddhism, and Jainism.

However, all of these systems or schools took shape under the direct influence of the Vedas, and the traditional division of these systems does not express either an actual essential difference between them or the true character of the impact made on them by the Vedas.[19] As we have said before, Vedic literature contains elements of opposing doctrines, materialist and idealist, with the latter predominant. We must therefore distinguish between two principal channels through which the Vedas influenced the subsequent development of Indian philosophy. Thus the Vedanta idealist conception borrowed from the Upanisads the notions of Brahman as the first cause of all the material objects and phenomena of nature; of *atman* as the absolute soul, the first cause of all the individual "consciousnesses" or souls; of *karma* as the substantial moral law, etc.

The formulation and solution of philosophical problems in the Upanisads (and in the Vedanta of the modern times, too) is extremely original.

For example, the Katha Upanisad formulates the fundamental problem of philosophy as the problem of the essence and correlation of life and death or, on a broader plane, the essence and correlation of the next world (the *atman*-Brahman world) and this one (the world of nature). The literary form of the exposition is the parable.

Let us give the substance of the parable.

Once upon a time a devout Hindus desired divine bounty. For this, he was prepared to offer a sacrifice of something which he held dearest of all. He had a son named Nachiketa. That son noticed that his father sacrificed to the gods those things which were not too dear to him, those from which he could part easily. The son knew that his father loved him very much. So once he had the idea that his father would have to sacrifice him. So he asked his father : "To whom will you give me?" The father evaded a direct answer. A little later the son repeated the question more insistently, but he did not get an answer. Soon he asked that question again. This time the father was so angry that he said, "To death I shall give you."

According to the customs of the country, having said, so, the father had to keep his word, so the son went to Yama, the Lord of Death. As the Lord of Death was absent, Nachiketa lived for three days and nights at his house without the usual courtesies of hospitality. According to the customs of the country, a guest is served by the master of the house and the whole household, who fetch water for him to wash, feed him, etc. When the Lord of Death returned home, he saw that Nachiketa had lived at his house without the pleasure of hospitality, and he said to Nachiketa in an attempt to redress the wrong done him : "Oh Brahman, you are an honourable guest, but in my absence you stayed in my house for three nights without a meal. Choose, therefore, three boons, one in respect of each of these nights as compensation. Oh Brahman, my salutation to you. Be good to me."

So Nachiketa asked the Lord of Death: "O Death, as the first of the three boons, grant that my father may be cheerful and free from anger and anxiety concerning me, and may he recognize and welcome me when I am sent back by you." And Yama said, "Let it be so!"

Nachiketa said : "The second boon that I ask is this. Tell me what I should do to get to heaven. I am eager to know the truth, for in heaven there is no fear, nor are you there, O Death, nor is anyone subject to old age. They have conquered hunger and thirst and they are merry and free from sorrow in heaven." Yama answered: "I shall tell you this, and you will be on firm ground which is hidden from men by darkness." And the Lord of Death told Nachiketa about the "divine fire"[20] which is hidden in man and which is our true credence altar. "The divine fire will lead you to life eternal,"[21] concluded the Lord of Death.

Then Nachiketa said : "This doubt exists. Some say when a man dies 'he exists' and some say 'he does not'. This I should like to know. Explain it to me. This is my third boon."

Yama replied : "Even the gods in ancient times doubted that point. It is very subtle and difficult to understand. Do not keep me to the boon but choose some other, O Nachiketa. Abandon that boon and release me from the obligation."

Nachiketa insisted : "I shall not choose any other boon, answer my question." The Lord of Death said : "Ask for sons and grandsons who will live a hundred years, for elephants, horses, gold and herds of cattle, a vast territory on earth, and a long span of life. And if you can think of some other boon of equal worth, ask also for that: wealth or a long life. O Nachiketa, be king of the wide earth. I shall make you the enjoyer of all your desires... All this I offer you, but do not ask about death."

But Nachiketa continued to insist: "All these things, O

Death, are not everlasting and only decay the vigour of man's faculties. The whole span of life is indeed short, so keep your chariots, horses, dance and music and merry making things with you. Man cannot be satisfied with wealth or enjoy long life, seeing you. That boon alone which I chose is fit to be craved.. O Death, tell me that which people doubt on, regarding the supreme life after death."

So in the end the Lord of Death had to answer the third question, saying: "Worldly objects give either joy or pleasure, and both bind man. Fortune is kind to him who chooses the joyful, but one who follows the pleasurable remains in delusion. The joyful and pleasurable lie before man. The wise man, after discriminating and examining them well, prefers the joyful, but the ignorant, due to greed and attachment, chooses the pleasurable." The Lord of Death praised Nachiketa for seeking wisdom and knowledge. The pleasures which he had offered Nachiketa had not tempted him. So Death continued : "The ignorant deluded by wealth never see the path of the hereafter. 'This is the only world and there is no other', thinking like this, such foolish men become my victims. The wise man abandons both joy and sorrows by meditation on the Self, that ancient illuminous one, difficult to perceive, subtle and unfathomable, who is seated in the heart cave in the body.[22] .... The Atman cannot be known through the study of scriptures, or by much learning or intelligence. He is attained by him whom He chooses. To him alone does the Atman reveal His own Truth.... One who has realized That (Atman) which is soundless, intangible, formless, undiminishing, tasteless and odourless, eternal, without beginning or end transcendental and unchanging, is released from the jaws of death.."

Swami Vivekananda, Aurobindo Ghose, and other outstanding Vedantists of the modern times keep reverting to this problem of problems : what will happen in the hereafter. Invoking the Katha Upanisad, Vivekananda writes that each time a person dies, a dispute arises : some say that he has gone for good, others, that he is still alive. Where lies the truth? The religious and philosophical teachings of all the peoples and countries contain a great number of answers to this question, Vivekananda goes on to say. At the same time there are attempts to erase the question itself. As long as death exists, however, all these attempts will be unsuccessful. We can freely talk saying that we do not see anything on the other side of the grave, that all our hopes must be limited to earthly life; we can be carried away by life struggle; everything that surrounds us, the whole world, may interfere with our leaving the narrow framework of our personal transient life...But as soon as we feel the coming of death, the question arises before us, time and again: "What is death? Is't it the end of all that we catch at so feverishly, as if all this were the most real of all the real things?" In a trice, the world is extinguished and disappears. At the edge of this gaping precipice, death, even the most hardened mind will be shaken, it will retreat and ask the inevitable question. The hopes and works of a whole life will be ruined in a second. Man lives by the desire to be happy; we catch at everything in the external world in the hope of finding that happiness. The youth at whom life smiles believes and is convinced that happiness is the whole world..... But high tide is inevitable followed by low tide in life. Everything is transient, pleasure and suffering, riches and poverty, even life itself. Everything passes. Aurobindo Ghose singled out the main subject matter of modern Indian philosophy in these words : What was before birth and what follows death—these are the questions.

This approach was not accident under the conditions prevailing in India. Jawaharlal Nehru wrote : "It must be remembered that the business of philosophy in *India* was not confined to a few philosophers or highbrows. Philosophy was an essential part of the religion of the masses; it percolated to them in some attenuated form and created that philosophic outlook which became nearly as common in India as it is in China. That philosophy was for some a deep and intricate attempt to know the causes and laws of all phenomena, the search for the ultimate purpose of life, and the attempt to find the organic unity in life's many contradictions. But for many it was a much simpler affair, which yet gave them some sense of purpose, of cause and effect, and endowed them with courage to face trial and misfortune and not lose their gaiety and composure...."[23]

The materialist ideas contained in the Upanisads were further developed in the Charvaka Lokayata system. Discarding idealism and mysticism, the materialists developed the following propositions : the substantial basis of all that is are material elements—water, earth, fire, air; only this world, this nature exists; the external world is independent of man; it can be changed, but only through physical action rather than through thought, magic, sacrifice, or prayer; there is no supernatural "purpose", nature is governed and directed by itself.

The Vedic literature is extremely rich and varied in its content. It has a great significance for the study of the history of philosophy, religion, law, psychology, ethics, aesthetics, language, natural science and, finally, of the forms of social life in ancient India. Many categories of modern Indian psychology, ethics and aesthetics can be traced back to the Vedic literature. Some psychologists, particularly the adherents of the Yoga schools, still continue to develop the theory of the Pranas. Vedanta, Buddhism, and other schools have worked out systems of ethical categories and developed "systems of conduct" using the Upanisad teachings of *karma, dharma* and *samsara* (the reincarnations of the soul). The doctrine of Brahman-*atman* as the source of the beautiful lies at the base of the aesthetic theories of the Vedanta. And so on.

The Period of Philosophical Sutras and Formation of the Philosophical Schools (Systems)

During this period, which lasted almost a thousand years (c. 5th century B.C.-4th century C.E.), the Upanisad literary form was gradually replaced by the *sutras*.[24]

The sutras are extremely laconic both in language and

content. Each sentence in the Sutras consisted of several syntactically loosely connected words and sometimes of one compound word only. A sequence of sentences made up the whole of the "thread" (*sutra*) of the exposition, and each sentence, a "node" or "bead" for memorizing the philosophical proposition expounded. In the course of the centuries, *bhashya*, or comments on the sutras, accumulated, one comment superimposed on another. Traditionally, the later thinkers, even the most outstanding of them, regarded themselves as mere interpreters of the ancient sutra cryptogrammes. The later interpreters, explaining the views of an earlier and therefore more authoritative commentator, introduced their own views in the doctrine, so that the sutra itself got lost among these accumulations and its original meaning became obscured. That was the source of endless scholastic polemics, which polished the logical niceties of an idea but at the same time sucked dry its essence.

During the early Middle Age (c. 4th–11th centuries), the force of the tradition of commenting was so great in India that not a single philosopher claimed that status of a founder of a new philosophy, although some of them were fully entitled to do so. Even the creator of the Advaita, which is the major philosophical system of objective idealism, the brilliant Samkara, modestly referred to himself as a mere commentator of the Vedanta.

In the course of time, during the second half of the Sutra period, the need arose for compiling précis of the basic propositions of the various systems, very short ones, without extensive commentaries but comprehensible to the erudite reader. That was start of the *karikas*—manuals expounding philosophical doctrines. In general terms, the first half of the first millennium of this era is regarded as the *karika* period.

The following nine systems or schools became best developed and most widespread in India : Charvaka Lokayata. Jainism, Buddhism, Vedanta, Mimamsa, Samkhya, Nyaya, Vaisesika and Yoga.

REFERENCES

1. All the Vedas have a Samhita, a Brahman, an Arnayak and Upanisads, but the author gives his own interpretation. —*Ed.*
2. *Yajus*—a sacrificial formula, dictum, or praise; *saman*—hymn.
3. According to some hymns, the initial matter produced out of itself the divine forces which in their turn built out of this initial substance nature and the whole world surrounding man as the carpenter builds the house.
4. The Vedic hymns have no names. Some scholars call this hymn, from its content, the hymn of creation, while others, the Nasadiya hymn, from its beginning (*Nasad* means "there was not"). See Theodor Aufrecht, *Die Hymnen des Rigveda,* bei Adolph Marcus, Bonn, 1877, S. 430; S. Radhakrishnan, *Indian Philosophy,* Vol. 1, p. 101.
5. The concept of *tapas* which frequently occur in the Upanisads originally meant "heat". By and by *tapas* came to mean in the course of time self exhaustion for the sake of other beings and later a special kind of asceticism in general consisting not only in continence, tempering the body, etc., but also in self-contemplation and concentration of thought.
6. A.L. Basham; *The Wonder That Was India,* Rupa and Co., Delhi, 1971, pp. 249-50.
7. "Concupiscence", the desire to manifest itself, the first movement of conscious will, must precede action. The word used here is *kama.* It later came to mean "love" and became the name of the god of love. Similarly, Gr. *Eros* and L. *Cupido* literally mean "desire".

   It is also important to note that thought ("the seed springing from the mind") is regarded in the hymn as a physical ability, that is, a property of matter rather than of spirit or soul.
8. S. Radhakrishnan, *op. cit.,* Vol. 1, p. 103.
9. Friedrich Max Muller, *The Six Systems of Indian Philosophy.*
10. Hesiod, *The Theogony,* translated by C.A. Elton, George Routledge and Sons Limited, London and New York, pp. 101-102.

11. *Filosofia y Letras.* Revista de la facultad de filosofia y letras. Tomo XXVIII, Mexico, Nums. 55-56, 1954, pp. 179, 180.
12. "The old title of the Atharva-Veda, 'Atharvangirasah', shows that there were two different strata in it, one of Atharvan and the other of Angiras. The former refers to auspicious practices used for healing purposes. The hostile practices belong to the Angirases. The first is medicine and the second is witchcraft, and the two are mixed up..." (S. Radhakrishnan, *op. cit.*, Vol. 1, p. 122).
13. See the Rig Veda, X, 129.
14. The Chandogya Upanisad (111, 13) gives, for the first time, a classification of the *pranas* ("breathings"). There are no precise data so far as to how the ancient Indians visualised all these *pranas*. There are numerous and often contradictory opinions about that. We follow the interpretation of *pranas* suggested by German Sanskritist Paul Deussen. But see *Gurshabad Ratnakar Mahankosh* for a detailed explanation of the *pranas*. – *Ed.*
15. *Prana* means breath in general or intake of breath. *Apana* is exhaling or breathing downward. *Vyana* is the intermediate breath, the interval between inhaling and exhaling. *Udana* is breath directing the stream of air upwards. *Samana* is inner breath uniting all the other kinds of breath.

    The Yogi later built their teaching of breath on this classification.

    The authors of the Chandogya Upanisad made an attempt to establish a functional connection between the kinds of breath, on the one hand, and the thinking and sensory processes in the human organism, on the other.
16. There is no generally accepted view of the etymology of the word Brahman. R.C. Zaechner writes : "Originally it seems to have meant prayer, and, by extension, a spell; later it is used as an equivalent for three Vedas, and still later as the sacred power underlying any sacred action" (R. Zaechner, *Hindu and Muslim Mysticism,* Schocken Books, New York, 1960, pp. 23-24). In this way Brahman became a substance or absolute devoid of any personal aspects. As opposed to the impersonal Brahman, theism appears only in the later Upanisads : "All this, whatsoever moves in this universe, is

indwelled by Isa," asserts the Isa Upanisad. Here a personal god is regarded as something superior to Brahman. The theistic tendency reaches the highest point in the Svetasvatra Upanisad and in particular in the Bhagavad Gita, where god announces through Krishna :

"This Universe the womb is where I plant Seed of all lives! Thence, Prince of India, comes Birth to all beings!".

17. S. Radhakrishnan believes that defining the ultimate reality in the words "Atman-Brahman" means characterising it from two sides, the subjective (Atman) and the objective (Brahman) (See. S. Radhakrishnan, *op. cit.*, Vol. I, p. 146).
18. The ways of knowledge, or the methods for "freeing" used by the Yogi, (Karma Yoga, Bhakti Yoga, Jnana Yoga, Raja Yoga), are discussed in the chapter on the philosophy of Vivekananda.
19. "Orthodoxy" in ancient India was defined more in social and political terms than in those of beliefs and convictions : the orthodox was expected to conform precisely to the rules of social relations, the laws of Varna, and Vedic rituals. Orthodoxy is *cila,* that is, conduct, rather than *craddha,* which means piety, offering sacrifices to the ancestors, and only in the last place, faith. In the philosophical views, Samkhya and Buddhism are often close to each other, sometimes much closer than the "godless Samkhya" and the "unconditional monism" (*anirbhedaadvaita*), and still both of these trends are included among the six orthodox systems, whereas Buddhism is regarded as heresy.
20. The "divine fire" is the soul which, according to the Katha Upanisad, is man's eternal essence.
21. This idea occurs in the other Upanisads, too. Thus, the Svetasvatra Upanisad says that, when the true nature of one's *atman* becomes a light, as it were, one sees in concentration the Brahman's true identity.
22. The reference here is to Atman as the absolute soul existing in man in the shape of an individual soul (the "inner Atman").
23. Jawaharlal Nehru, *The Discovery of India, Asia Publishing House,* Bombay, 1961, p. 86.

6 Survey of the Literature of Artha-Sastra and Niti-Sastra

I

The Early Schools and Authors of Artha-Sastra

Artha-Sastra is defined by Kautilya, the last and greatest master of the science, as the Branch of knowledge which deals with the acquisition and preservation of dominion. It is held, in other words, to comprise the art of government in the widest sense of the term. This definition is justified by the list of contents of Kautilya's *Arthasastra*—a work produced probably in the last quarter of the fourth century B.C. and the only surviving one of its class. The list comprises the branches of internal and foreign administration, civil and criminal law as well as the art of warfare. As regards the term Niti-sastra, it is used in the narrow sense of the science of polity as well as in the wider significance of the science of general morals.

From a number of quotations and references in later works we learn that there arose (probably in the fourth century before Christ) no less than four distinct schools and thirteen individual teachers of Artha-sastra. The loss of this fairly extensive literature is to be attributed to its supersession by the masterly treatise of Kautilya, which itself has been recovered from the oblivion of centuries by the fortunate discovery of a complete manuscript of the work and its publication by R. Shama Sastry in 1908. Among the old masters of the science special mention should be made of those of the schools of Manu, Brhaspati, and Usanas (sukra), and the two teachers Visalaksa and Bharadvaja, who are singled out for salutation and are quoted by later writers in different branches of learning.

The discussions of the ancient Artha-sastra authorities are centred in the first place upon a few basic concepts and categories. Such are the categories of the seven constituents of the State, the four traditional science (*vidya*), the four political expendients (*upayas*), and the six types of foreign policy (*gunas*) as well as the concepts of the State-system (*mandala*) and the king's coercive authority (*danda*). The early Artha-sastra masters themselves, as we learn from Kautilya's quotations, deal with such items as the scheme of the prince's education (based upon a comparative estimate of 'the four sciences'); the recruitment and selection of the ministers and the constitution of the ministerial council; the policy of a king's security against his sons, and that of a minister in the crisis of the king's death; the application of the king's coercive authority; civil and criminal law; the characteristics of the State structure (founded upon a comparative estimate of the calamities of the constituent element thereof); and the policies of the inter-State relations, in particular, those of attacking the enemy, waging offensive and defensive wars, and application of different sub-types of treaties.

II

The Arthasastra of Kautilya

In Kautilya's political nomenclature, a king's provision of security and prosperity (*yoga-ksema*) for his own people is conveyed by the technical term *tantra*, and his arrangement for keeping watch over the neighbouring rulers is expressed by another technical term *avapa*; and as such Kautilya's *Arthasastra* consists of two great divisions, the *tantra* portion comprising the first five Books (*adhikaranas*), which are divided into ninety-four sub-sections (*prakaranas*), and the *avapa* portion consisting of the next nine Books, which are divided into eighty-four sub-sections. The fifteenth Book consisting of a single *prakarana* may be regarded as somewhat outside the two divisions of *tantra* and *avapa*. An attempt will now be made to give a brief summary of the topics discussed by Kautilya under the above fifteen Books or *adhikaranas*.

Book One deals with the discipline and education of a king. He must be conversant with the knowledge of all the four *vidyas* (branches of learning), viz. *anviksiki* (metaphysics), *trayi* (the three Vedas, of course, including the fourth or *Atharva-Veda,* and also the Itihasa-Veda and the six Vedangas), *varta* (signifying pastoral pursuits, trade, industry, and commerce, *i.e.,* economics) and *dandaniti* (the science of polity or government). The whole of Kautilya's theory of polity is based on the proper and peaceful performance of the assigned duties of the four *varnas* (castes) and the four *asramas* (stages of human life). Kautilya states that a king who is severe in repression becomes a terror to his people, and one who is mild in the award of punishment is treated by them with contempt, while he who awards punishment as deserved is respected. So he thinks that *danda* should be awarded after full and just consideration, and it must not be awarded wrongly, nor allowed to remain in abeyance; for, in this case, it will produce the condition of *matsya-nyaya* or anarchy. On proper discipline and education of the king under experts and specialists depends his power of awarding *danda,* Unrivalled suzerainty can only be attained by a fully disciplined and educated monarch. The king is trained to control the six internal enemies, *viz.,* lust, anger, greed, vanity, arrogance, and jealousy. Kautilya next discusses fully[1] the institution of ministership, the necessity for creating ministers, their appointment according to their requisite qualifications, and the test of their honesty and loyalty by a method called *upadha* (allurement). The *buddhisacivas* or *matisacivas, i.e., mantrins* (counsellors and policy-makers), according to Kautilya, are more important than the *karmasacivas* or *amatyas* (executive functionaries and departmental heads).

Premising that deliberations (*mantra*) come first and administrative undertakings (*arambha*) next, Kautilya refutes[2] the views of some of the earlier teachers on the question of the adequate number of *mantrins,* which, according to him, should not exceed three or four. But he does not restrict the number of *amatyas* or *karmasacivas,* who constitute the so-called *mantriparisad* (the council of ministers). In matters of grave importance, Kautilya continues, all the *buddhisacivas* and *karmasacivas* should be convened together in a joint session, and the king should do what the majority decides: he should accept even the verdict of the minority, if it is deemed necessary and conducive to the object in view.

Kautilya's statecraft is mainly based on an efficient system of espionage. In the *Arthasastra* we find several classes of spices; the two main groups being the *samsthas* and the *sancarins*, the operation of the former being chiefly static and that of the latter mostly dynamic. These different types of spies should have a network of assistant workers and disciples having their sub-workers and sub-disciples for carrying on their secret business. The high State functionaries, including even the *mantrins*, were subject to their vigilance. The most interesting type of spies is the one called *ubhayaventana*, who was allowed by his own king to accept surreptitiously salary from his enemy, while engaged in collecting information about the latter's kingdom. The topic of espionage leads Kautilya to describe how a king should deal both with the groups of discontented, factious, ambitious, haughty, alarmed, and provoked persons in his own and the enemy's kingdom, and the princes of his household. Illustrating the manner in which detractors of the monarch should be silenced by the activities of spies, Kautilya advises them to tell the people assembled in the course of a public discussion how in the old days Manu, 'son of the Sun', was elected the first king by the folk suffering from anarchy; how in lieu of their one-sixth of the grain produce, one-tenth of their manufactured articles, and even cash money, Manu undertook the responsibility of maintaining security of people's life and property; how even the anchorites offered the king one-sixth of their gleaned grains; and how the king was to be the dispenser of rewards (as representing the God Indra) and punishments (as representing the God Yama); and how therefore the king should never be despised.

In the next place, a ruler is enjoined by Kautilya to keep a vigilant eye on the princes possessing, we are told, the characteristics of crabs who eat up their begetter. Observing that a royal family having no well-trained and well-disciplined prince perishes like a worm-eaten piece of wood, Kautilya advises the king to leave aside the wicked and untrained princes and to appoint instead of them a prince, whether or not the eldest, possessing the requisite princely virtues to the office of the commander-in-chief or of the heir-apparent. He should never install on the throne a wicked son, though he be the only son. Generally but not necessarily, the eldest son, should succeed to the sovereignty in circumstances other than dangerous. Kautilya even recommends a joint-family sovereignty (if the need arises) on account of its invincibility.

Describing next the king's daily routine, the author of the *Arthasastra* directs that the king must at once attend to all urgent calls of business and not put them off; for, when postponed, they may prove too difficult or even impossible to accomplish. Readiness for action is described as a religious vow for a king, and the root of all royal business is his enterprise. A king's happiness and welfare, it is said, depend on those of his subjects. The book concludes with an account of the precautions that are to be taken for the safety of the king's person in his household.

Book Two of the *Arthasastra* is a veritable mine of information about, the running of a bureaucratic system of government in an ancient Indian State. Only a few important features of governmental work carried on by this vast and heavy bureaucracy are briefly noted here. While describing the king's method of distribution of land under colonization to the cultivators, the author advises that certain lands, should be granted revenue-free and perpetually to specified classes of Brahmanas,[3] and that other lands, both arable and fallow, should be distributed to farmers only as life-tenants. By contrast, the king is forbidden by Kautilya to take away fallow land from those to whom it is given for bringing it under cultivation; and he is further enjoined to grant special privileges, immunities, and remissions to the cultivators, keeping, of course, an eye on the condition of his treasury.

While constructing a fort or a fortified town, the king is advised to arrange for storage of all kinds of oils, grains, sugar, salt, medicines, dry vegetables, fodder, dry fish, hay-stacks, firewood, metals, skins, charcoal, tendons, poision, horns, bamboo, barks of trees, strong timber, weapons, and armour which may last for many years. The Chief Treasury Officer (*sannidhatu*) has charge of treasuries, warehouses, storehouses, godowns, arsenals, and prisons. The Chief Revenue Officer (*samaharta*) deals with the collection of revenue from the seven sources, *viz.*, (1) forts and fortified towns, (2) the countryside, (3) mines, (4) cultivated fields and flower and fruit gardens forests, (6) pens of domestic animals, and (7) traffic-routes. He is in charge of all these heads of revenue and those of expenditure, *i.e.*, of all budgetary affairs. The king is directed by Kautilya to examine constantly the character of all departmental heads (*adhyaksas*) and their subordinates, such as accountants (*samkhyayaka*), writers or clerks (*lekhaha*), and coin-examiners (*rupa-darsaka*). It is further laid down that no chief officer should be allowed to hold his office permanently. Stating that it is hardly possible for officer directly dealing with government finance and revenue not to enjoy even slightly the taste of State money, Kautilya prescribes measures against corruption. Traffic in salt being a State monopoly, imported salt is highly taxed in Kaultiya's system, and adulteration of salt is punishable. For the protection of the community, the king should never allow import of useless and harmful commodities from foreign countries; but he should permit, without toll or customs duties, import of goods beneficial to the people and grain speeds not otherwise easily available in the country. Sale of commodities at the places (fields or factories) of their production is prohibited. The concluding portion of the book deals with the administration of cities under City Mayors (*nagarikas*), of which we may mention some principal features. The *nagarika* and his staff, it is said, should prepare registers of municipal holdings. Managers of charity houses should note the arrival and departure of heretics and travellers. Keepers of hotels, restaurants, and brothels should only entertain men of attested identity. Physicians, landlords, and householders are to report to the city officers about the diseases of the patients, the nature of the tenants, and the arrival and departure of strangers respectively. Towns people are to provide themselves with fire-extinguishing instruments and vessels filled with water. Dead bodies of human beings are to be taken out for cremation or burial through particular city-gates. The *nagarika* is to report to the king on nocturnal crimes committed in the city. General gaol deliveries should be provided for on the occasion of the king's conquest of a new territory, the installation of the crown prince, an the birth of a prince. Those among the prisoners who are very young, old, diseased or helpless are to be released on the days of the king's birth anniversary and on full moon days.

Book Three (*Dharmsthiya*) of the *Arthusustra* deals with the branch of civil law. The king is regarded as the final authority in judicial matters. He is assited in arriving at legal decisions by a triad of judges (*dharmasthas*), who actually try lawsuits in the company of some specialists in legal sastras (*vyavahara*). The author further describes the legal processes regarding statements of the plaintiffs and rejoinders of the respondents. The heads of law relate to marriage (including the different kinds of marriage, the question of proper and improper marital relations, widow remarriage, remarriage of males, dowry, divorce, etc.), inheritance and partition of ancestral property (including a discussion of different kinds of sonship), holdings, fulfilment of contracts, debts, deposits, pledges and mortgages, slaves and free labourers, partnership, revocation of sale and purchase, rescission of gifts, sale without ownership, and relation between property and its owner. In Kautilya's legal system, a girl of twelve and a boy of sixteen are treated as having attained majority. Regarding the law of divorce or dissolution of marriage, Kautilya rules that marriages contracted in accordance with the customs of the *brahma, prajapatya, arsa,* and *daiva* forms cannot be dissolved. Slavery is allowed in Kautilya's system under certain legal restrictions. It is no crime for the Mlecchas (non-Aryans) to sell or mortgage their own offspring, but an Aryan cannot be enslaved. The principle recommended by Kautilya for the guidance of guilds or unions of workmen and those who carry on co-operative work is that they should either divide their earnings according to the terms agreed upon, or in equal shares. Some topics of the law of crimes, such as violence, slander, assault, dicing, gambling with animals, are also dealt with in this context. In the cases of slander and assault, theft, violence, and abduction, even hermits and ascetics are not immune from the penalties of law.

Book Four named *Kantaka-sodhana* (removal of thorns or anti-social elements), deals with a number of miscellaneous topics. Those relate to : public protection against deceitful and fraudulent artisans and merchants; penalty for manufacturing counterfeit coins and for disturbing the currency; fraud in respect of weights and measures; remedies against providential calamities, *e.g.*, fire, flood, epidemics, and famine; protection from the acts of evil-doers living by secret and foul ways; seizure of criminals on suspicion, along with the stolen property, or in the act of theft; *post mortem* examination in the case of sudden deaths; eliciting confession from suspects by questionng or physical tortures; protection of the people from the oppressions of government servants; ransom or fine in lieu of mutilation of limbs of criminals, when ordered by the court; death-penalty with or without torture; outrage on girls; and punishment for transgression of social obligations. The high functionaries who try criminal cases are called *pradestrs,* and they are assisted in the trial by a tribunal or bench of three experts. In Kautilya's penal code, no Brahmana could be tortured for any criminal offence, nor could he be awarded the death-penalty; all that could be done in the case of an offending Brahmana is that he was to be branded with a mark on his forehead for his criminality and banished from the country. On the other hand, Kautilya does not make the king immune from punishment for violation of justice.

Among the topics discussed in Book Five of the *Arthasastra* are included the following : Secret measures against seditious ministers; replenishment of State officers in a financial emergency; emoluments for the royal *entourage* and other government servants; behaviour of the king's dependants towards him; consolidation of the kingdom after the sovereign's demise and similar catastrophes; and establishment of sovereignty of the single son of a king after his death. A few points under the above heads may be noted. A king may, in the interest of righteousness, inflict secret punishment even on his favourite courtiers and country chiefs. A king of attenuated treasury may collect money from the people even by unfair and despotic methods, such as the levy of benevolences (*pranaya*). But such demands for money should be made only once. Various pretexts for collection of money during financial stringency are also permitted. Kautilya, however, enjoins that only the wicked men and never the innocent should be victimized for such purpose. He rejects the view of Bharadvaja, who advises the minister to usurp the throne after his master's death. He declares instead that hereditary kingship in the single line of rulers should be preserved, since usurpation of the throne by the minister cannot be a righteous act, and it may also lead to popular fury. The minister should make even a wicked prince succeed to the throne, while asking the other ministers and members of the royal family to regard the new king as only a flag under which they themselves would be the real rulers.

The essential characteristics of the seven constituent elements of the State are first described in Book Six. Reference is then made to the six political expedients (*gunas*), *viz.*, peace (*sandhi*), war (*vigraha*), expedition (*yana*), neutrality or halt (*asana*), dubious attitude (*dvaidhibhava*), *i.e.*, peace with one and war with another, and alliance (*samsraya*). According as a king deals carefully or doubtfully or carelessly with these expedients, he attains the condition of augmentation (*vrddhi*), stagnation (*sthana*) or deterioration (*ksaya*) of his dominion. The author next defines the twelve constitutents of the circle of states (*mandala*), *viz.*, the *vijigisu* or the would be conqueror (in the centre), his immediate neighbour regarded as an enemy, the would-be conqueror's friend, the enemy's friend the friend's friend, and the enemy's friend's friend (the last five being in front); the rearward enemy, the reaward friend, the ally of rearward enemy, and the ally of rearward friend (the last four being in the rear); the mediatory king and the most powerful neutral king. Kautilya next defines the three kinds of power (*sakti*) of a king, namely, the power of deliberation, the power due to treasury and the army, and the power of energy, and their corresponding success.

Proper utilization of the six political expedients in the field of diplomacy is discussed in Book Seven of the *Arthasastra*. The king, we read, should strive intently to pass from the state of deterioration to that of stagenation and gradually therefrom to augmentation through in intelligent application of the six expedients. According to Kautilya, a king should always prefer peace to war in consideration of the immense disadvantages involved in waging war against an enemy, for war leads to wastage of human life, enormous expenses of money, sojourning in distant and strange lands, perpetration of cruel acts, etc. In case the *vijigisu* feels himself inferior to his enemy, he should try to enter into any one of the various *sandhis* described in this treatise. A king may march against an enemy in combination with his allies of superior, equal, or inferior status by agreeing upon his share of the spoils of war. The destruction of an enemy must be undertaken in an open fight even at a heavy loss of men and money.

A lively discussion on the several kinds of *vyasanas* (dangers or calamities) befalling a king and his kingdom both from within and without is the subject of Book Eight. A *vijigisu* is to consider them with respect to his own kingdom and that of his enemy. Kautilya endorses his teacher's view on the seriousness of the dangers to the seven constituent elements of the State in the following descending order: the king, the ministers, the country people, the fort (and fortified towns), the treasury, the army, and allies. To remove internal troubles caused by the *amatya* (minister), the king should keep the treasury and the army under his own control. Want of proper education and discipline is the cause of a king's vices due to anger and passion. The king is to guard against and provide for providential calamities, such as fire, flood, epidemics, and pestilence. A king is advised by Kautilya to avert financial troubles in the interest of the prosperity of his people.

The topic of leading an expedition by a *vijigisu* is dealt with in Book Nine. Before launching an invasion, a king should carefully weigh his own strength and weakness with those of his enemy. He should also consider the measure of his three *saktis*, the place and time for his march, recruitment of forces, possible troubles in the rear, loss of men and money, ultimate gain expected, and internal and external dangers that are likely to be encountered. Kautilya next describes the proper time for the enlistment of the six kinds of infantry: hereditary troops, mercenary troops, troops raised from corporate bodies, received from the allies, troops seduced from the enemy, and those enlisted from forest tribes. Kautilya thinks that though the Kshatriya army is better than the Brahmana one, which can be won over by prostration, the Vaisya and Sudra armies consist of very virile men, and they can be obtained in larger numbers. Before starting on an expedition. Kautilya is of opinion that success eludes the fool who consults possible internal and external troubles that may arise during his absence from his capital. A king undertaking a march should carefully weigh the profits likely to accrue therefrom and beware of the impediments to his expedition. Kautilya is of opinion that success eludes the fool who consults the stars too much. He next describes the methods of encompassing the death of seditious and hostile subjects. This is followed by an account of the use of strategic measures for averting all other kinds of political dangers, and a description of the remedies against providential visitations.

Book Ten concerns itself with war. During the king's absence in camp, the officer in charge of the capital city should strictly enforce the passport system so as to arrest armed men going out with writ. The king should protect his own army by all possible means during its march through difficult and dangerous paths, the soldiers being required to be looked after when afflicted by disease and pestilence or in any other emergency. Kautilya advocates treacherous fight if the *vijigisu* fails to cope with his enemy in fair fight. Other topics treated by him relate to grounds suitable for deploying the elephants, the horses, the chariots, and men, and the formation of various kinds of array on the wings and in that front. The services of unarmed labourers (*visits*) were to be requisitioned for examining camps, roads, bridges, wells, and river crossings for carrying machines, weapons, armours, food, and other paraphernalia, and for removing the wounded from the battle-field. All sorts of secret contrivances were to be laid under contribution; for example, the use of bravoes and traitors; setting fire to the enemy's camp; false announcement of burning down of the enemy's fort or of rebellion in the enemy's family or elsewhere. The author says, "The arrow shot by an archer may or may not kill even a single man, but the sharp intellect applied by a wise man can kill those lying in the mother's womb.'[4]

Book Eleven deals with economic guilds and political corporations in the shape of tribal republics, both being called by the generic title of *sangha*. The king is advised to acquire military aid from these *sanghas* since they are invicible on account of their corporate unity. A *vijigisu* is enjoined to secure the services of the *sanghas* by a careful application of the methods of conciliation and bribery, if they are favourably disposed towards him, and by those of dissension and punishment, if they are opposed to him. The seeds of dissension are to be sown among the hostile leaders of *sanghas*, and they are to be won over by engaging the services of beautiful women as spies.

Book Twelve describes the various Machiavellian contrivances which a weak *vijigisu* should use in fighting against a stronger one. When attacked by the latter, the former, it is observed, should either take shelter under a third superior king or resort to an impregnable fort. Aggressors are generally of three varieties : One contented with the surrender of the vanquished, one contented with the acquisition of his territory and wealth, and one seeking not only his territory, treasure, sons, and wife, but also his life. The battle of intrigue is to be adopted by the weaker king against the stronger invader by producing internal disturbances through the agency of spies. Secret methods are to be applied against the high State functionaries, princes, and chief army officers of the aggressor. Destruction of his stores and granaries is also recommended. The weak *vijigisu* may encompass the death of his enemy when entering the precincts of a temple for offering worship. The strong enemy should be made to accept, through a pretended friend belonging to the weak king's camp, a supply of poisoned food for use in his own capital city. How the weak king should achieve 'triumphant success' by bringing about the death of the stronger enemy by 'secret methods' is told at the end of the book.

In Book Thirteen we are first told how a *vijigisu* should sow seeds of dissension in the enemy's country before attempting to seize it; how in that act he should strive to enthuse his own men and frighten the men of his enemy by the proclamation of his own omniscience and his association with divinities; and how he should entice the enemy to come out with his entire family and his ministers to visit an improvised ascetic, and bring about his assassination at the time of the visit. Then follows a description of the *vijigisu's modus operandi* for besieging and storming the enemy's fort, which is made to serve as the pattern of the four steps to his attainment of the position of an imperial suzerain. The new conqueror should enjoy the fruits of his conquest by following the duties prescribed for a king, and seeing that the proper division of castes (*varnas*) and stages of life (*asramas*) is strictly adhered to by the people. A *vijigisu* should consolidate his new position by the creation of confidence in the mind of the conquered people. He should cover his enemy's vices by his own virtues and the enemy's virtues by doubling his own. He should bestow favours, remit dues, distribute gifts, and confer honours on the people conquered. A new conqueror should adopt the same mode of life, dress, language, and customs as those of the conquered people; he should show devotion to the local deities, and follow the festivities, convivial assemblies, and amusements of those people; he should award land grants, gifts of other properties, and immunity from taxation to learned men, orators, and religious people. He should introduce righteous customs and order full goal-deliveries.

In Book Fourteen Kautilya deals with certain recipes for the destruction of a king's enemies and for causing in them blindness, insanity, and various kinds of bodily diseases and deformities. Among these delusive devices are found certain medical formulas for making a man invisible to his enemies and providing him with the power of vision in night's darkness. Incamations are to be uttered for causing men and animals to fall asleep. Remedies are to be used against the application of poisons and poisonous drugs by the enemy to the king's own troops.

Book Fifteen give the plan of the entire work. *Arthasastra* is defined by the author as 'the science which treats of the means of acquiring and ruling the earth'.[5] This is followed by an explanation of thirty-two technical terms used by him in his work. In the concluding verses he says that this *Sastra* establishes and maintains the triad, *viz.*, virtue, wealth, and pleasure (*dharma, artha,* and *kama*), and sets down unrighteous acts detrimental to wealth (*artha*).

III

Kamandakiya-Nitisara

This treatise, belonging to the third century A.D., is based mainly on Kautilya's *Arthasastra*. In fact Kamandaka, at the beginning of his work, acknowledges Visnugupta (*i.e.*, Canakya or Kautilya) as his master and eulogizes him as the creator of the science of polity who has drawn from the great ocean of Artha-sastra the nectar of *Nitisara*.[6] This book is composed in an epic form, and old commentators regard it as a great *kavya*.

Kamandaka's *Nitisara* or the Essence of Polity consists of twenty cantos and thirty six sub-section (*prakaranas*) on special topics. A summarized list of its contents is given below. Canto

One : Subjugation of the senses and discipline under elderly teachers. Canto Two : Divisions of the branches of learning : establishment of the four castes and the four stages of life; and benefits of (the king's application) of punishment. Canto Three : Establishment of the rules of conduct. Canto Four : Perfection of the seven constituent elements of the State. Canto Five : The behaviour of the king and his dependants. Canto Six : Removal of the unsocial elements. Canto Seven : Security against the princes; and the king's self-protection. Canto Eight : Requisites of a king's *mandala* or circle of sovereign States; and conduct of that circle. Canto Nine; Various kinds of treaties. Canto Ten : Different kinds of hostilities. Canto Eleven : Various kinds of expedition, neutrality, duplicity, and seeking the protection of allies. Canto Twelve: Deliberation over policies. Canto Thirteen : The institution of envoys, and movements of ambassadors and spies. Canto Fourteen : The glory of strenuous effort, and the operations and afflictions of the constituent elements of the State. Canto Fifteen : The category of seven vices. Canto Sixteen : Expeditions; and the nature of aggressors. Canto Seventeen : Encampment of the army. Canto Eighteen : The category of four political expedients. Canto Nineteen : Examination of the strength and weakness of various divisions of the army; the duties of the commanders of the armies; security of the army during expeditions; and different kinds of treacherous warfare. Canto Twenty : The employment of elephants, cavalry, chariots, and infantry; proper locations for deploying them; award of prizes to the troops; various kinds of battle arrays; and righteous warfare.

It may easily be realized from the above summary of contents that Kamandaka is very indebted to Kautilya for his subjects. But he has omitted almost everything that is concerned with the actual reality of life in a State, such as administration, control of trade and commerce, and the administration of justice–in fact, those very things which impart to Kautilya's book an incomparable value in people's eyes. Kamandaka does not go much beyond the general maxims of *niti*. His book often delights in didactive maxims, which appear to be absent in Kautilya's treatise.

IV

Nitivakyamrtam of Somadevasuri

The *Nitivakyamrtam* or the Nectar of the Science of Polity, an interesting treatise on statecraft, was written in A.D., 959 by the Jain scholar Somadeva, the author of the romance *Yasatilaka,* in which also his vast knowledge of political science is in evidence. The work cited above consists of thirty-two discourses dealing with religious practices (*dharma*), wealth (*artha*), coveted worldly object (*kama*), the six internal enemies (*arisadvarga*), teachers of different lores (*vidya-vrddha*), metaphysics (*anviksiki*), the Vedas (*trayi*), agriculture, cattle breeding, trade (*varta*), the science of politics (*dandaniti*), counsellors (*mantrin*), royal priests (*purohita*), the commander of the army (*senapati*), ambassadors (*duta*), spies (*cara*), power of discrimination (*vicara*), vices (*uyasana*), the king (*svamin*), ministers (*amatya*), the countryside and its people (*janapada*). Forts (*durga*), the treasury (*kosa*), the army (*bala*), friends and allies (*mitra*), protection of the king (*rajaraksa*), daily duties of the king (*divasanusthana*), good conduct of a king (*sadacara*), good behaviour of the people (*vyavahara*), disputes (*vivida*), the six types of foreign policy (*sadgunya*), warfare (*yuddha*), marriages (*vivaha*), and miscellaneous items (*prakirnaka*).

Somadeva based his work mostly on the discussions of the topics in Kautilya's *Arthasastra*. But he takes more interest in moral maxims than in administrative and military matters, for he is anxious to teach all rulers how they should behave with their people. While accepting the Brahmanical *varnasrama* ideal as in the *Arthasastra* of Kautilya and other Niti-sastra, the Jain author prescribes the tenets of materialistic philosophy for kings, for whom ascetic practice are unbecoming. The pithy sayings of Somadeva are couched in simple Sanskrit written in a clear and lucid style.

V

Sukra-Nitisara

In the beginning of the book it is stated that Sukra himself compiled it, in an abridged manner, out of a ponderous load of earlier Niti-sastra matter. Internal evidence leads us to believe that the treatise may have been composed in its present form during the early mediaeval period of Indian history. The whole treatise consists of four chapters, of which the last has seven sub-sections (*prakaranas*). The first chapter deals with the duties and functions of princes, the second with the functions of the crown prince and other state dignitaries, and the third with general rules of morality meant to be observed by the king and his men. The first *prakarna* of the fourth chapter is concerned with the characteristics of the king's friends or allies, the second with the royal treasure, the third with arts and science, the fourth with customs and institutions, the fifth with the king's duties and functions, the sixth with forts, and the seventh with the soldiery. The book consists of both political and non-political portions, as can be ascertained from the above list of its contents.

The political part of the book deals with the State council, ministers, trade and commerce, public finance, jurisprudence, and international law. The non-political part comprises data for architecture, sculpture, and painting; manners and morals, pedagogy (including *vidyas* of different branches of learning, *kalas* or the fine arts, and literature); and economics (including statistics, prices, and wages). Hence it may be said that the *Sukra-Nitisara* is a socio-political and socio-economic work. It combines in itself the most salient features of Artha-sastra and Dharma-sastra, and even of Kama-sastra, to the exclusion of Moksa-sastra.

REFERENCES

1. *Kaut.*, I, 8—10.
2. *Ibid.*, I. 15.
3. Cf. *bhumichidra vidhana* in *Kaut.*, II. 2.
4. *Kaut.*, X. 6.
5. *Ibid.*, XV. 1.
6. *Kam.*, I. 2-6

7 Ethics of Arthashastra

In early India politics was considered one of the three or four major sciences. The school of Usanas (Shukra) goes so far as to suggest that artha is the only true science and that hence it takes precedence over the sacred law.[1] Most political thought of the time assumed the existence of a monarchical form of government, and politics was accordingly defined as the science of kingship. The arthasastra texts were intended as a political guide for the king and his ministers. Their scope is broad, embracing economic as well as political principles and including such subjects as public administration, foreign policy, techniques of warfare, civil law, and social structure. Their emphasis is on the need for sanctions capable of preventing social disorder. Anarchy is considered the greatest catastrophe that can befall mankind.

Whereas the dharmashastras considered government and the political process with reference to the ideals expressed in the Vedic canons, the largely secular analysis of arthashastra treats this subject more objectively. In the arthashastra literature the interests of the state, rather than the king's personal fulfilment,[2] are of foremost importance. Dharmashastra is of an essentially deductive nature; arthashastra, by contrast, introduces inductive reasoning and a greater realism. But the allegation that arthashastra differs from dharmashastra in that it is not dependent on the Vedas for validation must be rejected. To be sure, the authors of the arthashastras enjoy a relative intellectual freedom, and their contribution lies in the separation of political speculation from theology. But this need not and should not be taken to imply a repudiation of orthodoxy.

Very possibly the arthasahtra school was a reaction to the asceticism and despair of heterodoxy, an attempt to return men's thoughts to practical problems of social life. In the argument idealism tends to be subordinated to a philosophy of power politics and materialism. It has been suggested that the traditional belief that arthashastra is a science ancillary to the *Atharvaveda* is based on their similar view of the relation of means and ends; both have a concern with ends that over shadows attention to the methods employed. Kautalya, for instance, in his reluctance to allow dharmashastra to modify the goal-orientation of the efficient political system, is led to extol positive law. His arguments must have appeared to justify a radical departure from tradition.

Kautalya refers to at least four different doctrinal school,[3] and the names he mentions of early writers in the field agree with those we find in the *Mahabharata*, although the two works differ in conceptual scheme. It is apparent that arthashastra, in a simpler form, had existed since the fifth or even sixth century B.C. But the oldest formal treatise on government that remains is the *Kautaliya Arthashastra*. The manuscript, generally attributed to the minister of the first Mauryan emperor, Chandragupta, was discovered in the early years of this century at Trivandrum by R. Shama Sastri. A number of early sources attested to the existence of the treatise; Bana, the bard of Harsha's court, knew of a work on polity by Kautalya, and Dandin mentions the author of the *Arthashastra*.[4] Perhaps by their day the work had been lost. It remained hidden until our own time; the effect of its discovery on Indian scholarship was little short of revolutionary. (Since the ruling groups had an interest in limiting the circulation and preventing the popularization of the arthashastra treatises, it is not surprising that few of these works have survived).

In the arthashastra manuscripts both the Kautilya and Kautalya spellings appear, and the latter occurs in inscriptions of the tenth and thirteenth centuries. "Kautalya," it has been widely argued, is the correct Sanskrit spelling of the name of its author. The Kautalyalogist Ganapati Sastri maintains that his manuscripts support this form. Those partial to the *Kautilya* spelling include among their arguments the hypothesis that the name derives from *kutila* ("crooked") and that *Kautalya* is an attempt to cover up that fact. But, inasmuch as this "crookedness" was employed against the infamous Nandas, the author might actually have delighted in the name. And in the *Mahabharata* Bhisma says to Yudhishthira that "both kinds of wisdom, the straight and the crooked, should be available to the king," and proceeds to elaborate the subtle "morality" (the "dharma of distress") occasioned by times of emergency. This is simply the doctrine of *raison d'etat*, the power philosophy. The word may not have had the pejorative sense it has today—although the epic in another place states that the man who strikes below, the navel is "crooked and un. Aryan." At any rate, the comparative edition of the Patan folios based on the palm leaf fragments of the *Arthashastra* (dated on paleographic grounds c. the eleventh century A.D.), when published, will use *Kautlaya* as the preferred spelling.

References in the *Kamandakiya Nitisara*, the *Dasakumaracarita*, and the *Panchatantra* to "Vishnugupta" and "Chankya" indicate that Kautalya had other aliases. The personal name of the author was most likely Vishnugupta, Chanakya the patronymic, and Kautalya (or Kautilya) the name by which he was generally known. Legend not only connects Kautalya with Chandragupta as the latter's chief minister, but associates the two as early as Chandragupta's meeting with Alexander during one of the Punjab campaigns. The brahmanic sources for this period, the puranas, credit Kautalya rather than his king with the overthrow of Nanda rule. The *Mudraraksasa*, a drama of considerably later date, provides us with a similar picture of Kautalya as king-maker. But there is no mention of the Mauryan minister's having written a political treatise. It is of course possible that Kautalya compiled no more than a set of political aphorisms—and that he quoted these along with the maxims of other arthasastra writers, or that they formed the basis for an elaboration by a later scholar or statesman. Perhaps it is safest to say that the *Arthashastra* we possess includes additions and revisions by several later writers. "Vishnugupta" could be a redactor of a period as late as the fourth century A.D. rather than the minister of Chandragupta.

The social setting of the political commentary of the *Arthashastra* seems to antedate that of the early smritis. References to religion indicate the relatively recent appearance of Buddhism and Jainism,[5] and the persistence of Vedic ceremony. Lists of parallels in the accounts of Megasthenes, the Greek ambassador to Chandragupta's court, and the *Arthashastra* have been made. Similar descriptions of tax collection and highways, the palace, the bureaucracy and its functions, manufactures, the army, and precautions to be taken by the king for his safety suggest not only that the Mauryan king and the author of the *Arthashastra* were contemporaries, but that Kautalya is recommending much that he has already witnessed.

But these parallels are far from conclusive : indeed the later *Manusmriti* is closer to Megasthenes than the *Kautaliya* is. The Greek observer mentions a navy and regulations for dealing with foreigners—references one would expect to find in the *Arthasastra*. Megasthenes also suggests a less developed revenue system and a simpler commercial life than we find in the Indian work. But Megasthenes' dependability has been questioned; he is known to have had a vivid imagination and to have recorded much that he could not possibly have seen for himself. Further, he may not have understood the language of the Mauryan court very well.

Philological comparisons with Panini, the great grammarian who is said to have lived c. 350 B.C., have supported an early date for the *Arthashastra*. Vincent Smith, Jacobi, F.W. Thomas, Jayaswal, N.N. Law, J.F. Fleet, and Shama Sastri subscribe to the Mauryan date. But controversy over the date and authenticity of the *Arthashastra* is still active. Those who deny the association of its author with Chandragupta point out its reference to a small kingdom. Others argue that although the work does seem to reflect the needs of a small polity, the theory was meant to apply to monarchies of all sizes. Kautalya's treatment of the administration of justice points to a sizable empire rather than to a state of limited proportions, and on one occasion he refers to the dominion that stretches from the Himalayas to the ocean.

Those who ascribe a later date to the *Arthashastra* claim that the work may have been inspired by the teachings of the Mauryan minister, but that this does not necessarily mean that it dates from the late fourth century B.C. Their case is built on considerations of meter and language, the absence of reference to Chandragupta and to the royal title employed by the Mauryans, the silence of later works (puranas, Patanjali) regarding Kautalya's *Arthashastra*, and particularly Megasthenes' failure to mention Kautalya in his description of the Mauryan court. There is a reference in the treatise to China, although there is no evidence of contact between India and that country before the Han period, and in style and authorities cited the *Arthashastra* may be compared with the later work on erotics, the *Kamasutra*.[6] Jolly and Winternitz, who place the *Kautaliya* in the third century A.D., argue that the author was a theoretician and not a statesman. There is, in fact, little indication in the work that it creator led an active political life.

We know that the *Kautaliya* cannot have been more recent than the third century A.D., since authors of that period refer to it with admiration. And in no very convincing argument does it antedate 350 B.C. P.V. Kane's summary statement can be taken as representative of the most reliable scholarship on the subject. He writes that the work "has certainly an ancient atmosphere about it,.... all that has so far been gathered from it agrees with the traditional date of 300 B.C. and no cogent arguments have been yet brought forward that would compel us to assign it a date later than the above by six centuries."

Jacobi, in contradicting Hillebrandt's argument that the *Arthashastra* is the work of a school rather than a single author, cites the abundant criticism in the treatise of earlier works as evidence of a potent individuality. Kautalya attends to matters of practical administration, matters that would not generally absorb the deliberations of a school of political thought. The style of the *Arthashastra* is frequently similar to that of the bhashyas, which, in contrast to that of the sutras, is a style that suggests individual authorship. Jacobi claims that if the passages in the work which attest to the authorship of one man are removed, the metrical conclusion will be lost. And it was not unusual for writers to refer to themselves in the third person, as Kautalya does.

Certain of the provisions of the *Kautaliya* that are in agreement with the alter law books are probably modifications made by commentators on the *Arthashastra*, but because the work undoubtedly refers to the Mauryan period – although the date of composition may be centuries after Chandragupta – we can accept it as throwing light on the politics of the time and on the great preceptor. Possible the *Arthashastra* was written as a guide for the king of a modest realm who wished to become a great ruler. The Mauryas provided an example, and we may assume that whoever composed the text on statecraft had an extensive knowledge of Mauryan administrative and diplomatic procedures.

Kautalya is not seriously concerned with broad political speculation on the origin and nature of the state, and his originality is not to be found in the abstract theoretical realm. It is difficult to separate the myths he uses to justify techniques of government and methods of aggrandizement from the legitimate theoretical foundations. Radhakumud Mookerji suggests that in form the *Arthashastra* lies midway between the practical regulations of the Code of Hammurabi and the systematic theory of state and constitution in the political writings of Plato and Aristotle, combining the principles of government with a realistic consideration of the details of policy implementation and regulation. The treatise is, as its author explains, a compendium and summary of earlier arthashastra writings. Kautalya's main task was sifting and organizing this material, and resolving the ambiguities that characterized its disorderly state.

The fifteen books of the *Arthashatra* deal with the discipline of the prince, qualifications of the ministers, and duties of the king (Book 1); departments of government and general administration (2) ; civil law (3); criminal law (4) ; removal of dangers to the state, replenishment of the treasury (5); elements of kingship and policy (6 and 7); threats to the welfare of the state (8); military campaigns (9 and 10); corporations (11); theory of conquest (12 and 13); devices, magical and other, for advancing the interests of the state (14); general scheme of the study (15). Or, to classify further, Books 1, 6, and 8 relate to the theory of kingship; Books 2-5 to administration and law; and the remainder (7, 9-14) to war and diplomacy. A considerable portion of the *Arthashastra* is thus devoted to techniques for achieving universal sovereignty, a major theme of Hindu theory. Kautalya has seen to it that in the process no aspect of life should go unregulated.

Of the threefold ends of earthly life—dharma, artha, and kama (virtue, wealth, and enjoyment)—Kautalya assigns first importance to wealth and, anticipating the most outspoken of Western materialistic pronouncements, proclaims that the condition of righteousness is wealth. In his hands the concept dandaniti is broadened to reflect this materialism. Arthashastra becomes "the art of Government with a view to public acquisition." But although there is this emphasis on the material bases of the state, Kautalya, unlike many of his predecessors, defends the other branches of knowledge as useful in establishing security, the class basis of society, and discipline of mind. There is, in Indian philosophy, a hedonistic current that ridicules religion and ethics, but Kautalya is always aware of the instrumental value of religious rites and ethical norms in preserving the social structure.

The Vedas and later texts not properly part of the Vedas are considered sacred knowledge and hence source of dharma.[7] In the same spirit, custom and tradition are accepted as bases of law. But Kautalya gives the king the final word in determining what shall have the sanction of law in governing social relations. Even custom is subject to the king's interpretation. Dharma, in this radical conception of law, is brought more directly within the province of the monarch. Yet statute law must be compatible with the Vedas and the social order defined therein. The king's discretion is limited by Kautalya's warning of the dangers involved in any radical departure from custom. In claiming the highest authority for the royal edict, Kautalya shares the company of only one or two writers on law and polity. This elevation of the king's role as lawmaker is not in the mainstream of Hindu politics.[8] Kautalya's theory of law may have been influenced by Buddhist jurists who attacked the concept of sacred law, and by the fact that Mauryan kings exercised the legislative function.[9] *Rajasasana*, the king's law, was held to be sovereign in any dispute. But although the philosophy of expedience dominates the *Kautaliya*, an occasional passage suggests an acceptance of higher law and a Brahmanical outlook.

In the Initial book of the treatise Kautalya comments on the importance of each man's performing the duties of the station into which he was born. He supports the social order associated with the brahmans and justified by the varnashrama theory as long as Brahman religious practice and ideology do not get in the way of the interests of the state. Although Kautalya does not include the Brahman purohita among the essential officers of the state, he nevertheless continues to award preferential treatment to the brahmans. Kautalya championed the brahmanic social structure because he saw it as the best means of providing a balanced artha-dharma. It permitted a segment of the population to attain the spiritual life and provided for the more limited spiritual needs of the remainder of the population engaged in material production. Kautalya reminds us of Greek political thinkers in his conception of the polity as the framework within which the individual finds fulfilment and social institutions have their justification.

In the *saptanga* theory, an attempt to analyze and explain the political regime that replaced the tribal polity, Kautalya outlined the seven constituent elements of the sovereign state.

But it will be noted that the saptanga conception of the state is not actually an organic theory. The components are graded, and it is argued only that damage to one of the seven components of sovereignty might adversely affect the others. A true organic theory must await the later Gupta and post-Gupta age when internal dissension and external threat become a constant and serious menace to order. In *Manu* and in a late didactic portion of the *Shantiparva* the term *anga* is employed, and more is made of the analogy of the elements to the limbs of the body.

These components of sovereignty and the general tenets of government and colonization presuppose the ability to keep the population from returning to older tribal loyalties. Kautalya's fear of insurrection and of attempts to re-establish the tribal associations led him to emphasize the integrative as well as the goal-attainment function of the specifically political agencies, and to promote caste organization as an alternative to older patterns of coordination. At the same time he predicted that asceticism,[10] in transforming the people into a contemplative society, would undermine the necessary material foundations of community life. His main criticism of such forms of religious expression is that they are not economically productive. Thinking in terms of the state and its ends, he values asceticism primarily for its usefulness in espionage and intelligence activities; he recommends, for example, that spies be disguised as monks. Before a man could embrace the ascetic life he must have provided for those dependent on him. Kautalya is concerned that religion not be allowed to exert too great a strain on society. Dharma, he insisted, must be realized through artha.

Buddhism had questioned the relevance of action to man's salvation—action, the very essence of the class to which the Buddha himself belonged. And Buddhism warned against the seductions of material things. Although in the early sixth century B.C. the philosopher Carvaka had elaborated a materialist doctrine that rejected everything that could not be known through sense experience, and repudiated asceticism, ritual, mystic knowledge, and all conceptions of the supernatural, and although the school of arthashastra study was established by this time and capitalist enterprise had taken root, action in the "economic" sense of construction and acquisition had not yet developed as an ideal for the higher orders of Indian society. The traditional Brahman roles were actually closer to instrumental activity than were those of the Kshatriya class. The ritual had a utilitarian function, but the conditions and rules under which the ritual was performed had a symbolic rather than an intrinsic relationship to the sacred. Ritual represents a need to take action—in this instance by the manipulation of symbols. " Thus ritual is the expression in action, as distinct from thought, of men's active attitudes toward the non empirical aspects of reality." It tends also to reconstruct life and the universe in mechanical and even materialistic terms.[11]

The Kshatriya had traditionally found confirmation of himself in action *per se*, the direct relationship with other men, which found its fullest expression in warfare and governing. It was in the actual battle, rather than in the victory, that the warrior fulfilled his duty. This varna ideal may be contrasted with the function of the Shudra, *animal laborans*, who existed to satisfy the basic biological requirements of the community and was expected to resign himself to the drudgery of producing that which is immediately consumed. And it differs also from that of the Vaishya, who might be described as *homo faber*, the craftsman who creates the durable artifact—that which gives permanence to the world and makes it human.[12] In seeking an explanation for the materialism and realism of the arthashastra school and for the *Kautaliya* in particular, one is tempted to find in the dharma of the Vaishya class the model for economic action, which when extended to include the activities of building, maintaining, and augmenting the state, transformed Kshatriya action, pure action, into material gain.[13]

We have noted in earlier chapters that the challenge of the heterodox systems to Brahmanism, the erosion of older communal ties, and the need to control tribes and other groups incorporated into the Mauryan imperial state encouraged experimentation with new forms of social integration. For Kautalya the problem is not action so much as organization, the preservation of a consistent pattern of human relationships and the creation of new sources of power. Although Brahmanism could offer no design for the necessary structure of authority, it did suggest the principle of authority based on function. At the same time the state envisaged by Kautalya required the expansion of the area of the political to include many offices which had historically been performed by the brahmans but which could no longer be left to religion—particularly in a time of religious debate. The administration of justice, economic regulation, and the maintenance of internal order were to be incorporated into the political sphere—which in earlier times had been more or less confined to offensive and defensive warfare and patronage of the sacrifice. The demands of order and effective integration forced the area of state activity far beyond the classical confines of Kshatriya dharma.

It is possible that the *Arthashastra* was intended for a prince not himself a Kshatriya, and that this may have influenced Kautalya's conception of the nature and scope of royal power. Or the brahman author of the treatise may have been moved by the interests of his own class to extend the direct political influence of the priests. But although he mentions that ministers should be born of high family (which may mean simply that they should be of Aryan birth), he does not insist, as the *Manusmriti* does, that offices be restricted to members of the priestly class. Kautalya advises qualifying examinations supplemented by tests of character to ascertain loyalty, courage, and integrity.[14] The emphasis of the work is on the requirements of the state and public welfare, rather than the maintenance of positions of privilege. Kautalya was concerned with the development of an independent bureaucracy capable of providing the administrative structure for a stable empire spanning the length and breadth of the land. Such an organization was among the major accomplishments of ancient

China, but, with several notable exceptions, Indian political history was to be marked with less success.

Bureaucratization invariably modifies the traditional social structure. We know that caste privilege, especially in the area of legal rights, existed in the empire of the Mauryas, but it also apparent that a number of the grosser inequities had been reduced. The brahman no longer escaped with reproof or a token punishment for his crime. He continued to be favoured in many regards, but was dealt with more severely in his transgressions. It is not known whether Megasthenes' division of the "philosophers" into Brachmanes and Sarmanes represents a distinction that the Indians themselves made, though Fick thinks it very likely that the orthodox brahmans were differentiated from those negligent in discipline and more secular in their way of life. The tendency to relate punishment to the act rather than to the status of the offender indicates a departure from ascription. The law was often stern, and yet we are impressed with the greater justice of its administration. Kautalya recommends punishments significantly less harsh than those elaborated in the later smriti literature. On occasion he seems to speak out against cruel and inhuman punitive measures.

The author of the *Arthashastra* emerges as something of a champion of the shudras, espousing their rights as freeborn citizens, and going so far as to suggest that the sons of slaves should enjoy the status of Aryans. Kautalya, like the compilers of several of the law codices, sanctions mixed marriages in many cases. Generally, however, the tradition of the Vedas is accepted in the *Arthashastra*, and the king is charged with the preservation of custom and religion. This deference to the Vedic canon is inspired at least partly by Kautalya's sensitivity to the power of superstition and religion over the minds of men. It is difficult to assess the sincerity of his belief in incantation, spell, and magic. Often superstition and magic are enlisted in the service of the state and perform a frankly political function. The state is not beyond exploiting the natural gullibility of the people. The need to fake miracles suggests the importance Kautalya attached to retaining the charismatic element of authority.

There is an oblique reference in the *Arthashastra* to the state of nature, but no actual theory of the origin of government is developed. The passage is obviously official propaganda intended for use in justifying public policy and taxation, as well as in ensuring the loyalty of the masses and silencing "treacherous opponents of sovereignty." The monarchical state, which is basis of Kautalya's political speculation, originates in the unwillingness of men to tolerate the evils of anarchy. The difference between the agreement with Prithu and the compact Kautalya describes is sometimes compared to the difference between a social contract and a governmental contract that deals with definite arrangements between the king and his subjects. The contractual theory put forth in the *Arthashastra* is not meant to suggest limits to the royal authority. Kautalya rationalizes the king's authority in terms of service in return for grain and merchandise, but this contract is visited with spiritual sanctions and the office of the king is compared with the functions of the gods. It is likely that Kautalya looked on the state as an inevitable (and, in this sense, natural) device for ensuring the divinely ordained social order.

The theory of the state in the *Arthashastra* is actually little more than an analysis of the elements essential to the efficient operation of the political organization. Sovereignty is made to depend of seven properties. This is the saptanga theory, to which we have referred. At the head of Kautalya's list is the *svami*, or master, a term used instead of *raja* (ruler) to designate the head of the state, perhaps in order to allow the theory to apply to republics as well as to the monarchical state. It is evident that Kautalya considers the svami, the sovereign power, the most important of the seven components. Despite the significance he attaches to the role of the sovereign, Kautalya contrasts his position with representatives of other schools of arthashastra, each of whom championed a different aspect of the saptanga, in that he would give priority to whichever factor the times should dictate as being of most consequence. Kautalya is a pragmatist in his political approach. But he does commit himself to ranking the factors, for although there is no general agreement among arthashastra theorists as to the relative disadvantage resulting from the injury or destruction of the various elements in the sevenfold theory, Kautalya considers harm to king, official, and populace,[15] in this order, as the most serious misfortunes. Kautalya is no determinist in the sense of seeing social destiny as the toy of the gods. Because he believed in the ability of man to learn from his experience and to exercise his rational faculties, he devoted his treatise to the king as the architect of his time—not as the instrument of fortune.

The second element in the construct is the *amatya,* or administrative class; following Ghoshal, we shall distinguish the administrative officials from the advisers or chief ministers (*mantrins*), whom Kautalya limits to three or four in number. It is probable that originally the amatya was the clansman of the king. By Mauryan times these nobles had become his officers, the foundation of the bureaucracy. These two crucial constituents, the ruler and the official class, are followed by the rural and fortified (or urban) areas, the revenue (or treasury), the standing army, and the permanent ally of the state. Dharma is not included among the components of commonwealth. This list appears in the later treatises of Kamandaka and "Shukra," and in the *Manusmriti.* The theory, in which diplomacy is made an integral part of politics, is intended to show the necessary conditions for the effective functioning of the state. The king occupies a dominant and, in fact, sovereign position. Indeed, "state" and "king" are often used interchangeably. Kautalya's definition of sovereignty remains vague.

A primary source of the king's power is the devotion and allegiance of his people. The king is therefore advised to see no interest other than the interest of his subjects and to guard against their dissatisfaction. "In the happiness of his subjects lies his happiness; in their welfare his welfare." The basis of prosperity is the goodwill of the people. Kautalya does not speak of the rights of the people against the king, but he does regard the king as the servant of the people. There is no defense of arbitrariness, but Kautalya spots short of securing the rights of the citizen against the authority of the government, and, as in the theoretical outgrowths of Rousseau's ideas, the interest of the people must ultimately be identical with those of the state. Opposition to the king is seditious. The relation of king and subject is paternalistic. The state is obligated to protect the subject from transgressions on his rights by others. And not only life and property, but reputation as well, are safeguarded. The concealment of a daughter's premarital experience would cost the father a heavy fine. And woe to the bridegroom who did not advertise his defects (presumably physical).

Politics and Ethics

The reader often comes away from the *Arthashastra* with the impression that the work exhibits a complete indifference to ethical considerations. But as we have seen, side by side with ethical ideal and injunction there exists in ancient Indian theory a willingness to allow ends to sanction the methods employed in reaching those ends. Such political expedience is found in the earliest arthashastra schools cited by Kautalya. We might expect that when, as in the arthashastra school, the principle pervading political analysis and giving unity to the structure of the argument is altered, statements once accepted as merely descriptive of certain situations will take on new implications—as the doctrine of the survival of the fittest comes to justify expediency when the goal of political activity shifts to its own preservation and aggrandizement. When the state's military position was precarious, or when its security was at stake, any means of striking at the enemy was warranted. At such times the chivalric code was a luxury the state could ill afford. Nor is this policy of expedience and reason of state (*kutayaddha)* limited to the specifically arthashastra teaching. The counsel of Bhardvaja in the *Mahabharata* anticipates the dicta that later came to be known as Machiavellism. In (admittedly extreme) statements, it is argued that nothing should be allowed to frustrate the purposes of the king, and selfish ambition need be the only aim of policy.[16] Public interest has little place in this unblushing opportunism; the king need recognize no moral obligation—might and cunning are beyond such standards. "Right...leans on might as the creeper on the tree. Right is in the hands of the strong; nothing is impossible to the strong. Everything is pure that comes from the strong."

The advice of the brahman minister Kanika is similar. The warrior is told to be remorseless with his enemies, to speak softly but firmly, to be ever prepared and always alert, to trust no one, to employ all techniques that might further his purposes, to excite the fear of the timid, and to be guarded in his movements. The images of political life that appear from time to time in the *Mahabharata*, and especially in the *Shantiparva*, are of battlefield and jungle (matsyanyaya). "Without piercing the vitals of others, without achieving the most difficult feats, and without slaying creatures like a fisherman [slaying fish], no person can obtain great prosperity. Without slaughter no man has been able to achieve fame or subjects in this world. Indra, himself, by the slaughter of Vritra, became the *great* Indra...Animals live upon animals, the stronger upon the weaker....This has been ordained by the gods." And again : "A king desirous of prosperity should not scruple to slay son or brother or father or friend, if any of these seek to thwart his objects." Here is something of the old amorality of the heroic age. In the early Dharmasutras as well, political theory does not rely entirely on the scriptures for its authority. And, as several Indian scholars have pointed out, even in major religious works we find the search for a rational basis of politics, for a separate science of government. In Buddhist commentary, however, politics is returned to its subordinate position.[17]

There can never be a thoroughgoing divorce of politics and ethics for Kautalya; he never denies that the ultimate purpose of the state is a moral purpose, the maintenance of dharma. This is not say that the state has no justification of its own; and when morality does find a place in Kautalyan politics, expedience continues to be served. When Kautalya remarks that might and self-aggrandizement are more important than religion and morality, he means that moral principles must be subordinated to the interests of state in as much as the moral order depends upon the continued existence of the state. Kautalya is not above employing moral concepts either as a guise or because of their efficiency in securing appropriate conduct. Religion must, from the point of view of society, be judged in terms of its capacity to produce order. But had this not always been implicit in the relationship of Brahma and Kshatra authorities? Traditionally it was the religious proficiency of the purohita that determined the success of the king. Now, of course, the point had been reached where the brahmans must look to the state for the security of their interests.

For the most part, unscrupulous tactics are recommended only against those who would subvert and destroy the order on which society rested. Even in war, moral considerations may decide the outcome. In the *Arthashastra* war is no longer the sport of the kshtriya and legitimate in its own right. It has become an instrument of policy to be employed when all else has failed. Kautalya distinctly prefers means short of open conflict, but he is more concerned with the cost and the possibilities of defeat than with the moral and ethical aspects of the problem.

We have earlier remarked on the fact that dharma embraces both a natural and a moral order.[18] This fusion might in itself have encouraged a naturalistic ethic. We must remember that the concept of swadharma links moral good with fulfilment of caste function. The obligations of the king's personal dharma may necessitate certain acts which, of themselves, are not easily justified. Max Weber remarks :

> The problem of a "political ethic" has never preoccupied Indian theory and in the absence of the ethical universalism and natural right, it could hardly be otherwise. The dharma of the prince was to conduct war for the sake of pure power *per se*.... All political theory...

> went far beyond what was familiar and average practice for the *signores* of the early Italian Renaissance in these respects and was completely devoid of all "ideology" in our sense of the word.[19]

Danda itself provides at least a partial explanation for Kautlaya doctrine of expediency. The principle represents a bridge between morality and *raison d'etat*. Danda was nemesis for the king who misused its power as well as for subjects who offended against the moral order. "For punishment (danda), when awarded with due consideration, makes the people devoted to righteousness and to works productive of wealth and enjoyment; while punishment, when ill-awarded under the influence of greed and anger or owing to ignorance, excites fury even among hermits and ascetics dwelling in forests, not to speak of householders." But this quality of the royal power was easily eclipsed by the tremendous authority the coercive function assumed as guarantor of the dharmic system. The *Arthashastra* provides ample evidence that Kautalya understood the true significance of the two-edged sword of danda.

The fact remains, and it cannot be brushed aside, that in the first book of the *Arthashastra* Kautalya remarks that "the sole aim of all the sciences is nothing but restraint of the organs of sense. Whosoever is of perverted disposition and ungoverned senses will soon perish, though possessed of the whole earth bounded by the four quarters." The sentiment appears almost Buddhist in tone. A later excerpt may be taken as a fairly complete expression of the moral argument applied to political rule : "A wise king can make even the poor and miserable elements of his sovereignty happy and prosperous; but a wicked king will surely destroy the most prosperous and loyal elements of his kingdom." These statements are no attempt to disguise the political realism of the work and soften the harsh counsel to come. Kautalya here is very much the brahman minister, representative of the power essential to victory. For all his commitment to a philosophy of opportunism and force, Kautalya would not have limited might to mere physical mastery. Such may be the primary obligation of warrior and even king, but the *ultimate* power is spiritual.

It is the politically unrealistic exaltation of nonviolence and mystic self-trandscendence that Kautalya rejects. The world remains with us and must be conquered if the difficult task of conquering ourselves is to be successful. Self-mastery and world-mastery are interdependent. There is, however, the suggestion of a debt to the great philosophical systems of the "axial age." In the Buddhist tradition some men are already close to enlightenment at the time of their birth. They may choose to become either buddhas or chakravartins. The chakravartin, or world master,[20] must have achieved self-discipline; this is the condition of his success. The concept of a state spanning the length and breadth of the subcontinent under the rule of a chakravartin goes back at least to the tenth century B.C., but Buddhism gave the concept the special significance it has had for Indian history. The idea came to be understood as the hope that the sphere of interstate politics, the area of political activity subject only to the primitive law of survival, might be made more amenable to moral controls. Ashoka Maurya was the embodiment of this lofty principle.

Kautalya believed, no less than did the great emperor, that control of the senses is crucial to the king's effectiveness as a ruler. Indeed the principle that one should be able to rule oneself before attempting to rule others is a major premise of Indian philosophy, antedating its most famous and systematic statement in the *Republic* of Plato.

We have noted earlier the resolution of the dilemma of action in Krishna's counsel to the hesitant kshatriya knight. To act is not to commit evil if the act is performed in a spirit of detachment. Such a philosophy may have provided an adequate rationale for the traditional social role of the warrior class in the face of the new ethical and ascetic doctrines appearing at the end of the Vedic epoch, but for the emerging state there remained the practical problem of defense and material well-being. Action could not be disinterested if the state were to survive and prosper. Thus does the problem of *raison d'etat* develop—before its appearance in the West.[21] The statesman, faced with conflicting demands and feeling called upon to compromise traditional ethical principles in the interest of the state, may find justification for his acts in the knowledge that he has put the general welfare first. The ruler who remained faithful to the Kautalyan teaching could have such consolation; for the author of the *Arthashastra* the welfare of the state meant ultimately the welfare of the people, and the well-being of his subjects must be rated higher than that of the king himself.

Kautalya is aware that power must always be allied with shrewdness and restraint if it is not to be self-destructive. It is the element of cunning or, more positively, the sense of the situation, that has earned the brahman writer a sinister reputation in the minds of many. In discussing the traits of character indispensable to the king, he mentions "non-fatalism"—quite possibly as a criticism of attitudes of mind encouraged by Buddhism but incompatible with political life. The king must possess qualities of energy, among which he lists valor, impetuosity, agility, and dexterity. Immediately the tone of the work is set when Kautalya calls on the ruler to utilize "the opportunities afforded by the proper place, time and personal energy; [demonstrate] skill in discriminating between conditions which require conclusion of a treaty and manifestation of valor [*i.e.,* in determining when it is appropriate to pursue a policy of peace or war], letting off the enemies and curbing them, and waiting under the pretext of some mutual understanding and taking advantage of the enemies' weak points."

The state has a strong interest in encouraging civil morality; hence the ruler, who is an example to his people, cannot in his own conduct repeatedly challenge the bases of this morality. The ruler of unrighteous character is unable to rely on the loyalty and support of his subjects. "Which enemy is to be marched against—a powerful enemy of wicked character or a powerless enemy of righteous character?" asks Kautalya. "The strong enemy of wicked character should be marched against, for when he is attacked, his subjects will not help him, but rather put him down or go to the side of the conqueror. But when the enemy of virtuous character is attacked, his subjects will help him or die with him.... Hence, no king should give room to such causes as would bring about impoverishment, greed or disaffection among his people. If, however, they appear, he should at once take remedial measures against them."

Certainly it is as valid to judge a political thinker on the measure of what he sought to accomplish as it is to examine him in the context of later-day politics. Had not the Renaissance yielded Machiavelli, nor the nineteenth century Bismarck, if we were not sensitive to the arguments of reason of state, we would perhaps assess Kautalya in a kindlier light. Similarities in the theories of the Mauryan minister and Machiavelli have long preoccupied students of Hindu polity. (It has even been suggested that the Italian was inspired by the *Arthashastra*). But the validity of such a comparison is limited. Whereas Kautalya emphasizes the personal character of the king, and indeed sees the prince's capacity for righteous deportment as basic to beneficial administration, recommending that where possible he be exemplary in his conduct, Machiavelli is primarily concerned that the prince be able to inspire the loyalty of his people. In the *Discorsi*, he warns against arbitrariness and the dangers inherent in disturbing existing laws, remarking that security is what men want most. Private morality is valid only in the sphere of personal relations and not in politics, but the morality of the individual is closely linked with the interests and goals of the community. Machiavelli hoped that the state could elevate the man who, inspired by a public spirit, would rise above his natural weaknesses. Virtue thus became civic virtue, patriotism. Because righteousness as such is irrelevant to the realm of politics, men must learn "how not to be good."

Kautalya's greater concern with the life of the community and its role in shaping the institution of government is due not to his greater respect for man's moral nature and capacity for virtuous conduct, but to his acceptance of caste organization and the general noninterference of the state in the fulfilment of personal duty. Dandaniti exists to aid the processes of control and socialization, which are essentially the province of caste and religious institutions. Machiaveli's state exists to restrain man from the worst excesses of his own character. For Kautalya, the caste system (though still not fully developed) assumed the major burden of this regulatory function.

In the *Discourses* Machiavelli is intent on reviving ancient virtue as the basis of political society. He, like other Renaissance humanists, turned to the past in an attempt to find the foundations of the virtu that had motivated men to deeds of glory. But where corruption is the rule, the only hope for stability and cohesion is the prince. Loyalty to the leader must take the place of public virtue. In Indian theory there exists a myth that the king was originally named to combat some imminent danger to the order or to cope with some great need. (Likewise does the avatar appear in moments of crisis to ensure the preservation of dharma). The same concern for order and security inspires the *Arthashastra,* and the work is comparable to *The Prince* in its reliance on the *tyrannos* as the ultimate agent of stability and prosperity when the times are out of joint and social integration threatened. But where does Kautalya find *his* model of heroic virtu? The materialism of the arthashastra teaching must be supplemented with concepts and images of traditional Vedic belief.

With Kautalya we arrive at a new stage in the development of the principle of political authority. In Brahmanic theory the legitimation of power and the activities of the state had customarily been rooted in the ruler's duty of protection. The *Arthashastra* represents an important step in the direction of authority based on interest and concerns shared by all, authority which takes unto itself many functions previously reserved to institutions outside the state proper. But though caste appears to play a less important role in the treatise than in the law books or religious works (as we should expect), and though the state has entered into areas of regulation historically the prerogative of economic associations, tribes, or other social organizations, and has expanded its judicial and welfare activities, the primary intent was not to destroy the pluralism of Hindu society. Kautalya opposes any decentralizing tendency that would weaken the control of the state over the economic life of the community; the state is directly concerned with the accumulation of wealth, upon which its over all strength depends. It is true that the state he pictures has a strong interest in the values and sentiments of the people, and he is not above using religion for the purposes of the state, but he advocates no program of systematic indoctrination of the sort carried out in the regime of Ashoka. Nor does the state seek to eliminate the independent group life of the community and detach the individual from his old moorings. It is more appropriate to suggest that state policy constituted a greater threat to the tyranny of the group over the individual than to the freedom of the individual to pursue his own purposes as defined by custom and religious tradition.

The first step in the direction of what we have come to call totalitarianism may have been taken, but a wide area of autonomy remained with the many associations that composed society. The state's control over the thought and movements of the people could not in any sense approximate the regimentation of the modern totalitarian state with an advanced technological and organizational apparatus at its disposal. What Kautalya has done is to assert the importance of state participation in economic matters—active entry into the productive process, control of prices, interest rates, and licensing, and even supervision of occupations. All of which must, of course, amount to a significant weakening of one aspect of caste authority.

Montesquieu postulated that the central feature of tyranny was its basis in the isolation of the ruler from his subjects and the subjects from one another. Seen in these terms, the caste basis of Indian society served to fragment the population and insulate the masses against control by an elite. Caste, however, organized the people as well as divided them, creating groups along functional lines. Caste organization did represent a hindrance to the formulation of collective goals and, as such, constituted a challenge to the state-builder. Kautalya did not oppose the supporting and sustaining function of caste, as long as the general welfare was not prejudiced by narrow class interest. He advises the ruler, for example, to allow the people of a conquered territory to pursue their traditional way of life, retain their language, celebrate their festivals. And the king must not seek to cut himself off from the populace in splendid aloofness. He must actively seek their affection and be constantly alert to the main currents of opinion. Members of the community are encouraged, for their part, to think of themselves as subjects having in common a number of purposes that only the state can fulfill. Political authority, in the Kautalyan state, has become more differentiated from other forms of authority, and its scope has broadened immensely.

Kautalya was faced with the same need for political union in the face of disorder and external threat that confronted Machiavelli in northern Italy. In a sense, Mauryan India was itself in the throes of a renaissance, which would culminate in the enlightened rule of the emperor Ashoka. Belief stirred against belief, culture against culture; extensive discretionary powers were granted the ruler as the means for deterring disruptive forces, and authority was centralized as it had never been before.[22] The times called for flexibility, which in turn presupposed goal-directed collective activity. It is likely that with the increased gravity and expense of war the state would have found it more efficacious, when possible, to employ intrigue in meeting challenges to its authority.

Kautalya's opportunism—even if it does not represent the political position of the Mauryan preceptor—must also be seen in the context of brahman struggles with heterodox systems of thought. The very defense of brahman interests may have made the reappraisal of religious controls imperative. It was now to brahman advantage to seek the active cooperation of the state, to block any alignment of the state with heterodoxy, and to support the ambitions of political authority sympathetic to the brahmans. Perhaps it appeared to the brahman author of the *Arthashastra,* writing in a time of momentous change and declining power of old institutions, that the basis of the traditional code was forever lost, that matsyanyaya had become the characteristic of all relationships.

As Burckhardt has pointed out, Machiavelli viewed the state as a work of art—not as a product of nature working through man, or as part of the divine plan, but as the conscious creation of man, analogous to artistic fabrication. The *Arthashastra* can be characterized in the same terms. It is the art of government rather than a theory of the state that we find in the writings of the Florentine and the Hindu : both are preoccupied with techniques of achieving[23] supreme power, both are confronted with situations that make some degree of arbitrary government necessary. Both are concerned with the leader (*dux*), who establishes the authoritative role. Both (and this would follow) write from the vantage point of the ruler, and their treatises belong to the "mirror of princes" category of political literature.

The Machiavelli of *The Prince* is a political thinker engrossed with practical questions of the actual foundation of the state, the creation of a viable political order in the face of contention, timorousness, and debasement. The Machiavelli of the *Discourses* defends republican government as producing the most vigorous state once order has been established and secured. It is not inconceivable that, had Kautalya composed a "Discorsi" which assumed a condition of unity and strength, his emphasis would have shifted from *dux* to *rex,* the sovereign whose role is predetermined. We would have a work of the nature of the rajadharma literature, with all the safeguards against arbitrariness that the term implies. But there is little indication in the *Arthashastra* of any consuming interest in the development of a popular virtu, a mass public-spiritedness that could make possible a transition to republican institutions.

The approach to politics of Kautalya and Machiavelli has a definite empirical character and their theories rest on a naturalistic ethic. The good tends frequently to be that which contributes to the satisfaction of universal needs and desires. Security is one of the most important of these needs; it is the wish for security that bridges the private and public spheres of activity. The major function of the state is the provision of stability and security. Because religion itself depends on order, the state is justified in employing religion as a means for achieving stability. The constancy of human nature makes it possible for man to learn from history, but history is viewed by Kautalya and Machiavelli as a storehouse of examples, rather than as a dynamic process.[24] Kautalya is sensitive to the economic aspects of power, whereas Machiavelli works with more purely political concepts. Though rich in political maxims intended for broad application, Kautalyan theory is strongly pragmatic and adaptive. There is room in the argument for the unforeseeable. Unfortunate the king who does not constantly gauge the temper of his people, who does not estimate carefully his chances for success before acting, who does not seek advice from the experienced and the astute. In attempting to systematize the study of politics as a science in its own right and to treat the subject objectively, both Kautalya and Machiavelli were pioneers.

Perhaps Machiavellism is a characteristic of the transition from traditional authority to legal-rational authority—a development that failed to complete itself in ancient India, possibly because of a change in the legitimation pattern which served the interests of the monarchy without fundamentally altering the "sacred" structure. But problems of administering a large territory and conflicts within the normative system forced the initial break with the older principles of legitimation.

REFERENCES

1. Literally, the word *artha* means 'thing, object, substance,' and comprises the whole range of the tangible objects that can be possessed, enjoyed, and lost, and which we require in daily life for the upkeep of a household, raising of a family, and discharge of religious duties, *i.e.,* for the virtuous fulfilment of life's obligations." (Zimmer [441], p. 35). The word is pronounced art—ha.

2. The science of politics was, in the earlier stages of its history, known as *raja-dharma*. The term was, in time, replaced by *dandaniti* and *arthashastra* and, eventually, by *rajanitishastra*, or simply *nitishastra*. *Vide* Jayaswal [199], pp. 5f.
3. Manavah, Barhaspatyah, Ausanasah, Parasarah; he alludes to more than a dozen authors. B.C. Law, "A Short Account of the Wandering Teachers at the Time of the Buddha," in the *Journal and Proceedings of the Asiatic Society of Bengal*, XIV, No. 7, 399ff., has listed the names of forty-one wandering scholars whom he considers to have provided the precedent for technical and systematic manuals such as the arthashastra and nitishastra literature. Brihaspati and Shukra were venerated as the founders of the science of arthashastra. Works of the former school have been published by F.W. Thomas (*Brihaspatisutra*), and a relatively late version of the Shukra teaching has been edited by G. Oppert (*Shukranitisara*). *Vide* chapter 12 below.
4. Dandin parodies the arthashastra teaching. (The names Vishnugupta and Chanakya are generally understood to refer to Kautalya). A king is warned against rascals who promise much but can deliver little : they will say that, of the four royal studies, "theology, agriculture, metaphysics, are big and slow to show results. Leave them alone. Just study political science. Now Professor Vishnugupta has made a little epitome of this for the king—twenty-four thousand lines of poetry. Learn it by heart, apply it in detail; and it does what it promises.' 'Good,' says [the prince], and starts to study. He learns it (meanwhile growing old) and finds that book leading to other books. It can't be truly understood until the whole wordy mass is mastered. Well, suppose he does master it, later or sooner. The first result is that he no longer trusts anyone, even son or wife. Even for his own belly he must have just so much porridge, made of just so many grains of rice. For the coking of just so much porridge, he must be given just so much firewood, correctly weighed and measured.

   "Having risen from table... he must spend the first eighth of the day in listening to a complete statement of receipts and disbursements. While he is listening, a double amount is stolen by the knavish bureaucrats who have the wit to multiply a thousandfold the forty tricks of peculation taught by Chanakya." (*The Ten Princes,* transl. Arthur Ryder [Chicago, Phoenix paperback, 1960], pp. 202f.)

5. Kosambi [221] argues that the language of the glossators shows them to be Buddhists and Jainas and that they would have had no reason to adopt a forgery of the third or fourth century A.D. as genuine.

6. On the other hand, there are those who stress stylistic similarities with the Brahmanas and the Upanishads.

7. Kautalya goes so far as to include historical and administrative texts and even arthashastra literature in the category of "Vedas."

8. There is the possibility that the bureaucratic structure elaborated by Kautalya and the importance he attaches to the royal edict may reflect the influence of Hellenistic governmental practice. The regard for positive law and for the purposes of the state as ends in themselves also suggests a comparison with the legalist (or realist) school of Chinese political thought which dominated the Ch'in state in the third century B.C., although it is extremely doubtful that the great brahman writer can have known anything of this philosophy. The *Book of Lord Shang,* supposedly the work of Wei Yang (died c. 338 B.C.), is in some ways a Chinese equivalent of the *Arthashastra,* although the later does not have the same totalitarian implications, nor is it in substance a critique of the old order. The legalists, who took their inspiration from the *Book of Lord Shang,* set out to destroy hereditary class privilege and the feudal structure of China, and to challenge the traditional Confucian ideals and anything that was thought to detract from the strength of the state. In the place of the former values and institutions, these theorists and politicians advocated a rigid code of laws, a harsh discipline oriented toward service to the state, a Hobbesian psychology and naturalistic ethic, and a political policy based on expedience. *Vide* Dirk Bodde, *China's First Unifier* (Leiden, 1938); Moore [278], chapt. 2.

9. As the policy pronouncements of Ashoka's edicts indicate.

10. The reference is evidently to Buddhism. He does, however, recognize that the adherents of heterodox faiths constitute a force to be reckoned with, and he places the "heretics"

fairly high on the list of those whose affairs the king must be careful to attend to. (*Arthashastra*, I, 19, p. 41).

11. What Cornford says about the relationship of Olympianism and philosophy may have some relevance for the parallel development in India and may help explain why brahman ritualism, based as it was on the manipulation of the Vedic pantheon, could actually be a necessary step in the development of arthashastra ideology. "The type of philosophy to which an Olympian theology will give rise will be dominated by the conception of spatial externality, as *Moira* had dominated the Gods; and it will tend towards discontinuity and discreteness. Originating in an essentially polytheistic scheme, it will be pluralistic. It will also move steadily towards materialism, because, having no hold upon the notion of life as an inward and spontaneous principle, it will reduce life to mechanical motion, communicated by external shock from one body to another. It will level down the organic to the inorganic, and pulverize God and the Soul into material atoms." ([72], p. 123).

12. I have here borrowed the distinctions employed by Hannah Arendt [8] in her study of the various modes of activity and their relation to political life.

13. This problem was discussed in Chapter 9 above.

14. There is no discussion of the techniques for recruiting lower officials.

15. The people are not properly an element in the theory.

16. And such works as the *Manusmriti* and the *Shantiparva* hold that wars of aggression, if certain basic humanitarian rules are observed, are no less justifiable than wars to defend the kingdom.

17. The earlier discussion of the *Bhagavad Gita* pointed up the relativism in Indian thought, a relativism which is dictated by more than caste considerations and which extends to codes of conduct. This element, when it enters the realm of political philosophy, has proved more shocking to students than it has when it figures in religion and is characterized as "tolerance." The career of Lord Krishna, as it unfolds in the *Mahabharata*, exhibits what by other standards might be

seen as the most flagrant abuses. (It is interesting that two of the major roles he assumes, those of lover and warrior, are areas of activity where we might ironically admit that "all is fair.") There is no shortage of evidence that for all the syncretism and devaluation of the world in Indian belief, the social divisions it sustained (directly or indirectly) impeded the development of a universal ethic.

18. Such a principle is not unique to India. In Greece and elsewhere in the ancient world we encounter similar concepts which combine fate and justice and which, as rules, ordain what must be as well as what ought to be.

19. Elsewhere Weber, referring to the *Arthashastra*, says that "in contrast with this document Machiavelli's *Principle* is harmless." ("Politics as a Vocation," in Gerth and Mills [139], p. 124).

20. This concept (*cakravartin*, from *cakra*, wheel), which we have referred to on several occasions, was utilized by Buddhism to symbolize the universality of the Buddhist spiritual message. The wheel represents the Buddhist dharma. Although the emphasis on self-mastery reflects the influence of heterodoxy, it also has roots in the importance of discipline as the basis for proper fulfilment of caste function. The priests stood to secure their own positions and protect themselves by insisting on righteous behaviour buttressed by restraint and obedience. In brahman hands the idea of self-mastery seems to have been fused with the older Vedic belief that power could be communicated from the supernatural sphere to man (the Greek concept of *menos*) : self-mastery was a source of increased strength.

21. The dialogue that Thucydides (*History of the Peloponnesian War*, Book V, 84-116) represents as having taken place between the Athenians and the citizens of Melos is usually considered to be the first clear statement of the issue, but in classical Greece there was no distinct division between the ethics of national conduct and that of individuals, for man found his highest realization in the *polis* and could not rightly be considered apart from it. In India the separation was more sharply drawn, although Kautalya sought to relate state and society more closely, without destroying the regulative function of the caste order in the process. This

ambiguity complicates any attempt to label his thinking "solidarian." It is true that he worked to clear away impediments to the efficient operation of the political process, but he cannot be accused of actively striving to eliminate agencies that served to mediate between the masses and the governing elite.

22. Book V, chap. 11, of Aristotle's *Politics* (on methods of ensuring the stability of monarchies) suggests a number of rough parallels with Kautalya's advice to the ruler who would increase his power.
23. Acquiring and maintaining power. Machiavelli discusses the problem of preserving power and order in the *Discourses;* the creation of order holds his attention in *The Prince.*
24. There is a tendency among Indian scholars to credit Kautalya with a keener historical sense than the Arthashastra in fact reveals—or than we should expect, considering the nature of the Indian belief system.

8 Rationing in State Departments

The State in the Arthasastra follows in practice a strict policy of control over food consumption in the different branches of its administration. Articles of foodstuff and fodder are to be supplied for use by men and animals in the service of the State in measured quantities and proportions according to fixed scales. Where large numbers are involved as in the various State departments, average standards of maintenance are to be formulated, which can apply to all members of the consuming classes, for which they are intended, though they may not give satisfaction to individual tastes and appetites. To understand the value of rationing from experience in the field where it is at work is to pave the way for its application on a wider scale, if required. The State's scheme of rationing may as well be adopted by private employers of labour including dealers in various classes animals. The controlled rates may be taken as representing reasonably permissible limits of human and animal consumption to the extent of the employer's liability to feed their dependents. Rationing, to be in force is shown as a feature of the normal course of administration, and not as an indication of austerity connected with conditions of a chronic shortage of production. The State must be left with enough of its farm products to be disposed of through trade to earn a good return after consumption by its establishment, the limits of which must be prudently regulated. That actual physical needs are not overlooked is clear from the fact that separate scales are mentioned for men, women and children, as well as for different classes of animals based on an appreciation of their varying capacity for consumption. Thus it is advised that the ration for a horse must increase proportionately as it grows in age according to certain rates up to the fourth year, when the maximum scale is to be reached. The different elements of fodder have to be determined with an eye on, or an estimate of the physical requirements of the particular class of animals to be fed. In the case of a bullock, for instance it is said that in addition to a fixed share of cooked barely, it is to be give one *tula* of oil-cakes or ten *adhakas* of bran. That economy is one of the motives underlying the control policy may be easily admitted from the instruction delivered to the Superintendent of horses on the need for its observance in the distribution of the provision received from the stores. Rations for men and animals are to be distributed from the State's storehouse where are collected foodstuffs produced on royal lands, and those on private holdings representing the king's share as the agricultural tax to which he is entitled, etc. The king's store is under the charge of a Superintendent who works in the matter of the distribution of rations in co-operation with the Superintendents of horses and elephant respectively. As regards rations for human beings, different quantities are fixed for men, women and children, but what is specially significant is that a distinction is drawn between an Arya and an Avara, *i.e.*, a member of a low caste, in regard to shares of rations.

The distinction between an *Arya* and *Avara*, though not explicitly stated, may be presumed to be such a living factor in the related socio-economic system that the State is persuaded to regard it as the basis of preferential dietary provision. The existing inequality between the *Arya* and the *Avara* in their respective standards of living seems to be the justification of the State's discination in the rationing scheme. It has no policy of equalizing the differing standards by prescribing the same meals for both. The tables of rations adopted by the State may reasonably be supposed to be based on an average calculation of dietary requirements differing on grounds of sex and also of the age and social stratum to which the person concerned belongs. What is provided may be taken as the reductable minimum, since, for the State, economizing the consumption of its own resources of foodstuff, must be an aim constantly kept in view as the surplus is required for trade. It goes without saying that for the distributing centers it is essential to keep registers according to sex, age and caste, and of animals according to species and service. From the detailed figures regarding the numerical strength and composition of the army and the commissariat, as furnished by the Classical sources, some idea might be formed on a conjectural basis as to what could have been the total food requirements of the military departments of Chandragupta Maurya if the schedules of rations, contained in the Arthasastra, were applied. But even this estimate with its inevitable drawbacks, being limited to the Army only, would be incomplete since no figures are available for the other departments of the State.

Supply of provisions in some departments may be regarded as an item in the cost of production in the public sector in addition to wages to be paid to employees.

For the determination of quotas human beings, as already mentioned, are firstly divided into two broad classes, *viz.*, *Aryas* and *Avaras*; this difference may be supposed to be based on social and economic grounds. Secondly, both are subdivided into three categories each, *viz.*, grown-up men, women and children. This division is made on the ground that the rate of consumption by a man is to be taken as less than that by a woman, and also that children consume less than adults. Rations mentioned in every case are considered suitable or sufficient for one meal only.

It is to be noted that between an *Arya* and *Avara*, so far as the quantity of cereals to be distributed is concerned, there seems to be no difference, it being fixed for both at one *prastha* which is equivalent to 1/16 *drona*. Now the *drona* for servants is said to be different from the public *drona* by 12½ *mashas*. Thus a public measure is subject to a certain depreciation when its use is applied by the State to its employees. In so far as the difference is to be followed in the distribution of rations, an employee will receive them in quantities which are less by a certain percentage than if measured on the basis of the current public standard. Consequently the rations to which the employee's standard is applied will represent a smaller value in the market. Besides one *prastha* of rice, an *Arya* is entitled to ¼ *prastha* of *supa* (curry), as well as clarified butter or oil weighing 1/16 *prashta*. An *Avara* on the other hand is to have 1/6 *prastha* of *supa*, instead ¼ as fixed for an Arya, and 1/32 instead of 1/16 prastha of oil. There seems to be no provision for butter in the case of an *Avara*. According as a woman in an *Arya* or an *Avara* her total rations should be one-fourth of those fixed either for the *Arya* group or the *Avara* group of males as the case may be and one-eighth for children on the same principle of calculation. Thus rations are fixed on the understanding that a woman consumes one-fourth of what a male adult does and a child its one-eighth. Regarding the quality of the rice to the supplied, the selection is to be made in consideration of habits, service and rank. Out of *Sali* of different grades varying quantities of rice are produced, the finest of them being the smallest in quantity in comparison with the other varieties. Five *dronas* or twenty *adhakas* being taken as the common measure of *Sali*, the yield varies from twelve to five *adhakas* the difference between each preceding variety and the one following it being of one *adhaka* only. The first or the coarsest variety (*i.e.*, twelve *adhakas*), is meant for the consumption of young elephants, the second (eleven *adhakas*) of rude elephants, the third (ten *adhakas*) of elephants employed for riding, the fourth (nine *adhakas*) of those used for war purposes, the fifth (eight *adhakas*) of infantry, the sixth (seven *adhakas*) of military chiefs, the seventh (six *adhakas*) of queens and princes, and the eights (five *adhakas*) for the use kings. The rations, it will appear, comprise rice, salt, oil, or, in some cases butter as an alternative. References are also made to salt, sugar, curd and pungent substances required for the preparation of meat, fish, vegetarian (*saka*) and other dry (*sushkanam*) dishes. Different proportions of these ingredients are to be mixed up with flesh etc., of different quantities. It is not clear if these preparations are included among rations. *Supa* (soup, broth), also some kind of fat, oil or butter are separately mentioned in connection with rations when the *supa* cannot be made without either or both. Is prepared food to be distributed also? If so, what is the per *capita* consumption when the preparation consists of twenty *palas* of flesh dressed with half a *kudumba* of oil, one *pala* of salt, one *pala* of sugar, two *dharanas* of spices and a half *prashthaa* of curd? If greater quantities of flesh are used, the same ingredients are to be proportionately increased. Thus twenty *palas* of flesh serves as a unit for the calculation of the proportionate quantities of the different ingredients required to be used with it. These directions are probably given for the guidance of the royal kitchen or of any special kitchen run by the State for any particular establishment such as a military department. It should be noted that the utility of sugar, salt, pungent substances and curd as mentioned here is shown only in respect of the dressing of flesh, fried fish, etc. Whether a poor man's daily diet is to include these items is problematical. But the culinary instructions provided in this context are of some value in showing how it is seriously attempted to put a curb on waste and extravagance in the use of certain essential articles of food-value, to which a limit is set in pursuance of the State's policy of regulating consumption.

We may next proceed to consider rates of allotment for birds, animals etc., of different kinds. The typical animals mentioned are elephants, horses, camels, bullocks, buffaloes, boars, dogs, goats, asses, deer, birds include geese, herons, peacocks. In some instances differences in rations are to be supported on the ground of age or capacity as noted, for example, in the case of horses or elephants of different sizes. Rations for a bullock comprise one *drona* of bareley cooked with other ingredients as prescribed for horses, besides one *tula* of oilcakes or ten *adhakas* of bran; for a buffalo or a camel twice the above quantity; for asses and some varieties of deer half a *drona*, for an antelope one *adhaka*; for a goat, a ram and a boar half an *adhaka* or one *adhaka* of grain with bran; for a dog one *prastha* of cooked rice : for a *hamsa*, a heron and a peacock half a *prashta*: in the department of Superintendent of horses, for a colt, ten days old, one *kudummba* of flour mixec with ¼ *kudumba* of clarified butter, and one *prastha* of milk until the age, is six months. This quota is to be increased by a half in each successive month, in addition to one *prastha* of barley till it completes the age of three years when the provision will be further increased by one *drona* of barley which is to continue till the age of four years. This is the normal diet for a grown-up serviceable horse. For the best horse two *dronas* of rice (*sali, vrihi*), barley, panic seeds (*proyangu*), cooked *mudga* or *masha,* one *prastha* of oil, 5 *palas* of salt, 50 *palas* of flesh, 1 *adhaka* of broth (*rasa*) or 2 *adhakas* of curd, 5 *palas* of sugar, in addition to 1 *prastha* of *sura* (*liquor*) or 2 *prastha* of milk : quantities of some rations differ according as the horse is of large, medium or lower size. A draught horse is to be given the diet prescribed for the best horse. In the department of the Superintendent of elephants and elephant (of seven or eight *aratnis* in height) is to be given I *drona* of rice, ½ *adhaka* of oil, 3 *prasthas* of butter, 10 *palas* of salt, 50 *palas* of flesh, 1 *adhaka* of broth or 2 *adhakas* of curd, in addition to 10 *palas* of *kshara* (molasses), 1 *adhaka* of liquor, or 2 *adhakas* of milk : for elephants of a lesser height the diet is to be proportionately reduced. Additional rations are to be supplied in certain cases. Thus for elephants of the usual height the following must be provided : 1 *prastha* of oil for bodily treatment, a further 1/8 *prastha* of oil for the same use and for lighting purposes in the stable, 2 *bharas* of green feed and 2 ½ *bharas* of dry grass. In special cases additional rations are provided also for horses, consisting of one *prastha* of oil (for injection), 1 *kudumba* of oil for nasal use, 10 *palas* to soft grass, 20 *palas* of ordinary grass and haystalk or grass sufficient to cover an area of 6 *aratnis,* which is supposed by some to form a bedding for the horse. Special hygienic rations are distributed as suited to particular conditions of health. Thus a steed that has just given birth to a colt is to be provided for the first three days with 1 *prastha* of clarified butter : afterwards with one *prastha* of flour (*saktu*) and medicated oil for ten nights. The chapter dealing with the functions of the Superintendent of cows constants some particulars regarding rations for animals which are not the same as those noticed above to be found in the other relevant chapters applying to bulls, cows, mules, asses, buffaloes and camels whose rations are specified in the chapter dealing with the duties and functions attached to the office of the Superintendent of the Government Storehouse. But the particulars in the chapter on the Superintendent of cows are given in connection with the rights and duties of the cowherds, apparently those employed by the State, and these go to illustrate the manner of rearing heads of cattle'. Rations for a special type of bulls to be taken care of under the supervision of the department of cattle for their having a high speed and carrying capacity include half a *bhara* of meadow grass, one *tula* (100 *palas*) of oil cakes, 10 *adhakas* of bran, 5 *palas* of salt, 1 *kudumba* of oil, 1 *prastha* of drink, 1 *tula* of flesh, 1 *adhaka* of curd, 1 *drona* of barley or of cooked *masha*, 1 *drona* milk : or half an *adhaka* of sura, 1 *prastha* of oil or fat, 10 *palas* of sugar, with 1 *palu* of ginger as an alternative drink. Some of these are believed to have a special utility in ensuring serviceability of the beast of for which they are meant. The same items reduced in quantity are prescribed for mules, cows and asses. Double the quantity of the above commodities is fixed for buffaloes and camels. The diet of draught oxen and cows supplying milk is to be in proportion respectively to the duration of their service and the quality of milk yielded. Rations are thus determined not merely on the basis of what an animal actually needs for its bare sustenance, but also from the utilitarian point of view.

9 The Materialism of the Charvakas Lokayatikas

Brhaspati (c, 7th-6th century B.C.) is believed to be the founder of the Charvaka Lokayatika school and the author of its Sutras.[1] The Charvakas Lokayatikas are materialist philosophers. It would be a rude error, however, to restrict the Brhaspati line to the materialism of the Charvakas Lokayatikas. That would mean narrowing down the social basis of Indian materialism, belittling its significance, and distorting the actual history. The materialist tendency is actually inherent in nearly all the systems or schools of Indian philosophy, including the objective-idealist system of the Vedanta of the new times, which is shown in the second half of the present work.

To characterize the philosophical materialism of the Sutras period, it is important to single out the following general features :

- recognition of the fact that the external world, of which man is part, exists objectively and is therefore not a product of his brain but exists independently of any consciousness;
- recognition of the fact the external world manifests itself in a low-governed fashion, the low being capable of change only through physical action rather than through idea, magic, or prayers;
- negation of the existence of supernatural source; the view that the world develops spontaneously, without outside interference;
- recognition of man's perceptions of the object or phenomena of the outside world (sense experiences)

as the only source of knowledge;

- rejection of the view that knowledge is esoteric, innate, or intuitive (mystical);

- recognition of the fact that the nature of man's life and activity is determined by the conditions of his life and not by a deity.

Some of these features are inherent, in some form and to a certain extent, in many systems of Indian philosophy of the medieval period and even of the modern times.

It was Brhaspati who gave ancient Indian materialism it distinctive shape. Another outstanding representative, of this school was Bhishan. One of the most ancient *puranas*, the Padma Purana, says that certain man named Kanada discovered the great teaching called Vaisesika. Gotama compiled the Nyaya *shastras*, Kapila wrote the Samkya *shastras*, a certain Brahman named Jaimini expounded the greatest atheist teaching and a man named Bhishan, the despised Charvaka teaching, while Vishnu himself, to rout the demons, took the image of Buddha to preach the completely impious doctrine of Buddhism.

This passage from the Padma Purana is also quoted by Vijnana Bhiksu, a major representative of the Samkhya philosophy. Bhishan's name is mentioned in the Mahabharata (Santiparva and Salyaparva), in the writings of Manu, and so on. Expressing the hopes and moods of the poorest strata of Indian society, Bhishan was sharply critical of Brahmanism, the Vedic religion, and the ideology of the priests. The compliers of the Vedas, he said were hypocrites and swindlers. Invoking the Vedas, the priests dupe the simple people with meaningless, jumbles of words, living in luxury at the expense of the poor people bringing them offerings. Who the offerings for? Gods were non-existent and had never existed. Should there be offerings to the deceased relatives? But these became dust and needed no food. Just as a lamp that became extinguished would not be rekindled if oil was added to it, a dead man would not rise from the dead after a sacrificial ritual. Even if we assume that our dead relatives need food, why should we pass the food to the priests? Why should the priests eat the food if our dead ones are to be fed? That is about the same as feeding the people of one village while intending to feed those of another.

The Charvakas, rejected the idea of the existence of God, recognizing four material elements as the substance: earth, water, fire, and air. Combinations of these elements produce all objects and phenomena of nature, both material and spiritual. The soul is a body endowed with consciousness; the soul does not exist outside the body. Consciousness emerges from unconscious elements as their temporary combination in a specific form under definite conditions. In substantiating this proposition, Bhishan said that a man could not get drunk by eating some rice and a kind of molasses made of beetroot. A mixture of rice and molasses, however, is used to prepare wine on which man can get drunk. Consciousness is nothing but the result of a certain process of combining material elements. A man's death signifies simultaneous destruction of both consciousness and soul. A Charvaka named Ajita Kesakambalin (6th century B.C.) said that both a wise man and a fool die along with the body, both are dead, and have no existence after death.

The Charvakas decried religious superstition which kept the people ignorant and oppressed, and opposed their view of cognition as the result of sense perception to religious visions. This viewpoint of native sensualism certainly had its weak points. While recognizing sensations and perceptions to be the only source of knowledge, the Charvakas failed to realize the dialectical unity of the sensual and the rational elements in cognition. They viewed the results of man's cognitive activity in the form of abstract thinking as untrue or at any rate unreliable, containing elements of subjective arbitrariness and errors. The mind (that is, abstract thinking), said the Charvakas, did not exist without sensations and perceptions. Propositions and syllogisms were only possible on the basis of those data which were obtained through sensory channels. Moreover, abstract logical thinking (the mind) could not add anything to that which was given in sense perceptions. In other words, they failed to see the dialectics of the transition from cognition of phenomena to cognition of the essence, having a very limited and narrow conception of human practice and its role in the process of cognition. For the Charvakas, practice was the process itself of sense perception of the individual objects and phenomena of nature. The role of practice as the criterion of truth was reduced to the verifying activity of our sense organs.

It should be borne in mind, however, that the primary goal of the Charavakas was dealing a crushing blow to the ideology of Brahmanism. Jawaharlal Nehru wrote on this account : "The materialists attacked authority and all vested interest in thought, religion and theology. They denounced the Vedas and priest craft and traditional beliefs, and proclaimed that belief must be free and must not depend on pre-suppositions or merely on the authority of the past. They inveighed against all forms of magic and superstition. Their general spirit was comparable in many ways to the modern materialistic approach, it wanted to rid itself of the chains and burden of the past, of speculation about matters which could not be perceived, or worship of imaginary gods...[2]

The opponents of materialism (mostly the priests, the Brahmans) did not only persecute the materialist philosophers themselves, they burned their works, so that materialist literature (the literature of the Charvakas Lokayatikas) was almost completely wiped out. "Among the books that have been lost," Nehru points out, "is the entire literature on materialism which followed the period of the early Upanishads. The only references to this, now found, are in criticisms of it and in elaborate attempts to disprove the materialist theories."[3]

The Charvaka materialism is characterized by direct orientation against idealist and religious doctrines, the desire to prove the untenability of idealism and to denounce the falsity and deception of religion and its preachers. Thus the Charvakas' main purpose was denouncing. Brahmanist ideology rather than creating a consistent philosophical system.

The doctrine of the Charvakas Lokayatikas can be reduced to the following four propositions :

(1) Four material elements (*mahabhuta*) are the basis of all that is : fire, earth, water and air.[4] These elements are spontaneously active, with a force of their own (*svabhava*) inherent in them.

(2) Only "this world" (*loka*) exists; there is not hereafter or life after death;[5] that is, after man's death, his life is neither continued "there" (that is, in the Brahman-Atman world) nor revived "here" (on this earth). The Charvakas said :

> While life is your, live joyously :
> None can escape Death's searching eye;
> When once this frame of ours they burn
> How shall it e'er again return?[6]

The Charvakas criticized the religious idealist proposition that "consciousness is the property of the immortal soul", insisting that consciousness died with the death of man, while man himself disintegrated into the four basic elements. "Man is composed of four elements," they wrote. "When man dies, the earthly element return and relapses into the earth; the watery element returns into the water, the fiery element returns into the fire, the airy element returns into the air, the senses pass into space."[7]

(3) There are no supernatural (divine) forces. God is an invention of the rich to dupe the poor. Charvakas taught that the religion of Brahmanism, just as any other religion, was untenable and harmful, for it distracted the attention and strength of the poor towards worshipping imaginary gods, offering sacrifices to unknown forces, listening to abstract preaching etc. Religious writings were based on the fantasies of a certain group of persons materially interested in all this.

(4) There is no soul—in the sense in which the ministers of religious cults and, in agreement with the latter, the

philosophers used the term. It is matter that thinks, rather than the soul which is alleged to exist independently of matter.

(5) The law of *Karma* (requital for both good and bad deeds) is an invention of the adherents of religion employed also by idealist philosophers. The source of evil on this earth should be looked for in the cruelty and injustice existing in society rather than in the properties of human nature and inevitable sufferings said to be predetermined from on high.

(6) The only source of the knowledge of nature is sense perception. Only direct perception (through the five senses) gives man genuine knowledge (*pratyaksa*). Only that exists which can be directly perceived. That which cannot be perceived does not exist; it does not exist precisely for the reason that it cannot be perceived. By "that which cannot be perceived" the Charvakas meant first and foremost such religious "essences" as God, the soul, the heavenly kingdom, etc.

According to the Charvakas, sense perceptions can be of two kinds, external and internal. Internal perceptions emerge through the action of reason (*manas*). External perceptions are linked with the activity of the five sense organs.

Accordingly, knowledge itself is divided into two kinds or forms: the first kind is the result of contact between the sense organs and the objects of the external world; the second kind of knowledge arises through mental operations on the basis of sense data. *Elements of Materialism in the Nyaya Philosophy.*

The Nyaya (Sanskr. "rule", "substantiation", "method", "logical inference", "introduction to a subject", deduction", "logic in general") is a philosophical system or school that took shape approximately at the end of the 1st century C.E. Gotama (c. 3rd century B.C.) is regarded as the originator of the Nyaya philosophy. His Nyaya-sutra is basically a materialist work.

The Nyayiks mostly studied questions in epistemology,

or "the science of reasoning" (*tarkavidya*).[8] Their basic proposition is that the material world (nature) exists objectively and the existence of the external objects does not depend on the source of knowledge. The objects and phenomena of nature recognized by man through the five senses. Everything that is inaccessible to sense perception has no real existence. Therefore Brahma (God) does not exist either.

The sense perception of objects is regarded as the touchstone of the reliability (or truth) of our knowledge. Vatsyana (4th century C.E.), a commentator of the Nyaya-sutra, wrote that trustworthy knowledge was obtained from the coming in touch or contact (*sannikarsha* or *sambandha*) of the sense organs (*indriya*) and their object. This knowledge is called *pratyaksa jnyana* (sensory knowledge).

According to the Nyayiks, thinking capable of leading man to attainment of the truth, or "cognition in agreement with reality", is only possible in the presence of four elements: the subject of cognition (*pramatri*), the object of cognition (*prameya*), trustworthy knowledge (*pramiti*), and syllogism (*pramana*) as the means of cognition.

Nyayiks were mainly concerned with working out the instruments of cognition (the *pramanas*). Their teaching is therefore often termed Pramanashastra, or the science of the *pramanas*. Four kinds of *pramanas* were recognized in all: perception (*pratyaksa*), inference (*anumana*), comparison (*upamana*), and verbal testimony (*sabda*).

It is not our task here to consider the Nyaya philosophy in detail. We would merely like to point out that Nyayiks' sensualims was materialist in nature.

Endeavouring to bring out the similarity of the ideas of the Nyaya and the Charvakas, Ram Mohan Roy in his *History of Indian Philosophy* cites the historical legend to the effect that the first forms of this philosophy (Nyaya,— *V.B.*) was moulded by the hand of Brhaspati, so that men still speak of the cognitive abilitv (*buddhi*) of Brhaspati.

Later, in early Middle Ages, when Hinduism replaced the religion of Brahmanism and the attacks of the orthodox religion on materialism intensified, the Nyaya philosophy was penetrated by preachers of idealism and theistic attitudes (Vacaspati, Udayana, Vardhamana, and others). Various attempts were made to achieve a "logical proof of the existence of God", to spread the belief in the existence of the individual soul as a substantial being, etc. At the same time, Vatsyayana, Uddyotakara, and Visvanatha continued to defend the atheist line of Gotama.

It should be noted that the works of modern bourgeois scholars refer mostly to the medieval Nyaya or, to be more precise, its theistic and idealist additions. The situation is much the same with Vaisesika philosophical system.

Elements of Spontaneous Materialism and Dialectics in the Vaisesika

It is generally accepted in historical and philosophical literature that Kanada (c. 3rd century B.C.) was the founder of the Vaisesika school and the author of the Vaisesika-sutra. The final redaction of the sutras dates from some time not later than the 1st century. C.E.

Studies by Soviet Indologists have shown clearly that there is a distinct materialist tendency in the religious idealist system of the Vaisesika, a rational kernel under the idealist integument of the system, as it were. That is not accidental, for out of all the system of Indian philosophy the Vaisesika philosophy was most closely connected with the natural scientific views of ancient Indians.

The Vaisesikas proceed from the view that two worlds, the sensual and the suprasensual, exist objectively. 'They consider the supersensual world from dualist positions, and the sensual world, from those of materialism.

We shall restrict ourselves to a short exposition of the Vaisesika atomistic theory.

According to the Vaisesika-sutra, the development of the

sensual world is based on atoms existing in space; they are countless in number; they are also eternal. All that is consists of four basic elements : earth, water, light, and air. Accordingly, the atoms of which the elements consist are divided into four kinds : the atoms of the earth, the atoms of water, the atoms of light, and the atoms of air. *Akasha* (ether) has no atomic structure; it fills empty space between the atoms.

Atoms are impermeable, being indivisible. Their indivisibility is illustrated by the following example. Assume that we have separated the fibers of a cloth; we shall then obtain yarn. Proceeding in this way, we shall obtain cotton from the yarn, which may be divided into infinitely small particles. Finally, we come to a situation where these small particles of cotton can no longer be divided. These infinitely small indivisible particles are called atoms, and their combinations make up the world.

Comparing the atomistic theories of Democritus and Kanada, we find considerable discrepancies between them. According to Democritus, atoms are indivisible, immutable, qualitatively homogeneous, and distinguished from one another only by their quantitative properties—form, size, order, and position. This was the basis of the deterministic theory of the universe, which insists that every event is the result of necessity, and there are no accidental objects or phenomena in the world.

Epicurus, who continued the line of Democritus, gave the atoms the property of having weight, postulating also that the atoms had not only vertical but also "swerve" motion or deviation from the straight line. Thus necessity was complemented with accident; the motion of atoms was recognized to be free.

According to Kanada's theory, each atom is qualitively different from all others, possessing *visesa,* that is, unique specificity, of which there are as many varieties as there are atoms themselves.

According to Democritus, atoms are in eternal and continuous motion, whereas Kanada considers atoms to be immutable, inert, and devoid of inner motion. The motion of atoms, that is, their combination, separation and mechanical shifting, is due to external causes—the action of an external object. That is the "visual" cause. Apart from the visual (tangible or perceptible) cause, Kanada also postulates the existence of an invisible *(adrishta)* cause regarded as the ultimate cause of all atoms. The force of *adrishta* is natural, not divine.

Thus the Vaisesika atomistic theory should be described as a materialist one. Vaisesikas recognized the materiality of the world, regarding man's reasoning (consciousness or mind) as the product of material atoms.

The Materialism of the Samkhya Philosophy[9]

The founder of the Samkhya philosophical system and the author of the Samkhya-sutra was, as is generally believed, Kapila (c. 6th-5th centuries B.C.). The Samkhya-sutra was lost, so that we have to use later sources—Isvarakrishna Samkhya Karika (3rd-4th centuries C.E.), Vacaspati Misra's Samkhya Tattva Kaumudi (9th century), and others.

Kapila's primary principle is that the world is material. Matter (*prakrti*) is the basis of everything that is, it is omnipresent, eternal, and one. The motion of *prakrti* is just as eternal as *prakrti* itself. Primordially, *prakrti* has no outside cause, for matter (*prakrti*) has neither beginning nor end. Kapila wrote that the world was not created, and therefore there was no creator; the world itself was the cause of the world; the world developed gradually.

Kapila recognized the objective nature of the cause-and-effect links in nature, self-development of nature from the lower form to the higher. The first *sloka* of the Samkhya-Karika says that there is continuity in the development of the world from the lower to the higher... Nothing can arise out of something that does not exist........ There is a close tie between cause and effect. If that were not so, everywhere at any moment anything at all could arise. Each cause conditions a specific effect, and there can be no cause without an effect. The effect is always inseparable from the cause. Therefore any existence is conditioned.

Kapila used the materialist doctrine of the cause-and-effect links to substantiate his atheism and to criticize the religion of Brahmanism. He wrote that, if the first cause is God (Brahma) and the world is the effect, there is a discrepancy between cause and effect. There can be, however no discrepancy between cause and effect. The cause of this world is matter (*prakrti*). The universe is the result of modifications of matter.

As we see, Kapila uses the category of causality from the very start in the exposition of his philosophical views. That is not accidental. The point is that the position of Samkhya on causality were the decisive premise which determined its philosophical orientation. In criticizing Machism, Lenin pointed out: "The question of causality is particularly important in determining the philosophical line of any of the recent 'isms'.[10] As we see it, this idea of Lenin's is entirely valid, methodologically, relative to some of the oldest "isms".

According to the Samkhya doctrine, everything (any phenomenon) has its material cause. All relations between cause and effect are conceived in the sense that the latter is always present in the former.[11] The following are the Samkhya argument in favour of this.

There are two kinds of causes, material (in which the effect is latent) and efficient or productive (which helps the effect to manifest itself). If we accept, however, that the material cause does not contain the effect, the concept of "productive cause" loses in its meaning, for it has no object of action.

Assuming that an effect arises out of a cause in which it is not contained is tantamount to asserting that existence arises out of nonexistence, or something emerges out of nothing.

An effect must be of the same nature as the cause; they have the same basis. A cloth may only be made out of yarn (not out of milk); curds may be made out of milk (rather than out of yarn), etc.

The theory that the effect exists before it manifests itself is called *Satkarya-vada*.[12]

Thus Samkhya asserts that there are no effects without causes. Everything in nature has a cause of its own, including body and soul, sensations and intellect, which are "limited and dependent objects".

Only "the cause of all causes and effects", that is, *prakrti* (matter), has no cause. "....The products are caused, while prakrti is uncaused; the products are dependent, while prakrti is independent; the products are many in number, limited in space and time while prakrti is one, all-pervading and eternal."[13]

According to the Samkhya doctrine, prakrti consists of three forces or *gunas* – *sattva, rajas,* and *tamas*. *Sattva* is regarded as something light and illuminating; *rajas* motivating and mobile; *tamas*, heavy and restarting. Analysis of the Samkhya Karika shows that in effect *sattva* is potential consciousness; *rajas*, the source of motion, action, and development; *tamas* is that which restrains action and slow down development. These three *gunas*, constituting the basis of any object or phenomenon, are inseparably connected and mutually condition one another. They are connected as closely as flame, oil, and lamp wick.

The *gunas* are a kind of primary principles – mass (*tamas*), energy (*rajas*), and the conscious principle (*sattva*).[14] Everything in nature is charged, as it were, with these three principles. The interaction between them consists in that energy cannot exist without mass, while conscious phenomena do not exist without energy. How does an object or phenomenon emerge or is shaped, then? The process begins with individual particles of, the three forces, indifferently scattered through primary matter, being gathered together into wholes under the impact of natural affinity; this results in non-uniform pressure in various parts of matter, so that bodies, distinct from one another are gradually formed instead of uniform indifferent matter.

The emergence or formation of some object or phenomenon does not signify creation of matter, in the same way as the disappearance of an individual object or phenomenon does not mean destruction of matter. In the process of evolution, nature does not increase or diminish quantitatively. Matter cannot be either created or destroyed. The sum total of all matter – of all its actual or potential states – always remains constant. The elements of matter are in eternal motion which cannot stop for a second even; any material process, any growth or withering away is nothing but redistribution of matter, its transition from the past into the present and from the present into the future, or from potentiality to actuality. Redistribution of mass and energy engenders the entire diversity of the material world, the world of plants and animals.

The idea that matter (mass and energy) does not grow or diminish quantitatively but is merely redistributed in the process of emergence and destruction of individual objects and phenomena of nature, can be regarded as one of the strokes of genius of ancient Indian thinkers who anticipated later discoveries. In a most general form, this can be viewed as a distinct expression of the idea of the *law of conservation of the mass of substance* as it is known to modern natural science. It should be stressed at the same time that anticipation as one of the forms of perception of scientific truth was characteristic of many outstanding thinkers of antiquity. As Engels put it thinkers of the past brilliantly anticipated countless numbers of truths whose correctness is now proved scientifically.

Matter and the laws of the its evolutionary development are knowable. The ways or channels through which man receives knowledge of the objects and phenomena surrounding him are the five sense organs.

The entire infinite variety of matter is classified into five basic forms or essences : earth, water, fire, air, and ether,

Samkhya regards the process of world manifestation as ordered development of matter from the finer forms to the most dense ones which are referred to as "material elements" (*mahabhuta*). These "essences" are similar to the Greek "elements", with the exception that what in Graeco-Roman philosophy is referred to as the "fifth essence" (*quintessentia*) is called the first essence, or spatiality (*akaca*) in Samkhya.

We do not set ourselves the task of considering the interconnections and mutual relations between the *gunas* and essences, although this question is of great interest both on the epistemological and ontological plane. But we should dwell, however briefly, on the relationship between the *gunas* and *prakrti*. The point is that Samkhya is the first and probably the only philosophical school in India to make a serious attempt to formulate the philosophical concept of matter.

We know that there were materialists in Europe (such as Ludwig Feuerbach, for instance, who rejected the abstract speculations of Hegel) who negated the existence of matters as the being of "the general", calling it "an empty abstraction" and recognized matter only as the being of individual things. From this viewpoint, only individual things are genuinely material like this house, this tree, these leaves etc. That which is given in direct sense perception, that is, the individual sensual object, is indeed material.[15] This view, however, was deficient in divorcing the singular from the general, violating as it did their dialectic unity.

Philosophers of the Samkhya school were also guilty of divorcing the singular from the general but is very important to point out that they recognized the reality of both. In their view, matter (*prakrti*) exists in two independent forms, one general and one singular, and that was where the metaphysical gap lay.

Matter of the first form ("the general") is substance, the first cause of the world of objects; in it, the *gunas* are in a state of equilibrium, and it is therefore without qualities, which prevents man from perceiving it through the senses. It is therefore incognisable, but the incognisability results from its fineness rather than from nonexistence.

Matter of the second form ("the singular") is an infinite number of moving objects, phenomena, and events developing in space and time. The singular is accessible to the sense organs. It is knowable.[16]

The stumbling block for the Samkhya authors was the question of the origin of consciousness. Ram Mohan Roy believes that *purusa* was created by Kapila as an explanation for the origin of consciousness.

According to Kapila, *purusa* is the omniscient and extremely fine element which, as distinct from *prakrti*, possesses consciousness. *Prakrti* is the object or matter; *purusa* is the subject or consciousness. There are grounds to believe that Kapila was fearful lest this proposition of his should be given an idealistic interpretation. As distinct from *atman*, said Kapila, *purusa* does not create anything, it is passive; it is merely a passive witness; only *prakrti* is active, and so on. *Prakrti* is the subject of action; in the process of spontaneous development it comes in contact with *purusa* and ultimately cognizes itself; *purusa* is devoid of the ability for self-cognition.

The inconsistencies and errors of the Samkhya school relative to the origin and essence of consciousness were readily exploited already in antiquity by representatives of religious orthodoxy.

In the Middle Ages, Gaudapada, Vacaspati Misra and other commentators (or followers) of Kapila's doctrine made further concessions to idealism, recognizing the existence of soul independent of matter.

On the whole, an inconsistent position on this score gave rise to reproaches on the part of idealists for concessions to materialism as well as on the part of materialistically minded Indian philosophers. Thus S. Radhakrishnan criticizes Kapila for deviation from idealism : "If we admit the Samkhya view of prakrti and its complete independence of purusa, then it will be impossible to account for the evolution of prakrti. We do not know, how latent potentialities become fruitful without any consciousness to direct them."[17]

Ram Mohan Roy holds an opposite view of the Samkhya philosophy, indicating that its weakness lies in negating the historicity of development. Had the Samkhya philosophy asserted that at a definite stage in the development of the world, consciousness (*chaitanya*) arises out of things, while quantitative changes, reaching a certain phase of development, become qualitative changes producing new qualities, then the whole inconsistency (*asangati*) would have disappeared. Correctly criticizing the anti-historical (*metaphysical*) quality of the Samkhya philosophy, Roy regrettably commits an error himself, comparing Kapila's materialism to that of the French philosophers of the 18th century. The point is that the French materialism of the 18th century was a historical product of a qualitatively different epoch, and of a different class; it was different in its content.

Such is a brief characteristic of the materialism of the Samkhya school.

The Elements of Materialism in Jainism[18]

In the light of the problem considered here, the most valuable materials are to be found in the Jainist doctrine of being.

The basic premise of Jainism is that the ultimate basis of all that is substance, which can be extended and unextended.[19] Extended substance, in its own turn, is divided into living (*jiva*) and non-living (*ajiva*). The living substances, or the souls (*jivas*) have consciousness; these are the "subjects" in the philosophical sense, so to speak.[20] Non-living substances (*ajivas*) or objects are matter (*pudgala*), space, time, *dharma* (the condition of motion) and *adharma* (the condition of rest).

Matter (*pudgala*) is, according the Jainists, an eternal substance indefinite in terms of quality and quantity. It may grow and diminish in volume without addition or detraction of particles or elements; it may take any form and develop any qualities. Matter is the carrier of energy possessing two kinds of motion—simple or general motion (*porishpondon*) and the motion of gradual development or evolution. *Pudgala* is thus the physical basis of the world.

Everything that emerges, exists, and is destroyed, is referred to as material body by Jainists. The quantity of matter always remains the same ("it does not change"); what is changed are the material bodies, the things. The cause of the changes is contradiction or "differences in the identity" *(bhedabheda)*.

Jainists recognize two kinds of changes : (1) loss of old qualities[22] (*gunas*) and acquisition of new ones; (2) change of form. Changes in the world are due to disintegration or merging and combination of atoms.

Jainists worked out an atomistic theory of the structure of the universe. All physical objects, according to that theory, are the result of combination of gross and fine atoms (*pramana*). An individual atom (*anu*) is believed to be an infinitesimal quantity which has weight, however. Potentially, an atoms contains the whole thing; in other words, potentially it has taste, smell, colour, temperature, and tangibility. Because of the property of tangibility, homogenous atoms are merged, which ultimately results in the formation of an object or phenomenon.[23] Atoms also have such properties as being eternal, infinite, uncreated and indestructible. Consequently, matter also has these qualities, being an agglomeration of atoms.

In comparing the Jaina atomistic theory with that of Lucretius, one observes that Jainists believed each atoms to have two kinds of qualities, primary and secondary, while Lucretius attributed only one quality to it, the primary one. The secondary quality emerges, according to Lucretius, from the merging or combination of atoms.

One of the major differences between the atomistic views of ancient Greeks and Indians is that the Greeks endeavoured to explain quality in terms of quantity, while Indians did the reverse, explaining quantity in terms of quality.

Jainists believe *karma* to be material (*pudgalika*). In their view, *karma* represents matter in intangible form.

The Philosophy of Buddhism

Along with Christianity and Islam, Buddhism is known to be one of the three most widespread religions. The adherents of Buddhism have always endeavoured to give a profound philosophical substantiation to their teaching. Buddhism, however, is not exceptional in this sense: in India, many representatives of the dominant ideology have always believed that philosophy is the theoretical substantiation of religion, while religion is practical philosophy.

Buddhims strove to replace Brahmanism the religion of early slave-owning society in ancient India.

Brahmanism, as is well known, sanctified the estate structure of society (its division into the *Varnas*) and the dominant position of Brahman priests, who by that time became an impediment to social progress. Brahmans declared themselves to be above all other men and imposed on everybody a complicated sacrificial ritual which accompanied nearly every step a person made on this earth. They taught that in this as well as in the next world happiness could only be obtained through sacrifices of cattle, food, and melted butter to fire.

Buddhism rose against these senseless sacrifices and, in the first place, against him to whom the sacrifices were offered—against the God Brahma, declaring him to be non-existent. The cult of someone who never existed is truly meaningless.[24] To deal a final blow to Brahmanas and the institute of their property, Buddhists spoke against any property whatever and against the boundaries between the estates. In this connection they attacked the Brahmans' teaching of the soul : there is no soul, for if one admits the existence of a soul as an individual, there must also be personal property (where there is a self, there must be personal property).

Reflecting as it did the dissatisfaction of the free commoners and the lower urban castes, which were ruined and oppressed, Buddhism succeeded in winning the support of many oppressed people suffering from lack of rights, poverty, and hunger. In referring to early Buddhims, it should be noted that it succeeded, under the definite socio-historical conditions of the times, in expressing in a specific form the aspirations of the people for a better life.

The sacred texts of the Buddhists were gathered and given final shape some two centuries after Gotama Buddha's death. They were called *Tri Pritaka* (Three Baskets). Buddhism as a system is heterogeneous; there is a great number of schools, trends and directions in it. However, the way to an understanding of all numerous Buddhist doctrines lies through comprehending their philosophical basis.

Some scholars endeavouring to discover the essence of Buddhism proceeded from a consideration of the sutras—collections of aphorisms. But the sutras are very laconic, compressed; their aphorisms are abstract and unconnected, and this obscures the general meaning of the teaching, creating an almost unlimited possibility of arbitrary interpretations. Buddhists themselves interpreted the sutras in the light of some philosophical treatise (*Abhidharma*) or other. *Abhidharma* is the key to the knowledge of the Buddhist doctrine and the history of Buddhist sects, schools, and institutions. Without a knowledge of *Abhidharma*, it is easy to fall prey to artificial constructions. Some time in the past a kind of "pure Buddhist" standard was established, relative to which all other forms of this religion were declared to be a distortion, shamanism, etc. The result was that Buddhism had never taught much of what was imputed to it by its adversaries and what attracted many of its followers.

The division of Buddhism into schools and sects began as early as the 4th century B.C. The common foundation of all

Buddhist trends is this: the ultimate goal of life is salvation; ethical and religious experiences are the means of attaining that goal. To put it in modern terms, the ancient Buddhist atomistic theory assumed from the very outset a peculiar historical form of relativism. According to this theory, the whole of the world of things and phenomena surrounding man and man himself with his psyche and consciousness consists of atoms. But the atoms are not substantive; they are not the primary elements which exists eternally and whose essence is immutable. The world consists of an unlimited number of qualities (thing, objects, and phenomena). Each individual quality's existence has a beginning and an end. Compared to eternity, the length of life of each quality taken separately is an infinitesimal quantity. Any quality is in this sense a flare. Each atoms of which every quality consists is also an instantaneous flare (that is exactly the sense in which atoms are not substantial).[25]

Thus Buddhism does not recognize qualitative definiteness of objects and phenomena. This qualitative definiteness is illusory, for it does not exist in reality. Only infinitesimal (in magnitude and time) states (moments or "flares") exist, the carriers of which are *dharmas* ("carriers"), and we therefore cannot speak of any object or phenomenon as the subject of existence, that is, we cannot say that they actually exist.

Just as the light of a lamp appears a moving object to the observer, whereas in actual fact there is a new flare of light at each given moment, any other material element (*e.g.*, colours sounds, tastes, scents and tactile impression) is nothing but a chain of repeating flares.

The philosophical foundation of Buddhism is the theory of *dharmas*.[26] According to that theory, all that is, all nature is a single stream, a whirlwind consisting of elements (atoms). The life span of an element is infinitesimal or momentaneous ("a flare"), and everything which consists of them will sooner or later cease to exist, but that which really exists cannot cease. Therefore all phenomena of nature, both material and spiritual, cannot be called genuinely real being. The elements have their carrier, *dharma,* the eternal and immutable substance, which is the genuinely real being or essence of all phenomena.

There is no generally accepted view among Buddhists concerning the nature of that essence.

Sarvastivadins,[27] for instance visualise it as a personal carrier (*dharma*) for each of the elements (75 varieties of *dharmas* are believed to exist, all in all). According to Yogacaras[28] the whirlwind of elements of which the "illusory" internal and external life consists does not go back to a substantial carrier in the case of each element; there are no such carriers; all elements follow from a single common essence, from a "consciousness treasury".

The Madhyama school of Sunyavada[29] adhered to a third view. The founder of that school, Nagarjuna (1st-2nd centuries C.E.), believed, that Sarvastivadins and Yogacaras went to extremes and that their approach was one-sided. Generally speaking, all objects and phenomena of the surrounding world, he asserted, can be approached from four stand point :

(1) *"That"*[30] is, for we see it, hear it, touch it, smell it, or taste it, that is, perceive it in one way of another through our sense organs. In short, *"that" exists* (absolute *being*).

(2) *"That" is not* (absolute *non-being*), for that is ephemeral, transient, dependent on another "that", changes with each passing moment ("flash"), passes into another state, becoming some other "that"; the latter becomes a third "that"; etc., etc. *ad infinitum* ("the eternal stream or whirlwind").

(3) *"That simultaneously is and is not, i.e.,* it both exists and does not exist.

(4) *"That" neither is nor is not, i.e.,* it neither exists nor does not exist.

Declaring all these viewpoints to be one-sided and non-genuine. Nagarjuna formulated his own theory in opposition to them, which he termed the *theory of dependent origin* (*pratitya samutpada*). According to this theory, only that object truly exists which exists by itself, that is, not caused by some outside factor.

However, life shows that there are no phenomena without causes in the world around us, there are not absolutely independent things. The existence of any object or phenomenon of the material world always *depends* on certain conditions that are not directly connected with the object itself. What reality can we speak of, says Nagarjuna, when everywhere and at all time *that exists and this appears, the emergence of that produces this*. Dependent reality is no reality.

In replying to his opponents who hold that the world is real, as testified by our everyday experiences and reasoning. Nagarjuna says : experience and reason do not give us genuine knowledge. The evidence or data of our *pramanas* (the means of proof—sensations, perceptions, and syllogisms) is unreliable, for, to assert that the given perception is true we have to point out something which is true, and distinct from this perception. But is that "something" true in its turn? That will require proof. For that "something else" , if it is not true in itself, cannot make our perception true. But how are we to prove that truth of the "something else"? We shall require the existence of a third "something else", whose truth will have to be proved in its turn, etc.—the series is endless.

Nagarjuna wrote that the foundation of all that is cannot be said to exist (absolute being) and neither can it be said not to exist absolute non-being); it is something intermediate (*madhyama*)[31] amorphous, without cause, incomprehensible, and inexpressible, the only suitable word for it being the void (*sunya*). There is no *dharma* that is not *sunya*. But that is not needless emptiness, it is not a mystic nothing leading to nihilism.

S. Radhakrishnan,[32] as well as S. Chatterjee and D. Datta who concur with him, believes that, according to the Madhyamika view, "behind this phenomenal world there is a reality which is not describable by any character, mental or nonmental, that we perceive".[33] True, we would prefer to avoid using Kantian terminology here ("phenomenal" etc.), for that is fraught with the danger of modernization and a loss of the specificity of the Madhyamika doctrine; but the ascertaining of the fact that the Madhyamikas interpreted *sunya* as objective reality is of fundamental importance.

Thus *sunya* is objective, if transcendental, reality, the basis of unity (in Nagarjuna's terms, "coincidence") of matter and spirit, of object and subject, motion and rest, form and content, the singular and the general, the finite and the infinite. The dialectics of the general, particular and singular, of essence and phenomenon, etc. was the stumbling block for the Madhyamikas as well as many other ancient philosophers; they spared no effort to find a solution for this problem but failed.

In accordance with the division of all that is into two worlds—the world of phenomena (*samsara*) and the world of essence (*sunya*), the Madhyamikas based their epistemology on the existence of two truths, empirical (*samvrti-satya*), valid for the phenomenal world, and transcendental (*paramar-tha-satya*), valid for the *sunya*. They took notice of the antinomies of human cognition, the contradictoriness of concepts and the objective basis of this contradictoriness, but here, just as on the ontological plane, they failed to attain the dialectical level in handling the problem.

In is important to note that, although Nagarjuna uses such terms as "inexpressible", "unmanifested", "unknowable" relative to *sunya* as the "third" or "middle", he believes that *paramartha-satya* ("transcendental" truth) can be cognized, and the only way toward its cognition is knowledge of *samvrti-satya* ("practical" truth). As S. Radhakrishnan writes, according to the Madhyamikas "knowledge cannot be vindicated, even as the knowledge of phenomenon or appearance, if it were absolutely severed from the knowledge of nonmenal reality. Nagarjuna points out that without resorting to practical truth the transcendental truth cannot be attained."[34]

We have discussed mostly the progressive aspects of the

philosophical systems known as Nyaya, Vaisesika, Samkhya, early Jainism and Buddhism, their materialist tendencies and in particular their atomistic theories. This "one-sidedness" , is due, above all, to the need for showing, if only in outline, that there is a solid materialist and progressive tradition in India.

The atomistic theories of ancient Indians, just as those of other peoples of the remote past, reflected in the first place the confrontation between materialism and idealism, between dialectics and metaphysics. They were principally directed against the religious view of the world as a derivative of God the creator. "The Atomists," wrote Lenin, "are generally speaking, opposed to the idea of the creation and maintenance of the world by means of a foreign principle. It is in the theory of atoms that natural science first feels released from the need for demonstrating a foundation for the world For if nature is represented as, created and held together by another, than it is conceived of as not existent in itself...".[35]

A philosophical and sociological analysis of the theory and practice of Yoga will be given in the chapter on Vivekananda. Here we shall limit ourselves to a general characteristic of this school and its doctrine, and a consideration of the views of Patanjali (c. 2nd century B.C.), the systematiser Yoga ideas and founder of this school, concerning the problem of man.

The Sanskrit word *yoga* is used to denote a method for freeing oneself from fetters and oppression; uniting, combining consolidating, contracting; and a method for attaining unity, consolidation, etc. In prehistoric India this word was apparently used to denote causes and actions producing human suffering.

Throughout the centuries, dozens of Yoga doctrines and schools took shape, of which only 19 are believed to be independent and original.

In various Yoga schools the word *yoga* came to denote different phenomena and actions. Some regarded Yoga as a method of freeing oneself from suffering; others, as uniting man's individual soul with the absolute soul, *atman*, which, in their view, would mean the end of suffering; while still others saw Yoga as the process of separating *purusa* (consciousness) from *prakrti* (matter) and as the end of that process, that is, their separation itself, which simultaneously means release.

The Yoga-sutra (A Manual of Yoga) is the first major work of the Indian school of Yoga, which presents in the form of aphorisms the principles of Yogic teaching and also some practical advice (precepts) for attaining the ultimate aim of Yoga—liberating the soul from the bondage of the material world, including one's own body. It is believed that the author of the Yoga-sutra was Patanjali. For this reason the Yoga-sutra is sometimes called Patanjali-sutra, Patanjali's Yoga Aphorisms, etc.

The Yoga-sutra is divided into four parts (*pada*) : *the first part* is called *Samadhipada* and discusses the nature and goals of *samadhi,* or contemplative self-immersion; *the second part, Sadhanapada,* defines the means for attaining that goal; *the third part, Vibhutapada,* describes the inner aspects of Yoga and the significance of the extraordinary ("supernatural") abilities attained by Yoga; *the fourth part, Kaivalyapada,* deals with the nature and forms of "release".

In actual fact, Yoga is not a philosophy. Both in the remote past and at present Yoga is usually regarded as a definite practice of which the methodological foundation is the Samkhya philosophical doctrine. Evidence for this is found, for instance, in *Bhagavad Gita,* which was written several centuries before Patanjali's school came into existence. "The region of high rest which Samkhyans reach Yogins attain. Who sees these twain as one sees with clear eyes!"

According to the Samkhya doctrine, the world is material. Matter (*prakrti*) is the ultimate basis of all that is, it is eternal and one. The motion of *prakrti* is just as eternal as *prakrti* itself. The emergence of formation of any object or phenomenon does not signify creation of matter, just as the destruction of an individual object or phenomenon does not signify destruction of matter. Matter cannot be either created or destroyed. The totality of matter in all its actual and potential states remains constant. Patanjali comprehended and interpreted the Samkhya philosophy in the spirit of dualism : the material (*prakrti*) and the spiritual (*purusa*) are regarded as opposed principles that cannot be reduced to each other.

> Know thou that Nature and Spirit both
> Have no beginning! Know that qualities
> And changes of them are by Nature wrought;
> That Nature puts to work the acting frame,
> But Spirit doth inform it, and so cause
> Feeling of pain and pleasure. Spirit, linked
> To moulded matter, entereth into bond
> With qualities by nature framed, and, thus
> Married to matter, breeds the birth again
> In good and evil *yonis*.
>
> Yet is this—
>
> Yea! in its bodily prison!—Spirit pure
> Spirit supreme; surveying, governing,
> Guarding, possessing; Lord and Master still
> PURUSHA, Ultimate, One soul with me.
>
> (*Bhagavad Gita*, Chapter 13).

Under certain circumstances, material and spiritual principles may be interconnected, penetrating each other and forming infinitely diverse shapes, qualities, and systems. Man (a combination of body and soul) is one of the highest and most complicated material spiritual combinations (systems). The individual human soul (*purusa*) as a part of an absolute spiritual reality (*atman*) is immortal. Birth and death should be regarded from this viewpoint as changes in matter but not at all as "changes in ourselves" (in the soul). There is no death, there is "eternal" (in the soul). There is no death, there is "eternal" (very large or long) circle (reincarnation or *samsara*). However, large and long as the circle may be, it can arrive at an end or completion. The cycles of reincarnations performed by the soul "departure" for other side (for *atman*) and "return" to earthly life. Another departure and another return, etc., may ultimately end in the so-called full release (*moksa* or, in Buddhism, *nirvana*). That means that the soul attains through an enormous number of reincarnations a degree of purity from matter (*prakrti*) that after one of the departures to the other side it remains there, merging with the absolute spiritual reality and "being lost in it like a drop of water in an ocean".

Patanjali was one of the first ancient thinkers to formulate and elaborate on the idea that man is a system ("microcosm", or "the universe in miniature") consisting of four basic components – mineral, vegetable, animal, and human proper. Patanajali endows each of the components of man the system with objective existence, regarding them as independent entities. Accordingly, we should distinguish four levels or subsystems in man :

mineral man;
vegetable man;
animal man;
human man.

(1) *Mineral man.* At this level, man is regarded as a subsystem consisting entirely of the material of the mineral kingdom. The mineral kingdom is taken to mean here the whole of the inorganic world, the whole of the universe, including the "inanimate bodies' of this planet. On the earth and in space, all material bodies, from a sand grain on the shore of an ocean to the visible and invisible bodies of cosmic space, are interconnected, naturally emerging (breathing out) out of One (*ekam*) and naturally returning (breathing in) into one.

> That One breathed by itself without breath, other than it there has been nothing.

The mineral kingdom has always been in motion:

> All this was indistinguishable, fluid........
> Everything was in motion.

The initial source of the activity of the mineral man subsystem should also be sought for here. To understand the true essence of mineral man and determine the measure of his activity ("viability"), he should be considered in his relationships and interconnections with the environment consisting of an infinite series of large-scale and small-scale systems. The integrity and well-being of our human mineral subsystem depends, according to Patanjali, on the precision of our observance of the laws of the mineral kingdom. The mineral kingdom has a specific rhythm of life. On the planet Earth, the seasons change, the time of the day or night, and the rhythms of mineral life change accordingly. The rhythms have to be felt and known; they have to be complied with, for they ultimately determine the rhythms of man's entire life and activity in all its manifestations at all subsystem levels. The action of the cosmic forces and the rhythms of terrestrial and extra-terrestrial mineral life determine, for instance, the order of taking nourishment, that is, the order of "mineral fertilization" of the human man. Inasmuch as man is the universe in miniature, *all* minerals of the universe without exception must enter his body. In this sense, man must be an *omnivorous* being, that is to say, any limitations on the variety of foodstuffs are counter-indicated. There can be only one limitation : *moderation*. As for vegetarianism or dietetic nourishment, these are special cases (for sick persons mostly) and should only be recommended by a specialist (a doctor). The seasons signify and entail changes not only in the rhythm of terrestrial life in the broad sense but also in the rhythm of taking sustenance, and changes in the diet.[36]

In characterizing mineral man, it should be remembered that we do not deal with a simple combination of minerals. Mineral man is the highest product of the mineral kingdom, a living and active human subsystem subordinated to the laws of life and activity of man the system (human man). Raising mineral man to an absolute, that is, regarding him as an independent essence, Patanjali gives the following characteristic of his activity : he is alive, and yet he is passive, lazy, performing acts through force of habit, that is, he is only capable of doing that which he has been trained to do. It should be borne in mind at the same time that the "personality characteristic" of mineral man depends largely on objective causes. The objective causes are taken to mean the natural environment which, according to Patanjali, should be viewed systematically; the human man system is part of the planet Earth system, the planet Earth system is part of the universe system, etc. astrologists worked out special theories of causal dependence (and, to a certain degree, of predetermination) of the human man system (in the first place of the mineral subsystem) on the higher material systems. That was the basis for the horoscopes. As for the subjective causes, they emerge in the subsystem connections in the human man system.

(2) *Vegetable man.* With the mineral kingdom as its foundation, a higher organization of matter, the vegetable kingdom, emerges. The vegetable world is linked with the mineral basis not only through origin. It reaches with its roots into the soil consisting of minerals, it holds on to it firmly, extracting nourishment from it. It is linked with extra-terrestrial "mineral organizations"—the sun, the moon, the stars.

Vegetable life differs essentially from the life of minerals. First, plants are capable of *reproducing themselves*, bearing fruit and multiplying. *Living matter proper is something that is capable of multiplying and producing offspring.* Therein animate beings differ from inanimate things. A plant is the first form of living matter in the proper sense. Second, plants are more "active and enterprising" as compared to mineral systems. In India, for instance, wild plants can cover and destroy within a short period of time an abandoned house and even a town. Third, *the rhythm of the life of plants is different.* Plants respond in a different way to changes in the seasons and the time of day or night.

The vegetable man subsystem should be regarded in the first place as the finest and most mobile product the vegetable world. The human man must know and remember this constantly. With reference to the problem of nourishment, for instance, the human man should under all circumstances take into account his "vegetable man" essence. Changes of seasons entail corresponding changes in the mineral structure of plants. Thus meals consisting of plants (fruits, vegetables, mushrooms, berries) should include only those in season. The main drawback of the vegetable man subsystem is that it does not cultivate itself. The ability for "tending oneself' and aspiration towards self-perfection emerges at a higher stage—the animal stage.

(3) *Animal man.* The animal, as a higher organization of matter compared to the mineral and vegetable systems, could only arise in a highly developed mineral and vegetable kingdom. It imbibes the "refined product" of both. Patanjali stressed that the distinctive feature of the animal as a higher form of the living is its *mobility*. The ability to move (walk, crawl, run, jump, fly, etc.) enables the animal to enter upon most diverse links and relationships with the surrounding world. The form of activity is changed in a radical way. The animal can escape from an unfavourable factor by running away or, on the contrary, it may use favourable factors for satisfying its needs. Gradually, through selective overcoming of the environment, the animal works out a certain order in its behaviour. As it encounters the objects and phenomena of the external environment, the animal, in Patanjali's words, "learns to think" of what it has seen, to remember it, to become conscious of various situations and, accordingly, to introduce correctives in its behaviour. Even a tiny puppy will look at the end of a bench and feel that he must not walk further. The animals ability to find and achieve much of what is desirable and necessary in life, in which its ability for overcoming obstacles is manifested, was called cunning by Patanjali. "All animals have cunning." The animal man, as a subsystem of the human man, includes or synthesizes the basic properties of the two lower subsystems, the mineral man and the vegetable man.

(4) *Human man.* This highest subsystem is a synthesis and harmony of mineral man, vegetable man, and animal man. The vital properties of the systems being synthesized ("mineral pleasure", "vegetable pushing", and "animal cunning") become human here.

At the "human man" level, an individual *spiritual subsystem called purusa* (the soul) is introduced into the individual *material* subsystem. *Purusa* is part of *atman* (the world soul). *Purusa* as the individual soul enlivens the human man, endowing him with reason and making him capable of cognizing, reasoning, thinking, and acting in accordance with the convictions that are formed in him. *Owing to purusa, the activity of the human man rises to the highest level, the level of spirituality, for it becomes endowed with reason and soul.* The human man's potential is incomparable greater than that of any of the material subsystems listed above or that of all of them taken together.

The human man generalizes the life experiences accumulated by generations and assimilates the surrounding world, gradually freeing himself from the power of the spontaneous laws of nature. *He begins to act on the environment himself, changing it and subordinating it to his interests and needs.* He tills the soil, breeds cattle and practices various crafts. He can, for instance, take wild flowers and cultivate them, making them into a charming garden. He studies himself, directing his own life and cultivating himself. *He may cognize the laws of nature, the laws of life, not letting his future to become the product of chance.* In general, Patanjali concludes, the genuinely human life begins at the stage when inevitability disappears, the blind power of necessity ceases to rule, and the soul shakes off the fetters of *prakrti* (matter), thus becoming free.

We see that Patanjali's approach to man is cosmic and individual rather than social. From this standpoint, human society is a system consisting of the sum total of "individual systems", that is, of person, or "human men". Formulating this theory in modern terms, we should stress that social life (human society and its history) are considered in it as a mechanical agglomeration of individuals rather than as a specific form of the motion of matter (or "social organism"), and the essence of man is viewed as an abstraction inherent in a separate individual. In actual fact, as is well known, the essence of man is the totality of all the social relations. At the time in which Patanjali lived, he did not and could not know that, so had to ignore the course of human history and assume the existence of an abstract isolated human individual ("human man") connected with other similar individuals only with natural bonds on the plane of the spirit. It is therefore not at all surprising that, according to Patanjali, the theory of the laws and destinies of man's earthly life is the province of astrology. Patanjali was not without support in this belief. As we have pointed out above, astrology was a separate branch of knowledge in ancient India. And astrologers compiled all kinds of horoscopes predicting the future of individuals from the position of celestial bodies.

As we have seen characteristic of Patanjali is a the systems approach. For him, man is a self-moving, self-organized and self-directed system. There is, we believe, profound rational meaning in this approach, not to be missed by the modern science of man.

Vedanta

Vedanta (Sanskr. "the end of the Vedas") is an objective-idealist system (school). The supposed author of the Brahm-sutra is Badarayana. Historians of Indian philosophy believe that the Brahmasutra was complied between the 5th and the 2nd centuries B.C. Fraser puts the date at c. 4th century B.C. some European Indologists (Ritter, Jakobi, and others) believe the Brahma-sutra to date from the 7th-5th centuries B.C. Arthur Keith insists that Badarayana lived not later than the 2nd century B.C.

In the Brahma-sutra, Badarayana endeavoured to systematize from objective-idealist positions certain isolated philosophical ideas contained in the Upanisads. The Braham-sutra consists of four chapters. The first chapter discusses the theory of Brahman and explains its nature and relation to the world and the individual soul. The second chapter contains a critique of the theoretical opponents of the Vedanta – Charvakas, Jainists, Buddhists, and others. The third chapter deals with the ways and means (*sadhana*) of attaining Brahma-vidya (knowledge of Brahman). Contained in it are explanations of reincarnations, psychological and teleological discourses, etc. chapter 4 considers the results of Brahma-vidya.

The Braham-sutra consists of 555 sutras each of which contains two or three words. The sutras are rather vaguely worded and offer possibilities for extremely varied interpretations. The theory of the Vedanta was elaborated in commentaries each of which endeavoured to prove its compatibility with the texts of divine revelations (*sruti*) and the sutras. The authors of the principal commentaries (Samkara, Ramanuja, Madhva, Vallabha) were founders of independent Vedanta schools.

The first systematiser of the Vedanta philosophy was, as is generally accepted, Gaudapada (c.3rd-7th centuries B.C.). His Mandukya Karika is partially a commentary on the Mandukya Upanisad, but on the whole it is an original philosophical work. Gaudapada was greatly influenced by Buddhist writers, particularly the Madhyamikas, though he used the term Brahman for Nagarjuna's *sunyata*.

Mandukya Karika consists of four parts. The first part is a commentary on the Mandukya Upanisad. Recognizing the identity of Brahman and *atman*, Gaudapada characterizes "the order of reality", or the four aspects (states) of *atman : vaisvana-ra-atman – atman* as world consciousness in a waking state; *taijasa-atman – atman* in the state of sleep accompanied by dreams; *susupty-atman – atman* as consciousness in the state of deep sleep unaccompanied by dreams; *prapan-copasaman – atman* as consciousness outside the limits of all perception, relation, reasoning, definition, expression, etc., that is one that is characterized by extinction of phenomenal reality and constitutes the genuine nature of *atman*. The second chapter of the Mandukya Karika is devoted to proving the unreality of the world of experience. The third chapter considers in detail the Maya idea. The fourth chapter contains a continuation of the proof of the fact that the only reality is *atman*, uncreated, unalterable, immobile, immaterial. As for materiality, mutability, etc., all of that is mere appearance.

The basic proposition of Gaudapada's epsitamology are as follows : the world perceived by man in his waking hours is just unreal and illusory as during sleep; in the final analysis, there is no difference between the objects of experience and the ideas of these objects; both are equally illusory.

The major commentator of the Vedanta-sutra was Samkara (the 8th-9th centuries), and he may rightly be referred to as the founder of Advaita (non-dualist Vedanta).

Samkara believed that the foundation of all the phenomena of nature and society is an absolute, that is, a spiritual reality which is designated by the terms Brahman, *atman*, or Brahman-*atman*. Brahman is eternal, infinite, and amorphous; the categories of time and space, cause and effect, motion and rest, quantity and quality do not apply here. These categories, according to Samkara's teaching, are only characteristic of the world of phenomena, of nature and matter (*prakrti*).

How can the world, limited by certain boundaries and the cause-and-effect connection, be born of the infinite and causeless Brahman? In answer to this question Samkara said that only Brahman really exists, while the world of phenomena is merely the dreams and illusions of Brahman. Just as human dreams are in man's consciousness, so Brahman's dreams are in Brahman itself. There is no difference between Brahman and its manifestation, in this sense. At the same time there is no identity between them.

According to Samkara, Brahman eternally remains itself and cannot become "another", it cannot "transform itself" into anything, *e.g.*, into the objects and phenomena of this world. If that were possible, we would cognise absolute Brahman through knowledge of the objects and phenomena of the world surrounding us. But that would contradict the basic principle of the essence of Brahman.[37] If we assume, on the other hand, that Brahman does not manifest itself in this world wholly and entirely, but only partially, that will also have to be ruled out, for Brahman has no parts.

We see that the stumbling block of the inner logic of Samkara's proof is the attempt to speak of the Absolute while remaining within the reference frame of the concrete world "on this side".

The connection between Brahman and this world should, in Samkara's view, be regarded as the relation between an object and its properties ("the ocean and its waves") rather than as the relation between the whole and its parts. Our world is "Brahman's sleep" sometimes called Maya and sometimes matter, (*prakrti*). Maya is neither real nor unreal; it is appearance, or the "waves, bubbles and foam" concealing the Absolue, Brahman, from our view. There is water in the ocean, and we believe this water to be identical and one and the same (*abhinna*). In reality, however, water has many forms. It is due to the variety of forms of water that the waves, bubbles and foam are born in the ocean. Brahman and the world are one in the same way as the ocean is one, although it takes various forms—waves, bubbles, and foam. Thus our world (Maya), though founded on the Absolute, is not itself an absolute, and, as it has no substantive basis of its own, it cannot be true.

In this connection Samkara speaks of two objects of cognition—our world and Brahman.[38] Our world is cognised through *avidya*. That is a form of sensory and logical cognition which yields relative empirical truth (*aparavidya*). *Avidya* does not reveal the substantive basis of things; it is in this sense lack of knowledge, ignorance, or untrue knowledge. Samkara says that, just as we perceive a rope as a snake through optical error, so we take Brahman through *avidya*, for the world. *Avidya*, or lower wisdom, is opposed to *vidya*, or higher wisdom, which cognises the substance (Brahman) directly and gives man absolute truth (*paravidya*). *Avidya* disappears when *vidya* sets in.

The next major stage in the many centuries of the development of the Vedanta philosophy came with Ramanuja (12th-13th centuries). While accepting the basic propositions of Samkara's Advaita, Ramanuja at the same time imposed considerable restrictions (*vishishta*) on it.[39]

While for Samkara Brahman is a homogeneous impersonal Absolute and the world, an illusion, for Ramanuja Brahman is a person[40] including in itself the entire diversity of the material world, which, being a manifestation of Brahman, is real and not illusory. Brahman is the substance, while the world is an attribute.[41] The emergence of things (objects or phenomena) is viewed by Ramanuja as the manifestation of the world, and their destruction, as non-manifestation. Being destroyed, both matter devoid of consciousness and consciousness itself take the form of refined bodies, remaining the qualities of god.

The main difference between consciousness and matter is that consciousness is capable of enlightening itself (learning, enriching itself through knowledge) on the basis of its own existence, that is, it can be both subject and object. As for matter, it cannot enlighten itself, although it is the object of consciousness.

Inasmuch as Ramanuja does not oppose the concepts of "true reality" and "untrue reality" (appearance), he does not accept the division into knowledge (*vidya*) and non-knowledge (*avidya*), as Samkara did.

In the introduction to his commentaries on the Brahmasutra (I. I. I), Ramanuja sets forth the following fundamental theses. Those who, like Samkara, assert that the finite and true reality is simply being without attributes (*nirisesavastu*) are wrong. Reality without attributes is incognisable, and its existence cannot be proved by any mode of cognition.

Here are Ramanuja's arguments in favour of this viewpoint.

(1) All objects whose existence has been proved by various modes of cognition (*pramanas*) have attributes. Consequently, the existence of an object without attributes cannot be proved.

(2) The concept of attribute is always present even in intuition—both in the case of self-consciousness and in the object of intuition.

(3) In the case of direct knowledge (*pratyaksa*), both reflective (*savikalpaka*) and non-reflective (*nirvikalpaka*) knowledge has for its direct objects things characterised by definite attributes, with the sole difference that non-reflective direct knowledge yields an object devoid of some (through not all) attributes.

Ramanuja's main contribution to the Vedanta philosophy was his critique of Samkara's theory of untrue reality and untrue knowledge; his analysis of direct knowledge, which he divided into non-reflective and reflective; and his concretisation of the Brahman concept, as he believed that in Samkara that concept was too abstract and inaccessible to the broad masses.

The cause of human suffering, Ramanuja believed, does not lie in that this allegedly illusory world conceals Brahman from it and that, in cognising this "untrue world", we cannot obtain "true knowledge"; it rather lies in that Brahman is God, but we do not show enough love and loyalty to it (*bhakti*). According to the *bhakti* teaching, God is accessible to all, regardless of caste. Under the conditions prevailing in India at the time, this idea had a profound democratic meaning, as it sanctified the struggle against feudal and caste division.

REFERENCES

1. We shall therefore refer to the history of Indian materialism as the Brhaspati line.

2. J. Nehru, *op. cit.,* p. 100.

3. *Ibid.* The same idea is to be found in many other studies in the history of Indian philosophy. Debiprasad Chattopadhyaya, a prominent Marxist scholar, writes : "Apart from the mere mention of such lost treatises, what we now concretely possess are a few stray references to the Lokayata—views, or to its followers called the Lokayatikas, as preserved in the writings of those who wanted only to ridicule and refute the Lokayata... This philosophy had the misfortune of being known to us only through the writings of its opponents..." (D. Chattopadhyaya, *Lokayata. A Study*

in Ancient Indian Materialism, People's Publishing House, New Delhi, 1959, p. 7).

4. Hence one of the most probable versions of the origin of the name "Charvaka" : char "four", vak "word", that is, "four words".

5. *Loka* means "world", so that the ancient Indian materialists are sometimes called "Lokayatikas". Etymologically, the word *loka* means "that which is widespread among the people"; "that which is essentially secular".

6. S. Radhakrishnan, *op. cit.,* Vol. I, p. 281.

7. *Ibid.,* p. 273.

8. The Nyayiks were the creators of Indian formal logic. The story is current that during Alexander the Great's campaign in India Brahman priests described the entire system of the Nyaya logic to the Greek philosopher Callisthenes, who was in Alexander's army and later passed on this system to Aristotle. This logic was said to form the foundation of Aristotle's logical theory. This view gained wide currency at one time in Oriental countries. Modern scholars, however, reject it. Jawaharlal Nehru writes : "In fact Nyaya means logic or the science of right reasoning. It is similar in many ways to Aristotle's syllogisms, though there are also fundamental differences between the two. The principles underlying Nyaya logic were accepted by all other systems [of Indian philosophy. – *V.B.*] and, as a kind of mental discipline, Nyaya has been taught throughout the ancient and medieval periods and up to today in India's schools and universities..." (J. Nehru, *op. cit.,* pp. 190-191).

9. Indologists differ as to the origin of the name of this philosophical system. The word *samkhya* has two principal meanings : (1) count or computation; (2) profound meditation, reasoning, counting the pros and cons, struggle both in the intellectual and physical senses.

   Taking into account the first meaning, Gough explains the name Samkhya from the fact that in this system the principles of the Upanisads were listed. We believe that the scholars who reckon with the second meaning (like S. Radhakrishnan, Ram Mohan Roy, and others), have a better case. The meanings of the word Samkhya is close to Gr. *philosophia, dialektike*.

10. V.I. Lenin, "Materialism and Empirio-Criticism", *Collected Works,* Vol. 14, p. 153.

11. Let us point out that Buddhists, Nyayiks and Vaisesikas adhere to another view of this question. They believe that the effect does not actually exist in the material cause. Their argument is that if the effect existed in the material cause, there would be no need for the efficient cause. (If, for instance, the pot actually exists in the clay, what is the potter for?). The theory (*vada*) that the effect does not exist in the material cause before it is produced is sometimes called *Arambha-vada,* that is, the theory of the origin of the new in the effect.

12. Advaita Vedantists also adhere to the *Satkarya-vada,* with that essential difference that the transition of the cause into the effect is declared to be merely an appearance or illusion (*vivarta*). The following explanation is given here : if we saw a rope and took it for a snake, that does not mean that the rope had turned into a snake. Similarly, if Brahman created our universe, that does not mean that it actually became the universe that it created. Brahman (in this instance, cause) remains identical to itself and immutable, while the universe (in this case, effect) is merely appearance or illusion.

13. S. Radhakrishnan, *op.cit.,* Vol. II, p. 260.

14. S. Dasgupta (see *A History of Indian Philosophy,* Vol. I, Cambridge, 1922, pp. 244-245) interprets *sattva* as "intelligence-stuff"; *rajas,* as "energy-stuff", and *tamas,* as "mass-stuff".

15. This view has its sources in the nominalist tradition. In the Middle Ages nominalism, according to Marx, was the first expression of materialism which struggled against medieval scholasticism. The progressive thinkers of the 17th century (in particular Hobbes, Locke, and Spinoza in his theory of the individual things) also relied on nominalist principles in their fight against Aristotlean scholasticism. French materialists also turned to that tradition as an antidote to objective idealism.

16. *Pradhana—prakrti* in the state of equilibrium of the *gunas*—is just as unknowable as the Kantian thing-in-itself. *Prakrti* is knowable only in the state of nonequilibrium of the *gunas*, that is, what is knowable here is the dynamics of the *gunas* rather than *pradhana;* the transition from pure potentiality (*avyaktam*) to actuality (*vyaktam*) is cognised.

17. S. Radhakrishnan, *op. cit.*, Vol. II, p. 326.

18. What we have in mind here is not the religion of Jainism but rather the idealist philosophical system that took shape in the 6th-2nd centuries B.C.

19. Unextended substance is not considered in detail in Jainism. It is merely said to be "eternal, infinite, immobile, and amorphous".

20. The word *jiva* is used in different meanings in Jaina works : it denotes life, vitality, consciousness, and soul. *Jivas* are countless and varied. Because they recognised universals animateness of nature, Jainists worked out a classification of the souls (*jivas*) according to the criterion of "degree and kind of consciousness". For instance, the lowest class comprises the least perfect souls (in which consciousness is dormant) inhabiting the earth, water, fire, air, and plants (see Umasvama. Tattvarthadhigama-sutra, 2.22). Next come the souls of the animal world and man.

21. *Pudgala*—"that which is susceptible to combination and separation".

22. Jainists believed the primary qualities to be six in number : existence, pleasure, substantiality, cognisability, identity, and ability to have form.

23. The merging of atoms in aggregate states (*skandhas*) takes the following form : two atoms comprise a double *skandha;* a triple *skandha* is formed by the addition of still another atom (*anu*) to a double *skandha;* in the same way a fourth etc. are formed.

24. Although Buddhism was at its birth a religion without a god, later Siddhartha-Buddha himself was defied and declared to be a god. Moreover, there emerged the teaching of the coming to earth of a great number of gods or superhuman beings (the Boddhisattva).

25. Buddhists do not recognise spiritual substance either.
26. *Dhar* means to "accept" or "espouse"; *Dharma*—"carrier".
27. The adherents of the materialist trend in Buddhist philosophy.
28. The adherents of the subjectivist-idealist trend in Buddhist philosophy.
29. *Sunyavada*—a teaching on the void.
30. Some object or phenomenon of nature or the whole of the material world.
31. Hence the name *Madhyamikas,* followers of the middle path. See also the Buddhist source *Samyutta Nikaya* " 'Everything is' one extreme. 'Everything is not' is another extreme. The truth is in the middle." Truth is the coming into being without end.
32. S. Radhakrishnan, *op. cit.*, Vol. I, pp. 659 *et al.*
33. S. Chatterjee and D. Datta, *An Introduction to Indian Philosophy,* University of Calcutta, 1950, p. 146.
34. S. Radhakrishnan, *op. cit.*, Vol. I, p. 659.
35. V. I. Lenin, "Conspectus of Hegel's Book *Lectures on the History of Philosophy*", *Collected Works,* Vol. 38, p. 264.
36. Let us note, in passing, that raising the question of the role of rhythms in the universe and in man's life may be viewed as one of the brilliant anticipations of the ancient thinkers. Throughout the whole of the subsequent historical period, both in India and outside India, this guess concerning one of the most universal laws of the universe (along with the idea of universal cause-and-effect connections, of motion being an attribute of matter, of the mutual dependence of matter and consciousness, etc.) was substantiated and developed in science, art, and other forms of man's theoretical and practical activity. For instance, in art, the problem of rhythm in composition (in fine arts, architecture, fiction, music, theatre, cinema, etc.) remains the pivotal problem of creativity even now; in sociology we deal with the rhythms of the epoch; in production activity, with the rhythms of the work of enterprises, etc. We believe that this problem merits special consideration.

37. Samkara objects to any attempts to conceive the Absolute in the mind. The real is, in his view, outside of phenomena, and truth, outside of reasoning.

38. The idea of double reality is not an original feature of Samkara's teaching. As pointed out above, we also find it in Buddhist works (such as the Lankavatara-sutra or the Madhyamika Karika of Nagarjuna) and in Gaudapada's Mandukya Karika.

39. Hence the name of Ramanuja's philosophy, *vishishtadvaita.*

40. The god Vishnu, Shiva.

41. Brahman is the cause and the effect of the material world.

10 Textile Industry in India (300 B.C.—300 A.D.)

Weaving was an important industry in ancient India. The raw materials used were mainly flax, hemp, cotton, wool and silk. All textile fabrics are classified under four heads in Sanskrit dictionaries : *(i)* balka (bark-fibres), *(ii)* phala, made of hairs derived from fruits, *(iii)* kauseya (made of fibres derived from kosa, the cocoon) and *(iv)* rankava, made of hairs derived from ranku or deer; also known as 'lomaja'. Let us enquire into the textile industry which manufactured these fabrics into different types of cloth, fine and coarse from the coverings of beds and musical instruments and coarse fabrics to fine garments like 'dukula' and 'tasara'.

I. *Bark-fibres* : Ksuma was one of the most important bark-fibres manufactured into 'Ksauma' cloth, frequently met with in Sanskrit and Pali literature.[1] 'Ksauma' is, according to many scholars, linen made of Ksuma or uma (flax) and atasi (linseed).[2] He of course, doubts whether Ksauma meant linen because faced has long been used only for oil and not for fibres. But Kautilya[3] mentions 'atasi along with 'malati', 'murva', 'arka', 'sana' and 'gavedhuka' as fibre-yielding plants. Kulluka explains 'Ksauma' as a cloth made of 'atasi' fibre.

The queens of Dasaratha (Ksauma-vasanah) were clad in Ksauma, while welcoming Sita to their home. (Rama, Bala, 77, 15).Janaka offered Ksauma clothes during Sita's marriage, From this we may infer that Ksauma was a superior type of cloth, fit to be worn during festive occasions. Arjuna brought away valuable Ksauma clothes after conquering Uttara-Kuru beyond the Himalayas on the west. Susruta mentions Ksauma as one of the stuffs to be used for bandages.

Dukula was the usual name for the finest Ksauma. Kautilya mentions both Ksauma and dukula together in connection with the custom duties. 1/10th or 1/15th of the price was the duty to be levied for the goods of Ksauma, dukula etc. It seems that 1/10th is meant for the yarn and 1/15th for the finished product. Kautilya[4] refers to 'dukula' of Vanga as a white and 'soft fabric', that of Pandya or Pundra as "black and soft as the surface of the gem" and that of Suvarnakudya as "red as the sun" and "as soft as the surface of the gem, woven while the threads are wet and of uniform or mixed texture." He speaks of varieties of the same, "single, half, double, treble and quadruple". Such is also the Ksauma cloth, manufactured in Kasi and Pundra. Vanga, Pundra and Suvarnakudya, being accepted as East Bengal, North Bengal and Kamrup respectively, we learn from the above account of the *Arthasastra* that Bengal, Assam and Kasi were centres of manufacture of Ksauma and dukula in the Mauryan age. The use of the Ksauma cloth, evidently of coarser type, soaked in oil and thrown into enemies' camp after ignition for destroying them is also heard of in the *Mahabharata*.[5] The *Periplus*[6] refers to the import of linen into the ports of Western India, perhaps from Egypt; and this import, inspite of the fact that India herself produced flax or linseed fibre, as referred to in the *Arthasastra* indicates the large demand of Ksauma cloth in India in the 1st century A.D. The cultivation of atasi as a winter crop is referred to in the *Arthasastra*. The coarsest and thickest 'Ksauma' was called "atta", as attested by the Sanskrit dictionaries of the later period like *Amarakosa, Halayudha,* etc.

Sana (hemp) is another bark-fibre. Sanam, sanasuttam and saniyo are distinctly mentioned in the *Mahavagga* (1.30.4). Kautilya refers to 'sana' along with 'atasi' as wild fibrous plants and this indicates that 'sana' is other than 'atasi'. He directs the superintendent of arms to collect it for use as bow-string. 'Saniya' (hempen cloth) is also mentioned in the *Acaranga Sutra* (II.5.1). Susruta does not include sana-cloth for use as bandage, probably for its coarseness, but he recommends it for sewing up wounds. Manu[7] says that the girdle of a Vaisya should be made of sana threads. According to *Divyavadana*[8] sana-cloth was used by the cultivatsors. *Sanasutra,* which finds mention in the *Amarakosa* of the later period, means thread or string of sana and the commentators explain it as a string fit for fishing nets. Hence we may infer that sana was used for rough dresses of the common people and also for strings of the fishing nets or for surgical sewing.

Bhanga is another type of hemp. Buddhaghosa while commenting on the *Vinayapitaka*[9] says : "Some say that a single fibre of plant is bhanga but it is not. It signifies a thread spun of five fibres". This indicates that a pretty thick twist was used to weave into cloth. Bhanga is not mentioned in the *Arthasastra,* as a fibre-yielding plant but it might have been included within the generic term "balka". It is a field-crop, according to *Amarakosa* and it is mentioned in it immediately after 'atasi' and it may not be unlikely that both 'bhanga' and 'atasi' are related to each other in some respects, both being field-crops and yielding fibres. Sri J.C. Ray accepts the 'bhanga' of the *Amarakosa* as 'cannabis'. Watt says that 'cannabis' is wild in Kashmir and it is still cultivated there, both for its fibre and oil, and also throughout the Himalayan region from Kashmir to Assam.

The 'balka' of the *Arthasastra* denotes all fibres including coarser ones which were manufactured into ropes and bow-strings. The *Mahabharata*[10] mentions a list of fibres, evidently for ropes, viz. sana , rattan cane, munja grass, ballaja grass and skins and catgut. Manu (II) speaks of girdles, made of Kusa, asmantaka and ballaja as substitutes for munja, murva and sana, when these latter are not available. Guduchi, mentioned in Susruta has its aerial roots, yielding fibres, used as cords in surgery. From the above study we learn that flax, hemp and cannabis were plants yielding fibres which were used for bark-textiles in ancient India during the period.

II. *Seed-fibres* : Cotton is now the most important textile fibre, used for cloth almost everywhere. It was used even in the period of the Indus Valley culture, as attested by the remains of the woven material, found out at Mahenjo Daro.[11]

Herodotus[12] refers to clothes, made by the Indians, of wool grown on wild trees, meaning thereby cotton and speaks highly of Indian cotton. Its earliest mention seems to be in the *Asvalayana Srauta sutra* in connection with the material of the sacred thread of the *Brahmanas* and also in Panini, IV.3.143. Nearchus refers to cotton as "linen from trees of a more shining white". Cotton is mentioned in the Buddhist and Jaina texts.[13]

Kautilya gives us a full account of the textile industry. His reference to Aparanta (Konkan), Kalinga, Vanga (E. Bengal), Vatsa (Kausambi), Kasi, Mahisa (Jabalpur) and Madhura (Madurai) as seats of best cotton fabrics shows that cotton was produced and manufactured in different parts of India in his time. (II. XI). He mentions how cotton seeds were stored in time for cultivation and how trade in cotton and cotton-fabrics yielded revenue to the state.

Theophrastus[14] of the 3rd cent. B.C. and Pliny[15] compare Indian cotton plants to vines and Arrian[16] says that Indian cotton is brighter and whiter than that of other places. The *Acaranga sutta* (II.5) refers to expensive clothes made of blue cotton, of common cotton and of Bengal cotton. Manu attributes a special purity to cotton and so prescribes that a Brahmana should have his sacrificial thread, made of cotton. He regulates the operations of the weavers and washermen. Cotton cloth is mentioned in the *Ramayana* and the *Mahabharata*,[17] of course not frequently. The inscription[18] on Bhilsa Topes mentions the gift of a weaver (sotika), Damaka. Besides, we hear of a village called 'Karapasigrama' near Vidisa, noted for cotton and cotton-manufacture in inscriptions (Lud. Nos. 260 and 515). The name of this village is found in three inscribed labels on the railings of Sanchi Stupa No. I.

Cotton industry rose to its highest pitch in the shape of Indian muslins, held in high esteem and fetching high prices in Roman markets about the beginning of the Christian era. The *Periplus*[19] records that "Indian cotton cloth, the broad cloth called 'Monache'and that called 'Sagmatogene' and a few muslins" are exported from "the district of Ariaca" to East Africa. It speaks of the country of Arica as reputed for "cotton and cotton-cloths of the coarser sorts" with Barygaza as an outlet for exportation to the west. Barygaza was fed with muslins and ordinary cloths from Ozena[20] and Tagara.[21] It mentions muslins of Masalia[22]and also of "the finest sort called Gangetic"[23] which was definitely the product of North Bengal and exported through the mart called Ganges.[24] Warmington thinks that "from about 100 A.D. onwards much raw cotton was submitted to the looms of Alexandria and Syria". The mention of cotton-cloth and muslin in the Digest-list shows their entry into Alexandria en route to Rome by the sea route. The finds of post-Nero Roman coins in the cotton-growing districts of Maharastra indicate that cotton-products were exported to Rome from India.

The Tamil literature of the period of our review also speaks of cotton fabrics found in Kaveripattinam and Madura. The *Silappadikaram* (BK XIV, 180-200) describes the streets of Madura as being peopled over with cloth-merchants dealing in cotton fabrics. It speaks of Puhar where weavers dealt in fine fabrics, made of silk, fur and cotton. Argaru (Uraiyur, the old Cola capital) gave its name to a local variety of muslin. From the above study we may think that cotton industry flourished in India in the period of our discussion.

III. *Wool and hair* : The use of skins as clothing is shown by the term 'ajina', frequently met with in the Vedic literature and in the epics. Kautilya refers to a large number of animals from which skins and furs were obtained, *viz.*, a big lizard called godhi, leopard, lion, tiger, elephant, buffalo, rhinoceros etc. Hides were used as war-material. The trade in hides and fur was of much value. The *Periplus*[25] records that seric skins were exported through Barbaricum. Pliny[26] says that "the most valuable products furnished by the coverings of animals are the skins, which the Seres dye". The term 'seric' might have meant 'Cera' and if it was so, the skins or hides might have been Indian products, sent through the ports of the Cera kingdom. The *Mahabharata*[27]speaks of skins of martens and weasels, besides wool, silk and muslin, as presents to Yudhisthira from the Sakas, Tukhara and Kanka tribes.

The generic term for all woolen goods was 'rankava' or 'lomaja' (woollen and hairy). Ranku was proverbially a wild goat, perhaps the Himalayan Ibex. Blanket-making industry was developed in the border of India even in the Achaemenid period. Yaska refers to the "Kambojas who are called so because they enjoy blankets or beautiful things". This account of Kamboja reminds us of the condemnable practice of the northerners of the 'urna-vikraya', mentioned in *Boudhayana Dharma sutra*. Panini refers to different varieties of woollen goods, viz. pravara, pandu-kambala and panyakambala. From the *Mahabharata*[28] we learn that the Sakas, Tusaras and others, inhabiting the countries on the north and west of India presented the Pandavas with rankava, urnaja, kitaja, pattaja and fine cotton garments. The king of the Kambojas is also noted here[29] as bringing for Yudhisthira woollen cloth of various sorts, made of sheep's wool, fur of mice and other animals living in the holes, of the hair of cats, all inlaid with threads of gold. ("Aurnan vailan varsa-damsan jatarupa-pariskrtan/pravarajina mukhyamscha kambojah pradadau vahun//). The *Ramayana*[30] refers to carpets, made of the fleece of ranku, of sheep and of hares.

The *Arthasastra*[31] mentions woollen blankets of ten varieties, kambala (coarse), kauchapaka (used by cowherds), kulamitika (headdress), saumitika (a covering put over the hustings spread on the back of a bullock), turagastarana (husting on a horse), samantabhadraka (husting on an elephant), varnaka (coloured), talicchaka (bedsheet), varavana (a coat) and paristoma (a large blanket). Besides these, he mentions 'bhimgisi' (a blanket made up of eight pieces and black in colour) and 'apasaraka' both being the products of Nepal and some other blankets, made of the wool of wild animals, known as 'samputika' (trousers), caturasrika (a small rectangular blanket), lambara (a curtain or wrapper), pravaraka and sattalika (a blanket rubbed with a gem and smoothened while being woven).

The *Digha-nikaya*[32] mentions in the list of luxury goods : *(i)* gonaka (according to Rhys Davids, goat's hair coverlets with very long fleece), *(ii)* patika (white blankets), *(iii)* patalika (woollen coverlets), *(iv)* uddalomi (rugs with fur on both sides), etc. Elsewhere[33] it refers to blankets of feathers of owl. The *Mahavagga*[34] mentions a fluffy blanket called 'Kovaya'. Expensive clothes, made of fur and blankets are also heard of in the Acaranga sutra (II. 5) Gandhara and Kodumbara were reputed for valuable woollen clothes.[35] The Jat.[36] also mentions Kambala of Uddiyana (mod. Swat). Manu[37] speaks of 'Kutapa' which Kulluka explains as a soft blanket from Nepal. The *Divyavadana*[38] refers to 'Aparantaka', a class of cloth, evidently manufactured in Aparanta (N. Konkan). A shop at Surparaka is also mentioned in it as having dealt exclusively in this material, and this indicates its large demand in the locality.

The Graeco-Romans (Yavanas) obtained wool and woollen clothes in Indian markets like Kaveripattinam.[39] The *Periplus*[40] refers to the export of furs from Barbaricum which perhaps came from South India.[41] The 'marococorum lana', mentioned in Justinian's Digest-list of important goods is raw wool of the shawl-goat of the Karakoram region, exported to the Mediterranean world through the ports of the west coast of India.[42] From the above references we learn that wool-weaving was fairly developed in defferent parts of India during the period and this industry met the local needs and the foreign demands.

IV. *Silk* : Silk at present is of two kinds, wild and pure. Wild silk is the product of silk-worms feeding on the leaves of the forest trees. Pure silk is the product of the mulberry silkworms. Wild silk of India is derived from three species of worm, *(i)* Bengal 'tasar' worm, *(ii)* erandi or eri worm and *(iii)* muga worm. Bengal tasar worms are found in the forests of Bengal, Bihar and Orissa. Sometimes these worms are semi-domesticated, the eggs being gathered and put upon the leaves of asan, sal and haritake etc. Eri cocoons are reared in north Bengal. The product of the cocoon is spun and not reeled. Its fibre is more lasting than mulberry silk and tasar. The worm feeds on the leaves of eranda (castor-oil plants). Assam is famous for eri. *(iii)* Muga silk is the product of Assam. Its worms are most domesticated. They feed on the leaves of many plants, the most important being 'sum' of Assam.

The Mulberry silk is the product of Bombyx mori. The industry of cocoon-rearing is now carried on in the districts of Murshidabad, Rajshahi and Maldah. Four types of silkworm, all feeding on mulberry leaves are reared in Bengal,, *viz., (i)* nistari *(ii)* Chota palu or Desi, *(iii)* Bara Palu and *(iv)* China Palu.

Kauseya or silken garment is mentioned probably for the first time in Panini.[43] It is also referred to in the *Mahavagga*[44] in the Dighanikaya[45] in the *Acarangasutra*[46] and the *Jataka.*[47] The *Mahabharata*[48] speaks of two types of silk, 'Koseya' as kitaja and 'patta' as pattaja. The Sakas of the N. W. frontier regions of India brought as presents to Yudhisthira various garments including tasar and patta. The *Ramayana*[49] states that Rama and Sita were dressed in 'koseya' even at home.

The *Arthasastra*[50] mentions 'Kauseya', 'patrorna' and Chinapatta. It qualifies 'Chinapatta' as Chinabhumija', *i.e.,* produced or manufactured in China. Some scholars like Jayaswal[51] think that Chinabhumi does not mean China but the land of the Shin tribe of Gilgit area. Even if we assume that Chinamsuka or Chinapatta of the *Arthasastra* means silk-cloth imported from China, we can not deny that silk was an indigenous product of India much before the time of Kautilya, as evidenced by its reference at least in Panini.

The *Arthasastra*[52] states that 'patrorna' is obtained from Magadha, Pundra and Suvarnakudya and that it has its origin from the trees like Naga; Lakucha, Vakula and Vata. The 'patrorna' of a Naga tree is yellow, that of Lakucha is of the colour of wheat, that of Vakula is white and the rest is of the colour of butter. It adds that "that which is produced in the country of Suvarnakudya is the best". From this account we learn that South Bihar, north Bengal and Assam were the reputed centres of silk-industry in the Mauryan age. It may be noted here that 'Patrorna'is defined in the *Amarakosa,* (a dictionary written in the Gupta period) as a bleached or white "Kauseya" and is said to have been costly. The above report of Kautilya as to Suvarnakudya or Assam being the centres of this industry is confined by the Ramayana[53] which mentions Magadha, Anga, Pundra and "the country of the cocoonreareres" (Kosakaranam bhumi) as the names of the countries one passes through, while going to the east. Pundra is north Bengal and so Assam lying on its east is meant by the expression 'Kosa-karanam bhumi' Assam is still famous for the Eri or Muga silk.

It is difficult to determine when and how the mulberry silk was introduced in India and whether it was an indigenous plant or imported from outside. Some think that 'pattaja', referred to in the *Mahabharata,* stated above meant the pure or mulberry silk[54] as contrasted with the kitaja (Kauseya or tasar) and that it might have "come to Bengal via Kashmir as well as via Manipur" N.G. Mukherji, while writing on the 'Silk Industry of Bengal' says that sericultural industry of India is traceable not to China but to the Himalayan country, where the mulberry grows wild and that it travelled from north-west to south-east. Watt also opines that "in India the mulberry worm has been systematically reared for many centuries, though it seems probable that there have been two independent sources of the knowledge and stock possessed by India, viz, (a) Northern India, very possibly from Central Asia or Persia and (b) Assam to Bengal .... via Manipur". The word "tuda" of the *Amarakosa,* corrupted into tut or tunt in modern Indian vernaculars has been explained in *Bhavaprakasa* as mulberry. 'Tula' has been used in the *Arthasastra* in the same sense. The terms like 'palu' or palupoka used by the present silkworm-rearers of Bengal may be traceable to the Sanskrit word 'pallava' meaning leaves of the mulberry trees; and the mulberry trees; and the expression 'desi palu' indicates that this industry is indigenous to Bengal.

The *Periolus*[55] mentions that "raw silk, silk yarn and silk-cloth" were brought on foot through Bacteria from Thinae to Barygaza and were also exported to Damirica by way of the river Ganges. It also refers to the exportation of silk yarn and silk-cloth, through Barbaricum and Barygaza, which might have included indigeneous silk goods as well. This trade, we may infer, might have given an impetus to domesticated silk-industry in India.

It is interesting to note that silver and gold wires were used in brocade and embroidery. Megasthenes refers to gorgeous embroidered robes and fine muslins embroidered with purple and gold. Gold and silver robes are also mentioned in the *Mahabharata* (II) and *Ramayana.*[56] The *jataltas*[57] refer to golden turbans (Kancanapatta), used by kings and golden trappings for the use of state elephants[58] ("nage hemakappanavavase").

It is difficult to determine the technical aspect of the textile industry in India. "Among the finds at Mahenjo Daro were numerous spindle whirls in the houses, and that if (spinning and weaving were practised by the well-to-do and the poor alike) is indicated by the fact that the whirls were made of the more expensive facince as well as of the cheaper pottery and shell".[59] The technical terms like 'tantu'(warp), 'out' (woof) are found in the *Raveda* and the *Atharvaveda,* while 'tasara' (Shuttle) and 'Veman'(loom) are mentioned in the *Yajurveda* and these indicate that spinning and weaving were carried on as early as the vedic period. The use of separate terms for weaver, dyer and embroider indicates how specialisation in the textile craft was attained to some degree even in the Vedic age. The word 'tantuvaya' is implied in Panini's sutra "silpini chakrinah".[60] The place where the weaver plied his loom was known as 'avaya'[61] the loom as 'tantra'[62] and the shuttle as "pravanih".[63] The process of weaving is reflected in the *Mahabhasya* which states that the warp is stretched (astirnam tantram) and then threads are woven across it with a shuttle ("protamtantram"). The *Divyavadana*[64] gives us some idea of the different processes of ginning, cleaning, pressing, carding, spinning and weaving. Starching of yarn before weaving to increase the weight of woven clothes is also heard of .Kautilya allows 10% increase in case of cotton ½% in cases of linen and silk and 2% in case of wool.[65] Manu permits 10% increase in all cases (8.397).

The *Jataka*[66] gives us a graphic scene of the weaving operation. Women were occupied with carding cotton, as evidenced by the expression: "*Itthinam-kappasa-potthana-dhanuka*" in *Jataka*, VI., p. 41. Kautilya[67] prescribes that the state superintendent of weaving should employ women, mostly helpless in spinning etc. The *Milindapanho*[68] also reports that a lady herself had carded (pinjitam), pressed (Kunchitam), beaten (pattitam), cut (kantitam) and woven (vayitam) a wrapper.

Kautilya[69] gives us the following picture of the textile industry, how it was carried on under the supervision of the Superintendent of the Spinning and Weaving Department: "The Superintendent shall employ qualified persons to manufacture threads, coats (varma), cloths and ropes. Widows, cripple women, girls, ascetic women, women compelled to work in default of paying fines, mothers of prostitutes, old women-servants of the king and prostitutes who have ceased to attend temples on service shall be employed to cut wool, fibre, cotton, tula (silk?) hemp and flax. Wages shall be fixed according to the fitness of the yarn. Those who produce large quantities shall be rewarded with oil and emblic unguents. (*tailamalakodvartanaih*). Wages shall be cut short if the outturn falls short. The Superintendent shall closely associate with the workmen. Those who manufacture Ksauma, dukula, silk, woollen and cotton cloths shall be rewarded with special presents.... Those women who do not stir out of their houses, those whose husbands are gone abroad, those, who are cripple or girls may, when obliged to work for subsistence, be provided with the work of spinning out threads in due courtesy through the medium of maid-servants. Those women who can present themselves at the weaving house shall at dawn be enabled to exchange their spinnings for wages. Only such light as is enough to examine the threads shall be kept. If the Superintendent looks at the face of such women or talks about any other work, he shall be punished with the first amercement; and with the middle fine if he delays in paying the wages or if he pays for the work, not done. She, who, having received the wages, does not turn out the work, shall have her thumb cut off (according to Shama Satsry but Mr. Roy is more justified to explain the text "samdamsanam" as "fixing tightly an iron round the thumb" because cutting of thumb seems it be too harsh a punishment for a person, employed in spinning and weaving which becomes impossible without thumbs). The Superintendent shall closely associate with those who manufacture ropes and mail armour and shall carry on the manufacture of straps (varatra) and other commodities. He shall carry on the manufacture of ropes from threads and fibres and of straps from cane and bamboo bark. These are meant for war equipment and for fastening horses and other draught animals.

Now about washing of clothes. The Rgveda[70] tells us that "the god Pusan weaves woollen clothes and washes them". So washing and weaving developed as an art as early as the Vedic period.

Kautilya[71] regulates the operations of the washermen of the period. "Washermen shall wash clothes on wooden planks or on stones of smooth surface". Or they would be fined. They must not sell, mortgage or let out for hire others' clothes. Particular days were allowed to wash clothes of particular colours. They were not only to cleanse clothes but also to restore their colour. Manu[72] also frames rules for careful washing. He (Ch. X) tells us to cleanse tasar and woollens with alkaline earth, Tibetan shawls (Kutapa) with arista, fine silk with the pulp of a 'bael' fruit and linen with a ground paste of white colza seed (svetasarsapa).

The dyeing of textiles was also a subsidiary craft. Panini[73] mentions maddar (manjistha), lac (laksa) and indigo (nili). The dyeing of textiles was practised in the Mauryan period, as evidenced by the *Arthasastra* which mentions white, pure red, rose-red, and black woollens and furs of one uniform colour, such as black, dark-red and grey or of wheat colour or of straw colour. The *Acaranga-sutra*[74] refers to expensive clothes, printed with many patterns *abharanavichitra*) and to clothes which were dyed and rubbed with perfumes. The *Ramayana*[75] mentions the ladies of Ravana clothed in garments of variagated hues. Kusumbha was one of the prominent dyes used in ancient India. Kautilya refers to the cultivation of 'Kusumbha' in the Royal farms[76] for flowers which were, according to the commentator, productive of colouring material. 'Lodhra', mentioned in the Amarakosa was also used to dye silk with lac. Manjistha or Indian madder is also heard of in the *Arthasastra* as a red dye-stuff. The *Jataka*[77] refers to a variety of colours and to garments, rugs and curtains as dyed scarlet, orange etc. Even an umbrella is noted as red-coloured.[78] The word "cangavara" in two gathas,[79] used in the sense of a dyer's straining cloth removes our doubt. The word 'rajaka'[80] may be taken to mean both a washerman and a dyer. The *Jataka*[81] mentions a dyers' street (rajaka-vithi). Some other dyes like Kampilya, pattranga and nila (indigo) find mention in the Amarakosa.

The *Periplus*[82] mentions the import of purple. Indigo was an important dye-product of India, exported to western countries, as evidenced by the author of the *Periplus* (39) and Pliny.[83] The dye-manufacturer (rangakara) is also referred to in the *Milindapanho*, 331 in the *Ramayana*[84] and in *Manusmrti*.[85]. Hence we may infer that the art of dyeing was equally developed as weaving in this period. The archaeological evidences also confirm it. A piece of cloth has been unearthed at Bairat. It was used to wrap a few punchmarked coins in the early 2nd cent. B.C.[86] A few pieces of pottery with internal textile impressions of the Kushana period have also been discovered at Rangmahal. The materials used were cotton, linen and jute.[87]

The individual enterprise formed the basis of this craft as of others. Most of the artisans worked independently at their own houses.[88] The *Jatakas* mention 18 kinds of guilds including that of weavers.[89] The Nasik cave inscription[90] of the early 2nd cent. A.D. refers to an endowment of money, made by Usavadata to two guilds of weavers at Govardhana near Nasik and from this we may infer the rise of guilds of weavers elsewhere as well.

REFERENCES

1. *Ramayana*, II 6.7; *Mahabharata* (II. 27, 16), *Arthasastra*, II. XI. *Manu*, II. 41 and V. 141; *Divyavadana*, pp. 316, line-27, *Mahavagga*, 1.30.4 and *Acaranga sutra*, II. 5.1.
2. cf. Ray, J.C., *JBORS*, III, p. 187 f.
3. II. 17.
4. II, XI (AS = *Arthasastra*).
5. Udyog, 154. (Mbh = *Mahabharata*).
6. Secs. 39 and 49.
7. II. 41.
8. pp. 83 and 6.
9. 1.8.3.
10. Santi, 86.
11. cf. Mackay, *Further Excavation at Mohenjo Daro*, pp. 441-42, 591.
12. III. 106.
13. cf. *Acar.* sut. II. 5.1; *Bhagavati Sut*, 11.11 and *Tulika in Digha-Nikaya*, I, p. 7.
14. *History of Plants*, IV. 4.8-10.
15. Nat. Hist., XII, 38-40.
16. *Indika*, 16.1.
17. II. 49.23.
18. Lud. No. 331.
19. Sec. 6.
20. Sec. 48.
21. Sec. 51.
22. Sec. 62.
23. Sec. 63.
24. cf. *Schoff*, p. 258.
25. Sec. 39.
26. 37. 77.
27. Sabha, 49.23.
28. Sabha, 49. 22-25.

29. II. 49.3.
30. Lanka, 113.
31. II. XI.
32. I. i.15.
33. I. VIII. 14.
34. 8.1.36.
35. Jat. VI, p. 500 G.G.
36. IV. 352.
37. V. 120.
38. ed. Cowell and Neil, p. 316.
39. Pillai, 25.
40. Sec. 39.
41. cf. *Warmington*, 'Commerce between the Roman Empire and India', p. 157.
42. *Ibid.*, p. 160.
43. IV 3.42.
44. I. 30.4 and VIII. 1.36.
45. 1.i.15.
46. II. 5.1.
47. I, pp. 149 and 309.
48. II. 49-22.
49. Ayodhya, 37.89.
50. II. XI.
51. *Hindu Polity*, I, 212 n. 1.
52. II XI.
53. Kiskindha, 40.
54. J.C. Ray, *JBORS*, p. 216.
55. Sec. 64.
56. Sundara, 10.15.
57. IV 404 and V. 322.
58. cf. Strabo, XV, I. 54 and 69.
59. *Mohenjo Daro and the Indus Civilisation*, I, p. 32.

60. VI. 2.76.
61. "avayanti asmin", III. 3.122.
62. V. 2.70.
63. V. 4.160.
64. VII, p. 83 (21-25).
65. AS. IV.I.
66. VI, p. 26-G. 105.
67. II.XXIII.
68. IV. 6.10.
69. II.XXIII.
70. X. 26.6.
71. IV.I.
72. VII. 396.
73. IV. 1.42, IV. 2.2 and VIII. 3.97.
74. II. 5.
75. VI. 7.
76. II. XVII.
77. VI, p. 279—GG. 1223-6.
78. Jambonadam chattam, Jat, VI, p. 218. G. 934.
79. Jat, V, p. 186, GG. 219-220.
80. Jat, VI; p. 276, G. 1197.
81. IV, p. 81.
82. Sec. 36.
83. 35, 25-27.
84. II. 83.15.
85. IV. 216.
86. Sahni, *Archaeological remains and excavations at Bairat,* pp. 22-23, pl. IV (a).
87. cf. Rydh, *Rangmahal,* pp. 201-2 p. 52 (5-12).
88. Jat. VI. 189 and *Patanjali,* I.4, 54.
89. cf. R. Davids, *Buddhist India,* pp. 90-96.
90. *E.I.,* VIII, pp. 81-85.

11 The Textile and Weaving Technology in Ancient India Upto-1200 A.D.

Regarding weaving and textile technology in ancient period, we find stray and cryptic references from literary, archeology and foreign records. As regards art and crafts the Vedic Aryans knew how to weave tine cloth and knew sewing. The wool was obtained from sheep (*avi*) for spinning and weaving and hence *urna* is used to denote sheep and *avika* sheep's wool. The word *ajina* denotes generally the skin of an animal *e.g.*, a gazelle, as well as that of a goat (*aja*). The use of skin is shown by the adjective 'Clothed in skin' in the *Satapatha Brahmana* and the turrier's trade is mentioned in the *Vajasaneyi Samhita. Otu* denotes the 'woof' in weaving and corresponds to *tantu* the wrap. In the process of weaving a shuttle (*tasara*) was used. The weaver is named *vaya* and the loom *veman*. A wooden peg (*mayukha*) was used to stretch the web on, while lead was employed as a weight to extend it. The work of weaving was probably the special for women. In the *Panchavimsa Brahmana, Satapatha Brahmana* and the *Rgveda* the female weavers are mentioned as *Vayitris* and *Siris* Respectively. A metaphor in the *Atharvaveda* personifies Night and Day as two sisters weaving the web of the year, the night, serving as warp, the days as woof. In the *Atharvaveda tantu* appears properly to mean 'thread' and in particular the 'warp' of a piece of weaving.

In the *Satapatha Brahmana* the warp is called *anuchada,* the woof paryasa and tantu being the 'Threads. Tarku (spindle) is known only in Vedic literature from two mention of it in yaska's *Nirukta*. In the *Rgveda* and *Yajurveda Samhita* Tasars denotes the weaver's shuttle and *tuna* in the later samhita and Brahmana denote the 'fringe' or trimming of a garment.

The word *Pravara* or *Pravara* denotes a 'covering' or woollen cloth in the *Brihadaranyaka upanisad*. In the *Brahmanas*, the word *Pracinatana* denotes the warp of a piece of cloth. In the *Rgveda* and later the most usual word for clothing is *Vasas*. Clothes were often made of sheep's wool and the God Pusan is called a weaver of garment. The garments work were often embroidered and adorned with gold. Among the technique, which can be regarded as traditional in India, in the sense of their ancient practice, are embroidery, hand-painting, resist-dyeing and brocading.

The Vedic and Buddhist literature mention several other varieties of cloth, though there is some doubt about the materials from which they are manufactured. Such as *Barasin* cloth manufactured from the fibres of the *barastree* (red-flowered rhododendron). *Dursa* or *dussa* a variety of woollen cloth. *Maitryani* and *Taittiriya-Samhita* and *Sankhayana Arnyaka* mention *ksauma* and saffron-coloured *ksauma* garments (*Kausumbha paridhna*). *Kauma* has been translated as a variety of silk though in later literature it is used for linen. In the *Satapatha Brahmana* and the *Maitrayani Samhita* Pandya was worn by the kings at sacrifices and it has been suggested by some scholar as an unbleached or dyed cotton or silken stult, *Tarpya*, according to the commentators on the *Katyayana Sranta Sutra* and *Satapatha Brahmana* suggest it to be a linen garment, or one thrice soaked in ghee or one made of the *trpa* plant. Goldstiicker and Eggeling are inclined to translate the word as silken garment.

The word atka in the sense of a garment occurs in the *Rgveda* and is also translated by Roth, Lugwig, Grassmann, Zimmer and others as a garment. It was interwoven or embroidered with gold thread. The *pesas* was gold embroidered cloth with artistic and intricate designs. The making of such a garment was a regular occupation of women as is indicated by the word *pesakari*, the female embroidered figuring in the list of his victims in the *Yajurveda*.

The *Jatakas* show that the Craftsmen were organised in eighteen guilds including the wood workers, the smiths, the painters, and the rest expert in various crafts. The works of weaver of embroiderer (*pesaskarasippa*) as well as of *nalakara* 'the basket maker' because these professions were in the hands of the aborigines, were considered as low professions and both weavers and basket-makers were relegated to the class of despised castes.

In the *Mahajanaka Jataka* cotton, silk, linen and kotumbara cloths are described. Spinning and weaving seem to have been fairly common in the period of the jatakas. Thus according to the *Tundila Jataka*. There were cotton fields in the neighbourhood of Benaras. Women looked after the proper up keep of such fields and were known as 'keeper of the cotton field (*Kappasarakkhiya*) as mentioned in *Mahajanaka Jataka*. Some technical terms as regards spinning and carding are also mentioned. In a story it is mentioned that the woman spun (*kantitva*) fine thread (*sukhumasuttani*) and made a ball (*gulam*) of it. Bow for carding cotton is also mentioned (*Kappasepothanadhanukam*). In the time of Buddha Cotton produced in Benares was used in the manufacture of cloth. Buddhist literature is full of references to the cloth of Kasi (*Kasi Kuttama*); it was at places termed as *Kasiyani*. The cloth of Benares was so famous that the commentator of the *Mahapinibbana sutta* commenting on the term *Vihita Kapasa* (Calendered cloth) modern Hindi-*Kundikiyahua*) with which the mortal remains of a world ruler were covered, calls it the cloth of Benares (*Kasikavatta*), which on account of the fineness of its structure did not absorb oil. This fineness of the structure of Benares cloth (*Varanaseyyaka*) is also given in the *Majjhima Nikaya*. The Commentrator praises the cloth of Benares because in Benares according to him fine cotton was produced; the women spinners and weavers were clever and the water (for bleaching) was soft. Both obverse and reverse sides of the cloth of Benares were soft and smooth fine silk was also produced at Benares. The Buddha had permitted the use of *Kauseva-Prayara* or silken *Chadar* to the *bhikkus*.

Linen (*Ksauma*) was also common and ordained as one of the cloths for making *civara* of the *bhikkus*. It is also mentioned in the *Mahavagga* that the blankets were made from *Ksauma* and wool. Five hundred blankets of this material were presented by the king of Kasi to Jivaka Kumarabhrtya who in his turn presented them to the Buddha *Kotumbara* was also a variety of cloth, the nature of which has not been explaind. It is, however, possible that it might have been some woollen or barken or cotton staff manufactured in the country of Audumbaras, the word *Odumbara* and *Kotumbara* being synonymous according to Pryzluski.

For woollen staff the word *Kambala* has been used in the Buddhist literature. In the Jatakas the scarlet *pandukambala* of Gandhra is praised (*Indagopakanannabha gandhara andukambata*). The country of Sivi was famous for its shawls and the *siveyyaka* dussa is praised in the *Mahavagga*. It is also mentioned in the *Mahavagga*. It is also mentioned in the *Sivi Jataka* where king of Kosala is said to have presented one Dasabala with a cloth piece from Sivi costing hundred thousand pieces of money. The word *dussa* still found in Hindi and Panjabi *dhussa*, which is used for a particular type of woollen Chadar. Another variety of cloth which might have been manufactured from wool was known as *Vahitika* which was sent by Ajatasatru to Prasenjit, who in his turn offered it as present to Ananda. This cloth measured sixteen hands in length and eight in width. The use of *namtaka* (Hindi namdar) 'felt' and 'Kojava', 'flutty blanket' being luxurious woollen goods, was forbidden to the *bhikkhunis*.

Besides these varieties, cloth made from hemp (sana, Hindi San) and *bhaga* were also produced. A cloth from the fibre of bhag-tree is still produced in the Kumaon district of U.P. and is known as *bhageta*. The following cloth were forbidden by the Buddha to his disciples-cloth from *Kusa* grass (*Kusa-cira*), bark (*balkala*), wood (*phalaka*), human hair (*Kesa-Kambala, bata-kambala*), the feather of an owl as clothing, the strips of deer-skin (*ajinksip*) and cloth made from fibrous stalks of *mandara*. The bhikkhus were also allowed the use of loom (*tantaka*) with shuttles (*vemaka*), strings (*vatta*), tickets (*sataka*) etc.

As regards the implements employed in sewing the needle was known. *Thimble (pratigraha)* was also used to avoid needle pricks. It seems that gold and silver were employed for manufacturing thimbles chief for wele-to-do; for the bhikkhus thinbles made from bone or conch-shele etc. were only prescribed. Sassors (*Batthaka*) were also known, and as the sassors and thimble were prone to be mislaid small bag (*avesana vitthaka*) was used to hold them.

There are little direct information about the way in which weaving as an industry was organised in ancient India, but there is evidence of weavers' guilds and also of the Centralization of commodity production in market-towns. *Kautilya's Arthasastra* (Late 4th Century B.C. to Late second cen. B.C.) has a Chapter devoted to the superintendent of weaving in what appear to have been the court workshops. Here, employment seems to have been on a casual basis, payments being made according to fixed piece-rates. There it is stated that superintendent of weaving shall employ qualified persons to manufacture threads (*sutra*), coats (*varma*), cloth (*vastra*) and ropes (*rajju*). The materials employed for spinning were wool (urna, fibre (*balka*) cotton (*karpasa*), tula hemp (*sana*) and flax (*Ksauma*). Windows, Cripple women, girls, mendicant or ascetic women (*pravrajita*), women compelled to work in default of paying fines (*daudapratikarini*), mothers prostitutes, old women-servants of the king, and prostitutes (devadasi) who have ceased to attend temples on service shall be employed to out wool, fibre, cotton, panide (*tuta*) hemp and flax, wages shall be fixed according as the threads spun are fine, coarse (sthula, *i.e.*, big) or of middle quality, and in proportion to a greater or less quantity manufactured, and inconsideration of the quantity of thread spun, those (who turn out to a greater quantity) shall be presented with oil and dried cakes of myrobalan fruits (*tailamalakodyartanaih*). Those who weave *Ksauma Dukula,* silk woollen and cotton cloth shall be encouraged by presenting them with perfumed garlands of flowers. They may also be made to work on holidays (tithisu) by payment of special rewards (*prativapadana manaih*). Wages shall be cut short if, making allowances for the quality of raw materials, the quantity of the threads spun out is found to *fell short*. Weaving may also be done by those artisans who are qualified to turn out a given amount of work in a given times and for a fixed amount of wages. The superintendent shall closely associate with the workman. Those who manufacture fibrous clothes, raiments, silk clothes, woollen clothes and cotton fabrics shall be rewarded by presentatives, such as scents, garlands of flowers, or any other prizes of encouragement.

Various kinds of garments blankets, and curtains shall be manufactured. Those who are acquainted with the work shall manufacture mail armour.

Those women who do not star of their houses (*anishkasinyah*), those whose husbands are gone abroad, and those who are cripple or girls may, when obliged to work for subsistence, ·be provided with work (spinning out threads) in due courtesy through the medium of maid-servants (of the weaning establishment). Those women who can present themselves at the weaning house shall at down be enabled to exchange their spinning for wages (*dhanda-yetanavinimayam*). Only so much light as is enough to examine the threads shall be kept. If the superintendent looks at the face of such women or talks about any other work, he shall be punished with the first amercement. Delay in paying the wages shall be punished with the middle most amercement, likewise when wages are paid for work that is not completed. She who, having received wages, does not turn out the work shall have her thumb cut off. Those who mis-appropriate, steal or run away with (the raw material supplied to them) shall be similarly punished. Weavers, when guilty, shall be fined out of their wages in proportion to their offences. The superintendents shall closely associate with those who manufacture ropes and mail armour, and shall carry on the manufacture of straps (*yaratra*) and other commodities. He shall carry on the manufacture of ropes from thready and fibres and straps from cave and bamboo task, with which beasts for drought are trained or tethered. Silk mentioned in the *Arthasastra* is referred to in the *Mahabharata* as Kitaja which was the product of cina and vathika.

Cotton cloth was extensively used in the period of the 1st Century A.D. In the *Divyavadana* mention is made of the growth of good cotton and its plantation (Karpasa vata). The softness of cotton-wool (Karpasapica) was appreciated, and in the *Divyavadana* the softness of the body of Upagupta is compared with cotton wool. Cotton wool was purchased from the market and after ginning it (*tam parikarmayitya*) the yaru of even structure and fine quality was spun. The weaver (*Kuyinda*), while engaged in weaving cloth, packed and gathered the cloth and yaru *(aviciravicirakam)* and with raised head (*abhinirmayodudhasasiraskah*) and with the clapping movements of hands and feet (*sphatitampanipad)* began the-weaving operation. The weavers wife sat preparing the warp (*tasarikam Kartum arabdha*) with the help of well prepared and good quality staren *(divyasudha*).

Silk was also used and silk goods were manufactured extensively. In the *Divyavadana* the silk is indicated by the words *pattamsuka, cina, kauseva* and *dhanta-patta.* In the absence of any other information it is difficult to distinguish between these varieties of silk, *Pattamsuka* may indicate plain white silk; *cina* as its name indicates, was imported from China : 'Kauseya seems to be the true silk obtained from the cocoons spun by the silk-worm feeding on mulberry leaves; and *dhauta patta* seems to be worked silk. *Pataloka* or variegated silk *vicitra patolaka,* has been mentioned.

Woollen cloth was manufactured and generally known as *Kambala.* The term *dusya* (modern *dhussa*) in this age seems to have been applied to costly woollen cloth. It is related in the *Divyavadana* that in uttarakuru there were *kalpadusya* trees which yielded the *kalpadusya* variety of woollen cloth. It is also mentioned that a Matanga woman wore uncalendered dusya cloth *(anahata dusya).* The *Kalpa-dusya* trees was also supposed to produce the rolls of woollen cloth known as *tundicela* from which *Kalpadusya* pieces of various sizes and of blue, yellow, red and white colours were obtained. Sometimes fine cloth of mixed texture was also woven from the admixture of wool and the fibres of *dukula, ksoma* (ksauma) or linen manufactured from the bask-fibre of *Linium Usitatissium* was also extensively used. Huge sheets of flaxen cloth (*sanaka*) measuring eighteen hands length wise and twelve hands and four digits breadth wise are mentioned in the *Divyavadana.* At another place a weaver is shown wearing a flaxen *dhoti* (*sanasatika*). The farmers also were flaxen *dhotis (sanasati) phalaka*-cloth made from the fibres of certain fibrous fruits is also mentioned in the *Divyavadana.* 'Cloth of gold' was known as *haryani* or *hirivastra* and *valyaja* grasses and blankets made from the hair of the camel, goat and from human hair are also mentioned there. In *Divyavadana* shawls richly brocaded and embroidered with precious stones (*suvarna pravarakah)* were known. *Pandu (*a type of cloth) *dukula* yellowish cloth woven of the fibres of *dukula* are mentioned in *Divyavadana. Aparantaka,* manufactured in Aparantas or Western countries, was also one of the varieties of cloth. In the *Lalitayistara Puspapatta* (flowered cloth) is mentioned; but it is difficult to say whether floral patterns printed, woven or embroidered are meant. There were also regular shops as mentioned in the *Divyavadana,* which stocked cloths of different varieties. There some, however, which specialised is stocking a certain kind of cloth. Thus there were shops at Sopara which exclusively dealth in the cloth imported from kasi (kasika-vastravary) and also shops which stacked *phuttaka* cloth which might have been printed muslin. These was a regular street of cloth merchants at Modura who stocked different varieties of cloth, woven cotton, thread laces, and hair of silk thread kept in bundles, each bundle containing hundred pieces. In the post town of Kaveripattinam, as stated in the *Silappadikaram,* there were weavers (*karukas)* who combined in themselves the functions of a middlemen and dealt in fine fabrics made of silk, sur and cotton. The *Amarakosa* contains interesting information about the costume and the textile materials of the Gupta age, though terms are not always clearly explained. Different types of materials :

(a) *Valka* (made from the task fibres), which includes ksauma etc.

(b) *Phala* (made from the fibre fruits),

(c) *Kauseya* (silk),

(d) *Rankava* (made from the hair of a goat). There is a species of goat called 'rang' which flourishes in the steppes of the high pamir platean. It artereds a very fine 'shawl wool.' It is mentioned in the *Mahabharata,* felts were also manufactured from the fine wool of the *ranku* goat, for the cloth fresh from the loom the following words have been used: *anahata* (uncelandered), *hisprayani* (fresh from the loom), Fantraka (woven on the loom), and *nayambara.* After the both was bleached it was known as *udsamaniya,* one of the varieties of silk is called *Patrorna* in the Amarkosa. Perhaps it was some kind of wild silk; *Ksirasvami,* a commentator of the *Amarkosa,* calls it silk spun by the insects feeding on the leaves of Banyan and *lakuea* (a kind of bread or fruit tree). Costly bleached silk is known as *mahadhana.* According to Devardhigam (middle of the fifth century) varieties of silk is technically called *vidaya.* Patte was woven from the Patta yarn, presupposing thereby that patta was a astain kind of silk yarn. *Dukula* according to Amarsimha was a synonym of Ksauma (linen) and the line covers were known as *nivita* and *pravrta.* It seems that of same larger date all this bleached materials were being classified as *dukula.* The commentator of the *Acaranyasutra* (11th century) explain *dukula* as cloth made from cotton, manufactured from Gauda.

Susruta mentions the following cloths for use as bandages, vol. *Ksauma* (linen), Karpasa (cotton), *avika* (woollen), *dukula* (fine linen), *Kauseya* (tasar, or wild silk) *Patrorna* (fine white silk), china-patta, (Chinese silk).

REFERENCES

1. Marshall, J. H. Mohenjodaro and the Indus civilization. Vol-1, 1973, New Delhi.
2. Rao, S.R. Lothal & The Indus civilization, 1973.

3. The Allchins, Birth of Indian Civilization, 1968 Cambridge.
4. Medonell and Keith, Vedic Index of Names and Subjects.
5. Herodotus, 'The History'
6. N.R. Banerjee, Iron in Ancient India 1965.
7. R.S. Sharma, Light on early Indian Society and economy, Bombay 1966.
8. S.K. Maitoi, Economic life of Northern in the Gupta period, 1957, Callcutta.
9. Fleet, Inscription of the early Gupta king and there successors, 1970.
10. R.N. Soletore, life in the Gupta Age, Bombay, 1943.

12 Indian Culture and The Industrial Age

A living culture, such as the Indian, with an ancient past, cannot wipe out its traditions in regard to ideas and modes of life; nor can it turn a blind eye to the contemporary changes invading it from without or emanating from within. Indian culture is noted for its adaptability. Through the ages it has been adjusting itself to differing conditions and circumstances. All the great minds of India have stressed the need for growth through change. Speaking of the forms of poetic art, for instance, Kalidasa says that the old forms are not necessarily good because they are old, nor the new ones bad because they are new. The myth of different codes for different ages was evolved and the technique of changing the current standards was also agreed upon. For example, it was conceded that a great leader or an assembly of elders could initiate a change. A place was also given to the freedom of thought and action as prompted by one's conscience.

It is true that on certain periods there were setbacks to Indian culture. At those times people forgot the essentials and tended to cling to the non-essentials of culture. But at everyone of such crises, before the spirit of culture could be obliterated, there came about a renaissance inspired by a sage or a group of sages. The first two such instances known to Indian history are the appearance of the Upanishads and that of the Buddha. It is by such renewals that Indian culture has managed to live, while almost every other ancient culture disappeared long long ago.

The coming of the West to India, after the Industrial Revolution, did make a great difference. The modern Western civilization made the Indian intellectual capitulate to its power, and those who brought it did not care to understand the soul of India's culture. Both the Western teachers and their Indian converts believed that Indian culture was a primitive one, and that the salvation of India lay in renouncing it. But things began to change when some of the European scholars discovered Sanskrit. Some of the ancient texts of India that came to be discovered served to dislodge, to some extent, European dogmatism. In India too great reformers and spiritual leaders arose, Ram Mohan Roy, Ramakrishna and Vivekananda were among the pioneers of the present Indian renaissance. Mahatma Gandhi of course, is the one whose influence has been the most pervasive, and who in-liberating India from her political subjection also gave her back her dignity.

As long as India was unfree, she had no charge of her own destiny. The problems of poverty and illiteracy remained unsolved. It is but natural that the leaders of the people who fought for independence and won it, and who are now in charge of India's destinies should bend all their energies to a speedy solution of those problems. They feel that there is no alternative to the industrialization of India. Hence the five year plans do accord a primary place for the starting of industries and for increasing production.

The question, now, is whether industrialization and increasing urbanization will not make for an utterly secular view of life. That would naturally militate against the traditional culture of India which is essentially religio-philosophical or spiritual. Will not the omnipotent machines take the place of God? Will not man, in his preoccupation with earning and spending, neglect the culture of his soul will he continue to believe that there is a soul that survives death and that its ultimate destiny is spiritual freedom?

If along with the attempts to make India materially prosperous, the Gandhian ideology, which is in fact the ideology of Indian culture, is not forgotten, then the evils of industrialization are bound to be mitigated. Some of the non-essential, and even harmful, institutions that pass under the cloak of Hinduism will go; and it is good that they go. Such are casteism and untouchability. The fast changing conditions of life are such that no one who is caught in them will be able to practise untouchability, apart from the fact that it is against the law. So also, the observance of all caste rules is next to impossible. Any one who has studied the evolution of the caste-system in India would know that the rigidity and inelasticity that has crept into it for the past one thousand years have not served the best interests of Hindu society. Hence, if under the stress of modern condition, casteism breaks, it will not do any great harm to Indian culture. What the well-wisher of India would want to see is that the fundamental religio-philosophic ideas are not thrown into the limbo of oblivion.

This is not likely to happen, if the leaders and intellectuals of India are vigilant. In a recent article entitled 'Religion today in India' I came to the conclusion that the religious state of the Indian nation is pretty sound at present. One of the many evidences I gave in that article was the statistics relating to the number of local engagements in the city of Madras announced in a leading daily newspaper in a particular week in March-April 1995. It was found that out of a total of 324 items announced 215 related to religious meetings as against 109 which were of a non-religious character. In regard to these data, I also made this observation *viz.* that not all religious meetings are announced in the press and that at some of the non-religious meetings the speakers do very often introduce religious topics in their speeches.

One of the basic features of Indian culture is that it permits substitution of forms provided they express the spirit. When the Vedic sacrifices fell into disuse the Agamic rites took their place. Quite early in the history of Indian culture, animal models were substituted for actual animals in the sacrifices. Even though many may not offer the formal *sandhyavandana* (twilight prayers) today, the practice of praying and worshipping is on the increase. The institution of *bhajana* (group-singing of devotional songs), for instance is very popular now even in cities and towns. On the *Ayudhapuja* day formerly people used to offer formal worship to the instruments of production and distribution such as the plough and the ox-cart. Now to these have been added the tractor and the motor-car.

There is a general indifference towards religion, it must be confessed, among students in schools and colleges. This is due more to the absence of proper training than to any other cause. The implementation of the recommendations of the University Education Commission of 1948-49 under the chairmanship of Dr. S. Radhakrishnan will go a great way in reorienting the minds of students. It has been my experience that the student community responds handsomely if a proper approach is made to their minds.

The mass media of communication that science and technology have placed at our disposal ought to be used for educating the people at large on the right lines. The leisure that increasing industrialization yields to the average worker, if properly utilized, will be a great blessing. Appalling poverty, except in exceptional cases, is a stupendious obstacle to the pursuit of the higher values. It is futile to preach religion to empty stomachs. In so far as industry seeks to remove poverty, it will prove to be one of the essential conditions for the growth of culture.

The University can and ought to play its legitimate role in the cultural revival of our people. In two ways it can help : (1) by reordering collegiate education, and (2) by giving an active and constant lead to the people. Education should be not only for bread-winning but also for soul-making. The University should not be content with being an ivory tower; it must go to the masses and let them have the benefit of the light of knowledge. It would also be good if there is cooperation between the universities and the *Ashramas* in the matter of educating our people. While the universities should impart to them the correct view of life, the *Ashramas* should guide them to the proper way of life. And it is a basic teaching of Indian culture that a view, however correct it may be, will be futile if it does not lead to exaltation of life and the way of life one leads will end in a *cul de sac* if it is not informed by true vision.

13 Intercourse with the Outside World

1. China—upto the T'ang Period

It has been described in a preceding chapter[1] how, during the first three centuries of the Christian era, Buddhism, and along with it Indian culture, had spread over Central Asia and obtained a definite footing in China. As centuries rolled by, the power and influence of Buddhism gradually increased in China and, as before, Buddhist monks of Central Asia, of sundry nationalities, took part in the missionary activity.

The monks of Kuchi took a leading part in the propagation of Buddhism in China from the fourth century A.D. The greatest of them was Kumarajiva whose life remarkably illustrates the wonderful religious and cultural internationalism of the period.

Kumarayana, the father of Kumarajiva, was born in a respectable family of hereditary ministers to an Indian state. He, however, abdicated his rights to this high office in favour of his relatives and went to Kuchi. The king of Kuchi cordially welcomed him, and he shortly rose to the high position of *Rajaguru* or royal preceptor. He married Jiva, a princess of the royal family who had fallen in love with him. Soon after the birth of her son Kumarajiva, Jiva became a Buddhist nun and, when her son was nine years old, took him to Kashmir. Here Kumarajiva studied Buddhist literature and philosophy under a teacher named Bandhudatta and attained great proficiency in a variety of subjects. After completing his studies, Kumarajiva, with his mother, visited a number of renowned Buddhist institutions in Central Asia, and obtained high reputation as a Buddhist scholar. He then returned to Kuchi.

Shortly after, hostilities broke out between Kuchi and China. A Chinese force besieged Kuchi which surrendered after a brave fight. As was customary in those days, the victorious Chinese general took the renowned scholar Kumarajiva to China. This happened in A.D. 383. Kumarajiva remained with the ruler of Ku-tsang in Kan-su for nearly fifteen years. The Chinese emperor repeatedly invited him and he proceeded to the capital in A.D. 401. From that date till A.D. 412 Kumarajiva worked and stayed in the Chinese capital. He devoted his whole energy to translating Buddhist texts and interpreting Buddhist religion and philosophy. He translated more than one hundred Sanskrit texts and was the first to interpret Mahayana philosophy in China. His great command over both Sanskrit and Chinese, and vast erudition in different branches of philosophy, made him eminently fit for this task. His translations were a great improvement upon those of his predecessors. Many scholars from different parts of China became his disciples and he may be justly regarded as having ushered in a new epoch in the history of Buddhism in China.

The fact that Kumarajiva was taken all the way from Kuchi to Kashmir by his mother for purposes of education shows the high position held by that region in the then Buddhist world. It was, therefore, quite in the fitness of things that learned Buddhist monks of Kashmir should play the leading part in the propagation of Buddhism in China. It is said that the Buddhist scholars who went to China from Kashmir during the fourth, fifth and sixth centuries A.D. far exceeded in number those who went from the other parts of India taken together. Among these Kashmirian scholars special mention may be made of Sanghabhuti (A.D. 381-384),[2] Gautama Sanghadeva (A.D. 384-397), Punyatrata (A.D. 404), Vimalaksha (A.D. 406-413), Buddhajiva (A.D. 423), Dharmamitra (A.D. 424-442), and Dharmayasa (c. A.D. 400-424). Two of them, Punyatrata and Vimalaksha were collaborators of Kumarajiva, while Dharmayasa was a pupil of Punyatrata. They all engaged themselves in translating Buddhist texts into Chinese and expounding Buddhist philosophy, and received high honours from the people as well as the officials.

More importance attaches to another Kashmirian scholar Buddhayasa. He was born in a Brahmanical family but became a Buddhist monk. After completing his studies he proceeded to Central Asia. The king of Kashgar had invited three thousand Buddhist monks to a religious ceremony and Buddhayasa went with them. He made a profound impression on the king and was invited to live in the palace. Kumarajiva met him there and studied some sacred texts with him. When, after Kumarajiva's return to Kuchi, this kingdom was invaded by the Chinese, its king appealed for help to the king of Kashgar. The latter started with his army for Kuchi leaving the young prince in charge of Buddhayasa. Buddhayasa was very much upset by the news of the fall of Kuchi and the deportation of Kumarajiva. He stayed in Kashgar for ten years more and then went to Kuchi. A year later he went to China and worked with Kumarajiva. After the latter's death he returned to Kashmir. He was a man of strict principles and never accepted any present even from the Emperor on the ground that it was unbecoming for a monk to do so.

Reference may also be made to another noble son of Kashmir, namely Gunavarman. He was born in the royal family, but became a Buddhist monk. When he was thirty years old, the king of Kashmir died and he was invited by the ministers to ascend the throne. Gunavarman refused and retired to a forest life. He then went to Ceylon and preached Buddhism. Later he proceeded to Java and converted the king and his mother to the Buddhist faith. At this time Java was attacked by hostile troops and the king asked Gunavarman whether it would be contrary to the Buddhist law if he fought against the enemy. Gunavarman replied that it was the duty of everyone to punish the robbers. The king then fought with his enemy and won a great victory. Gradually, through the efforts of Gunavarman, the Buddhist religion spread throughout Java. The name and fame of Gunavarman had now spread all over the Buddhist world. In A.D. 424 the Chinese monks of Nanking requested their emperor to invite Gunavarman to China. Accordingly the Chinese Emperor sent messengers to Gunavarman and the king of Java. Gunavarman embarked on a vessel owned by the Hindu merchant Nandin, and after visiting different places on the way, reached Nanking in A.D. 431. The Chinese Emperor himself went out to receive him and put him up in a monastery called Jetavanavihara after the famous monastery of that name in Sravasti associated with the hallowed name of Buddha. Gunavarman died there within a year, but so great was his industry that even during this short period he translated no less than eleven Sanskrit texts into Chinese.

A number of learned Buddhist monks from other parts of India also carried on missionary activity in China. Among these may be mentioned Gunabhadra (A.D. 435-468) of Madhyadesa (Central India), Prajnaruchi of Banaras (A.D. 516-543), Upasunya of Ujjayini (sixth century), and three monks Jnanabhadra, Jinayasas and Yasogupta (sixth century) from Eastern India (*i.e.*, Bengal and Assam. Three others, Buddhabhadra, Vimokshasena and Jinagupta hailed from the North-Western frontier. The first two claimed descent from the Sakya family of Kapilavastu. It is said that when Kapilavastu was attacked by Vidudabha,[3] king of Kosala, four members of the Sakya clan disobeyed the Buddha's law of non-violence and fought with the enemy. For this offence they were expelled, and two of them, proceeding west, became rulers of Uddiyana (Swat Valley) and Bamiyan (near Kabul). Vimokshasena claimed to be the descendant of the first, while Buddhabhadra, who was born at Nagarahara (Jelalabad), was probably a descendant of the second. When Buddhabhadra was in Kashmir, a Chinese monk, who accompanied Fa-hien to India, came there and requested the Buddhist community to send a learned scholar to China. Buddhabhadra, who was selected for this purpose, went to China *via* Burma and Tonkin and collaborated with Kumarajiva.[4]

The third Jinagupta, was born in Gandhara and was the pupil of Jnanabhadra and Jinayasas, mentioned above. They reached Ch'ang-ngan (A.D. 559) where a monastery was built for them by special orders of the Emperor. Owing to political troubles they were forced to leave China (A.D. 572). On their way home they stopped in the country of the Turks at the request of their king. Jinagupta's teachers died there, but he stayed on till 581 doing missionary work and translating Buddhist texts. He returned to China in 585 and died in A.D. 600.

We may refer, in some details, to a few other Indian monks who did missionary work in China, as their lives offer special points of interest.

Dharmakshema, born in Central India, went through Kuchi to Western China which was then an independent principality. He was engaged there from A.D. 414 to 432 in translating Buddhist texts. He wanted then to return to India, but the local ruler refused him permission lest he might go to other Chinese kingdoms. Dharmakshema, however, defied the order and proceeded on his journey only to be murdered by the ruthless king in A.D. 433. This is a strange, though fortunately a solitary, instance of barbaric cruelty, untempered by Buddhist piety.

Of all the Indian monks who went to China, probably no name is better known in India than that of Paramartha. Born in Ujjayini he became proficient in all branches of Buddhist learning and probably settled down at Pataliputra. At that time a Chinese mission sent by the emperor Wu came to the king of Magadha and requested him to send a renowned Buddhist monk to China. The king was probably the last Imperial Gupta ruler Vishnu-gupta. He selected Paramartha who took with him a large number of Buddhist texts and reached China in A.D. 546. Although political troubles interrupted his work in A.D. 557, he stayed on till his death in A.D. 569 and translated no less than 70 Buddhist texts.

Dharmagupta, another famous monk, was born in Lata (southern Gujarat) and studied with some learned teachers in the Kaumudi-sangharama at Kanauj. He stayed in the royal monastery named Devavihara in Takka (N. Punjab) for some time, and then proceeded towards China. He followed the overland route through Afghanistan, staying on his way at Kapisa (Kafiristan), Badakhshan, Wakhan and Tash Qurghan. He spent two years at the royal monastery of Kashgar and proceeded by the northern route. He passed through Kuchi, Agnidesa (Qara Shahr), Turfan and Hami. These were all flourishing seats of Buddhism and their monks were eager to profit by the learning of the great Indian monk. So after staying a year or two in each of these places Dharmagupta reached Ch'angngan in A.D. 590. In addition to the usual activity of translating Buddhist texts, he is said to have composed a treatise giving minute geographical details of all the countries visited by him, and even noting down such topics as their system of government, social and economic condition, including food and drink, dress, education, manners and customs. Such a book from an Indian author would have been a unique literary production, but unfortunately no copy has survived.

The Indian monk who obtained the greatest celebrity in China was Bodhidharma. He was the third son of an Indian king (probably the Pallava king of Kanchi). He is almost a semi-mythical figure, and various miracles are attributed to him. He was received by the Emperor Wu, and is credited with the introduction of the contemplative form of Mahayana into China. He visited China in the second quarter of the sixth century A.D. Reference may also be made to Vinitaruchi, a Brahmana of South India, who reached the Chinese capital in A.D. 582 and translated two works into Chinese. He then proceeded to Tonkin and founded the Dhyana School there.[5]

The activities of Indian missionaries in China during the fourth, fifth and sixth centuries A.D., which have been briefly described above, had a great effect upon the Chinese. In the first place, it aroused greater interest than before among the Chinese for Buddhism and Indian culture. Secondly, it whetted the desire of the Chinese to know Buddhism at first hand and come into direct contact with Indian culture by visiting India.

The career of the great Chinese scholar Tao-ngan, who flourished in the second half of the fourth century A.D., illustrates this new spirit in China. Born in a family famous for its erudition in Chinese classics and strong devotion to Confucianism, Tao-ngan became a staunch Buddhist and read Buddhist literature with the help of able teachers. He studied critically the Chinese translations of Buddhist texts, corrected them, and compiled a series of commentaries in order to explain the true meaning of Buddhist philosophy and doctrines. His scholarship and mastery over the sacred texts attracted a number of Chinese from all over the country. He trained them thoroughly and sent them to different parts of the country to preach Buddhism.

Tao-ngan also wrote a book on India in order to encourage the Buddhist monks of China to visit the Holy Land. This bore fruit and quite a large number of them undertook the long and perilous journey. Their main objects were not only to learn at first hand the true doctrines of Buddhism and the correct principles of conduct to be observed by the monks and the laity, but also to collect Buddhist texts and sacred relics, and acquire merit by visiting the holy places associated with the Buddha.

A party of five monks under the leadership of Fa-hien started for India in A.D. 399. They met on the frontier another group of five monks who had started a little earlier, and travelled together for some time. At Tunhwang the district officer supplied them with the means for continuing the journey. Fortunately Fa-hien has left a detailed record of his travels, and this gives us an insight into the objects of their journey, the difficulties of the road, and the condition of Buddhism and Indian culture in Central Asia. The objects of the journey have been stated above. As regards the difficulties of the road, we may quote the following extract describing vividly the perils of the desert—"(Travellers) who encounter them perish all to a man. There is not a bird to be seen in the air above, nor an animal on the ground below. Though you look all round most earnestly to find where you can cross, you know not where to make your choice, the only mark and indication being the dry bones of the dead (left upon the sand)."

We are further told that "the difficulties which they encountered in crossing the streams on their route, and the sufferings which they endured where unparalleled in human experience."

Fa-hien entered India through Kashmir and travelled all over North India. He stayed at Pataliputra for three years, learning Sanskrit, reading Sanskrit books, and writing out the Vinaya rules. At Tamralipti, again, he stayed for two years writing out his Sutras, and drawing pictures of images.

Of Fa-hien's companions, one died on the way and several went back to China at an earlier stage. Another was so deeply impressed by the dignified conduct of the Indian monks that he resolved to stay in India. "He sadly called to mind the imperfections of the monks in China and prayed that in future births he might be born in India alone".

Fa-hien, however, whose original purpose had been to secure the introduction of the complete Vinaya rules into China, returned there alone. He embarked on a large merchant vessel from Tamralipti and after fourteen days reached Ceylon. Having stayed here for two years and collected a number of Sanskrit works not available in China, he took his passage in a merchantman bound for China. Fa-hien has vividly described the perils of the sea and how he narrowly escaped a watery grave. At last he landed in China in A.D. 414.

After his return to China Fa-hien, along with the Indian monk Buddhabhadra, mentioned above, translated some of the works he had brought from India. He died at the age of 88.

Of the monks of the other group who joined Fa-hien, Pao-yun studied Sanskrit in India and translated Sanskrit Buddhist texts on his return to China.

Soon after Fa-hien and Pao-yun, another group of fifteen monks led by Che-mong started for India in A.D. 404. Nine returned from the Pamirs, and one died of fatigue. The remaining five visited India and made a collection of Buddhist texts. Three died on the return journey and Che-mong reached China in A.D. 424 with only one companion.

In A.D. 420 Fa-yong started with 25 Chinese monks along the northern route of Central Asia and reached India through Kashmir. After having travelled all over Northern India they returned by the sea route.

Names of several other Chinese monks who visited India during this period have also been preserved, but no details are known.

Simultaneously with the new enthusiasm for visiting India, we notice a growing practice of inviting Buddhist scholars to China. In this matter also the initiative was taken by Tao-ngan, the great leader of the new movement in China. He invited a large number of scholars from Central Asia. His example was followed by others, and as we have seen above, in connection with Paramartha and Gunavarman, even the Emperors sent envoys and formal invitations for bringing the renowned Buddhist teachers from India to China.

Reference may be made in particular to two instances of royal solicitude for the cause of Buddhism. In A.D. 518 Sung Yun, an envoy, with a Chinese monk, was sent on an embassy to the western countries by the Empress Dowager of the Great Wei dynasty to obtain Buddhist books. Fortunately we have a detailed account of this embassy. They passed through Central Asia to the Huna kingdom and visited Udyana and Gandhara. They procured altogether 170 volumes, all standard works of the Mahayana sect. Emperor Yang of the Sui dynasty (A.D. 605-617) also sent a mission to Central Asia and India.

These facts and the high honours shown to Indian teachers on their arrival in China by all ranks of people, from the Emperor downwards, reveal the great hold that Buddhism and Indian culture had over China.

This is confirmed by what we know of the development of Buddhism in China. The kings of the Eastern Tsin dynasty, like their predecessors, were great patrons of Buddhism. Two of them built four large monasteries, each accommodating one thousand monks. During the rule of this dynasty (A.D. 317-420) 17,068 Buddhist institutions, great and small, were founded all over China, and 263 volumes of Buddhist texts were translated into Chinese. Under the foreign Wei dynasty, which ruled over the northern part of China from A.D. 386 to 534, Buddhism made rapid progress. Even before this period one of their chiefs had issued an edict in 335 in which he said : "As Buddha is a foreign god it is in the fitness of things that I should worship him. When a thing is found perfect and faultless why should they still stick to the customs of the ancient dynasties? My people are called barbarians. I grant them the privilege to worship Buddha and adopt the Buddhist faith if they like to do so."

Such an attitude on the part of the ruling family naturally gave great impetus to Buddhism. Many Wei kings were themselves devout Buddhists and copied, recited, and explained sacred texts. The first ruler Wu-ti (A.D. 386-407) is said to have founded 15 *chaityas* and two monasteries, erected 1,000 golden images, and entertained every month 3,000 Buddhist monks in a religious assembly. Altogether 47 big monasteries were built by the Wei Emperors and during the period of their rule more than 30,000 temples were constructed by private families. The number of monks and nuns exceeded two million.

The rulers of the Northern Ts'i dynasty, which succeeded the Wei in A.D. 550, were also great patrons of Buddhism. One of them copied 12 Buddhist texts with his own hand and regularly maintained 3,000 monks. Another erected a *chaitya* in gold. Another ruler sent in A.D. 575 a Buddhist mission to the Western countries in search of Sanskrit books, and it brought back 260 texts, though the dynasty was overthrown by that time. It was during their rule (A.D. 550-577) that Buddhism was introduced among the Turks. A Chinese monk took courage to go to the chief of the Western Turks, named To' po Kaghan (A.D. 572-581), and told him that China was prosperous and mighty for having favoured Buddhism.

Thanks to his teachers the Kaghan adopted Buddhism, observed its rules of conduct, and made regularly the *pradakshina* (circumambulation) of the *stupas*. He built a monastery and sent an ambassador to the Ts'i emperor for securing Buddhist books. At his request the *Mahaparinirvana-sutra* was translated into Turkish by a Chinese scholar.

Buddhism was equally favoured by the ruling dynasties of South China, *viz.*, the Song (A.D. 420-479), the Ts'i (A.D. 479-502), and the Leang (A.D. 502-557). The Chinese official history gives details of the personal activities of various rulers by way of copying Sanskrit texts and reciting them, founding monasteries to accommodate monks, and erecting golden statues. One of them lived like a monk, and prohibited the killing of animals either for sacrifice or for food. As usual, the work of translating Buddhist texts into Chinese was continued throughout this period with the help of Indian scholars.

An important landmark in the history of Buddhism in China was the foundation of a monastery at Lu-shan by Hui-yuan, a disciple of Tao-ngan. This attracted numerous Buddhists from all over China and their number is said to have exceeded one thousand. Hui-yuan selected 17 disciples including two Indian scholars—Buddhayasas and Buddhabhadra—and founded a school known as "The School of White Lotus" It introduced the 'cult of Amitabha,' based upon the Mahayana philosophy. This new doctrine plays an important role in the modern Buddhism of the Far East. The Lu-shan school made a positive contribution to Buddhism which may henceforth be regarded as a living force in the life and culture of the Chinese.

The meditative form of Mahayana was introduced in China by Bodhidharma, as noted above. One of his disciples Chi-k'ai, founded a new school, called T'ien-t'ai according to the name of Chi-k'ai's place of residence. He made a new classification of Buddha's teachings and Buddhist literature, and attempted a syncretism of the different forms of Buddhism. His views were accepted by all and henceforth the Chinese respected and studied both Hinayana and Mahayana without being troubled by any sense of contradiction. Chi-k'ai's teachings met with great success in Japan which follows his syncretism even today.

During the rule of the Wei dynasty (A.D. 386-534), whose patronge of Buddhism has been referred to above, no less than eight embassies from North-Western India were sent to the Imperial court in China. The Chinese official history gives the following list :

Country	*Date of Embassy A.D.*
Ki-pin	451, 502, 508, 517
Kia-pi-sa (Kapisa)	503
Pu-lu-sha (Purushapura or Peshawar)	511
Kan-ta (Gandhara)	511
Kia-shih-mi (Kashmir)	511

The identification of Ki-pin is a matter of dispute among scholars. Pelliot, in agreement with S. Levi, held that prior to A.D. 600 Ki-pin denoted Kashmir, and after that date it designated Kapisa. Rapson and Sten Konow, however, identified it throughout with Kapisa. Dr. P.C. Bagchi endorses the views of Pelliot after an elaborate discussion of the problem, giving full reference to previous writings on the subject. Dr. L. Petech, the latest writer on the subject, thinks that Ki-pin was used by Chinese historiographers, from the very beginning, to denote Kapisa and the adjacent country politically associated with it, though the Chinese Buddhists applied the name to Kashmir from the second to the early seventh century A.D. In his opinion "the two traditions run for centuries parallel to each other, and to a great extent ignoring each other."[6]

If Ki-pin denoted Kashmir, the separate mention of the two countries is difficult to explain. If, on the other hand, it means Kapisa, similar difficulty arises with regard to the second name in the above list. The third and fourth names also denote politically the same region. Petech thinks that "perhaps the local governors or tributary princes had sent embassies of their own".

Embassies were also sent from other parts of India. A king of South India, for example, sent an ambassador to China during the period A.D. 500-516.[7]

2. China—T'ang Period

The T'ang dynasty ruled in China from A.D. 618 to 907. This period constitutes one of the most glorious chapters in the history of China. The whole of China came under one political authority whose power once more extended over Central Asia. The intercourse with India and the influence of Buddhism and Indian culture reached the highest peak in China during the period. Thousands of Indians—missionaries, merchants and others—thronged the principal cities in China, and more Chinese monks and royal embassies came to India in the seventh century than during any other period.

The fame of the Nalanda University[8] was now at its height and it came to be the great international centre of Buddhism which attracted Buddhist monks from all over Asia. The Chinese Buddhists also shared the general enthusiasm for studying at Nalanda, not merely Buddhist philosophy and literature, but also other subjects like Brahmanical philosophy, mathematics, astronomy, and medicine. They were encouraged by the Emperors who gave them all facilities to undertake the journey.

The first Chinese monk to visit India during this period was Hiuen Tsang who played the most distinguished part in establishing Buddhism on a solid footing in China, and improving the cultural relations between that country and India. Born in A.D. 600 of an orthodox Confucian family, he became a Buddhist monk at the age of 20. Not being content with the existing translations of Buddhist books in Chinese, he decided to visit India. He started in A.D. 629 by the northern route in Central Asia. He reached Kapisa (Kafiristan) in A.D. 630 and during the next fourteen years travelled all over India.

He stayed two years in Kashmir and for shorter periods in other places, for studying the Buddhist texts. He also resided in Nalanda, on different occasions, for a total period of two years, and learnt the Yogachara system from Silabhadra, the famous monk who presided over the institution. Hiuen Tsang was highly honoured by the great Indian rulers Harsha-vardhana and Bhaskara–varman, as noted above.[9] He left India with a large number of books and images at the beginning of A.D. 644 and, proceeding along the southern route in Central Asia, returned to China in A.D. 645.

Hiuen Tsang has left a long account of his travels, giving details of the various Indian kingdoms visited by him. This book, *Si-yu-ki,* forms an invaluable source of ancient Indian history, and has been frequently referred to in this volume. It also gives us a graphic picture of the condition of Buddhism in India and all the territories outside it through which the traveller passed.

Hiuen Tsang left India almost in a royal procession. Harshavardhana gave him a big elephant with 3,000 gold and 10,000 silver pieces for defraying his expenses, and his numerous books and images were entrusted to the military escort of a king of North India called Udhita. As the elephant was drowned on the way, and he could not secure means of transport for his books, he halted at Khotan and sent a memorial to the Chinese Emperor. After referring to the extreme hardships of the journey over more than 50,000 *li,* he returned, he said, with a mind satisfied with the accomplishment of his vows. "I have beheld the Gridhrakuta mountain, worshipped the Bodhi tree; I have seen traces not seen before; heard sacred words not heard before; witnessed spiritual prodigies, exceeding all the wonders of Nature." This passage from the petition shows the devout spirit with which Hiuen Tsang regarded Buddhism and everything connected with it.

The Emperor sent a gracious reply. "I pray you come quickly," he said, "that we may see each other." He also sent instructions to his officials at Khotan and other places on the way to help Hiuen Tsang with guides and conveyances. As Hiuen Tsang approached the border of China, the Emperor asked the Governor of the western capital to send proper officers to receive him. Hiuen Tsang arrived in a boat by way of a canal and received a unique welcome. The news of his arrival spread fast and the people came in large numbers to behold and pay homage to him. The streets were so crowded that wen he wished to disembark he could not advance and had to pass the night in the canal.

On his arrival at the capital Hiuen Tsang received a royal ovation. According to his biographer, "the Emperor and his court, the officials and the merchants, and all the people made holiday. The streets were crowded with eager men and women who expressed their joy by gay banners and festive music." Such an honour is usually reserved for kings and generals on their return from a victorious military expedition. That Hiuen Tsang was thought worthy of it on account of his prolonged visit to India speaks volumes not only for the great veneration which the Chinese had for Buddhism, but also for the new angle of vision which contact with Indian culture had inspired among the Chinese.

Hiuen Tsang spent the remaining years of his life in translating Buddhist texts, and training his pupils. He founded a new school of Buddhist philosophy in China which carried on his work after his death. His book *Si-yu-ki* or 'Record of the Western countries' gave a strong impetus to the love of Indian culture in China. His personal influence with the Emperor was probably at the root of the new policy of establishing political relations with the Indian rulers.

Hiuen Tsang translated altogether 74 different works consisting of 1,335 chapters. He had, moreover, drawn a vast number of pictures, and written out with his own hands copies of various texts. He died in A.D. 664 and was buried in the Western capital. But in A.D. 669 his remains were removed by order of the Emperor to another place where a tower was constructed in his memory.

The noble example of Hiuen Tsang induced the Chinese monks to visit India in large numbers. Chinese texts have preserved the biographies of sixty monks who visited India during the latter half of the seventh century A.D. The greatest among these later pilgrims was I-tsing. He left by the sea route in A.D. 671 and having passed several years at Sri-Vijaya, an important centre of Buddhist learning in Sumatra, arrived in A.D. 673 at the port of Tamralipti in Bengal. He stayed at Nalanda for ten years (*c.* A.D. 675-685), studying and copying Buddhist texts. He returned to China with a collection of 400 Sanskrit manuscripts containing more than 50,000 *slokas.* He translated a number of texts and compiled a Sanskrit-Chinese dictionary. Fortunately we still possess his book entitle *"A Record of the Buddhist Religion as practised in India and the Malay Archipelago."* In this he has noted in detail the rules of monastic life as practised in India, a subject in which he evidently took a special interest. He also wrote a biography of about sixty Buddhist monks who visited India. Almost all of them were associated with China, though many of them were natives of other lands such as Korea, Samarkand and Tushara (Turk) country. This biography shows the international position of Buddhism in Asia and indicate its influence in outlying countries like Korea. The fact that about sixty Buddhist monks came to India from China in one generation, shows the frequency of such pilgrimages in these days, though most of them have not been probably recorded.

The seventh century A.D., which saw the arrival of so many distinguished Chinese monks in India, also witnessed the journey of noted Indian Buddhists to China. The earliest was Prabhakaramitra, a famous scholar of Nalanda. Born in a royal family of Central India, he took to the life of a Buddhist monk and studied at Nalanda. He was later appointed a Professor there and his disciples became famous scholars in course of time. Starting with the disciples, he reached the country of the Western Turks and taught Buddhism to their Chief. The Chinese ambassador at the Turkish court invited him to China, but the Turkish chief would not let him go. At last, at the request of the Chinese Emperor, the Turkish ruler accorded the necessary permission, and Prabhakaramitra reached China in A.D. 627. He was engaged in translating Buddhist texts there, and 19 scholars were appointed by the court to assist him in his work. Some translated his words into Chinese, some verified this translation, while others wrote it down. Another group copied it and high officials, under the orders of the Emperor, examined the final redaction and supervised its execution. Prabhakaramitra died in A.D. 633.

Another Indian scholar, Bodhiruchi, went to China in A.D. 693 at the request of a Chinese envoy, probably at the court of a Chalukya king. A regular Board was set up to help Bodhiruchi in translating Buddhist texts. It consisted of both Chinese and Indian scholars. The latter included Brahma, an ambassador of the king of Central India, and Isvara, a chief of Eastern India. The Emperor himself was occasionally present when the translation was being made and took down notes with his own hand. Sometimes the queen and other ladies of the palace and the high officials of the court were also present. Bodhiruchi translated fifty-three volumes, and died in A.D. 727.

Vajrabodhi, son of Isana-varman, king of Central India, was a famous scholar at Nalanda. He was the teacher of the Pallava king Narasimha-varman II[10] at Kanchi for some time and then proceeded to Ceylon. The king of Ceylon sent a mission to China for presenting a sacred Buddhist text and other objects to the Emperor. Vajrabodhi accompanied it and reached China in A.D. 720. Vajrabodhi propagated the mystic doctrines of Buddhism known as Tantrayana and translated a number of texts on the subject. This had great effect and the cult was popularised in China. Vajrabodhi died in A.D. 732. His work was continued by his disciple, Amoghavajra, who was with him in China. In 736, Amoghavajra came back to Ceylon but returned to China ten years later with 500 texts. Between A.D. 746 and 771, he translated 77 texts. He died in A.D. 774.[11]

It is unnecessary to describe in detail the visits of other individual monks; and we may now refer to the development of political relations between India and China as evidenced by the despatch of embassies from one court to the other. Mention has already been made above[12] of Harsha-vardhana's embassy to China in A.D. 641 and of three other Chinese embassies, the first under Liang-hoai-King, the second under Li-y-piao and Wang-hiuen-tse in A.D. 643, and the third under Wang-hiuen-tse in 646. Wang-hiuen-tse was sent a third time in A.D. 657. A Brahmana thaumaturge (probably a Tantrik named Narayana-svamin), who claimed that he possessed the secret of prolonging life, was sent to China by an Indian king at the request of the Chinese Emperor.[13] As the Emperor was not satisfied with his skill, he was sent back with Wang-hiuen-tse. The envoy also carried presents offered by the Emperor to various Buddhist shrines in India. He was sent a fourth time to India in A.D. 664 in order to bring back a Chinese pilgrim whom he had previously met in India. Wang-hiuen-tse wrote an account of his travels in India, but the book has been lost and only a few extracts from it have been preserved in other works.

Reference has already been made to an embassy to China sent by Yasovarman, and the exchanges of envoys between China and Kashmir have also been related above.[14]

Many other embassies are also referred to in the T'ang history which has preserved a systematic account of the political relations between China and different parts of India. This may be summed up as follows :[15]

In A.D. 717 the Emperor awarded the title of "king of Pu-lu (Bolor)" to the local chief Su-fu-sho-li-che-li-ni (Subhasri). In 719 the king of Bolor, Subhasri, sent an ambassador to the Emperor to express his gratitude for the award. In 720 the title of "the king of Bolor" was awarded by the Emperor to the local chief Su-lin-t'o-i-che (Surendraditya?). In 731 the title of "the king of little Bolor (Yasin)" was awarded to Nan-ni by the Emperor. In 733 the king of (little) Bolor, Mo-kin-mang, sent a noble named Cha-cho-na-se-mo-mo-sheng to thank the Emperor for the award. In 741 the title of "the king of little Bolor" was awarded to Ma-hao-lai. In 745 the king of little

• Bolor sent a Buddhist teacher named Kia-lo-mi-to (Kalamitra) to pay respects to the Emperor.

The political condition of Kapisa, Gandhara and Uddiyana was uncertain in this period. The two latter kingdoms were certainly dependent on Kashmir. We know from the Chinese official history that in 720 the title of the "king of Wu-ch'ang (Uddiyana)" was given to the local chief by the Emperor. The king of Gandhara sent an ambassador to China in 758 with presents to the Emperor. The title of "*tegin*" was awarded to the chief of Kapisa in 720

The king of Kapisa sent an embassy to China in 710 and again about A.D. 750. In A.D. 751 the Chinese Emperor sent a mission under Wu-K'ong to escort back the Indian ambassador from Kapisa. On his arrival in India, Wu-K'ong was converted to Buddhism. He spent several years in Kashmir, visited the holy places and returned to China in A.D. 790. No less than six embassies were sent from Ki-pin to China between A.D. 619 and 750. Ki-pin has been identified with both Kapisa and Kashmir,[16] but as already noted above,[17] it referred to Kapisa from the seventh century A.D.

As early as 692 a representative of king Ti-po-si-na (Devasena) of Central India came to pay respects to the Emperor. The envoy must have been the same as Brahma (Fan-mo) who assisted Bodhiruchi in 693 in the work of translation. In 741 the son of the king of Central India came to pay respects and he was given a Chinese name Li Ch'eng-ngan.

In 692 representatives of the king of Eastern India, Mo-lo-pa-mo (Malavarman?), and the king of Western India, Sha-lo-yi-to (Siladitya), came to China to pay homage. We do not know who Malavarman was but the other king was certainly Sīladitya III of Valabhi who reigned at the end of the seventh century. In 692 the king of Northern India, Na-na, the king of Central India, Ti-mo-si-na, and the king of Southern India, Che-lu-ki-pa-lo (Chalukya Vallabha), sent ambassadors to the Emperor.[18] The Chalukya king, reigning in 692, was Vinayaditya. The king Sha-li Na-lo-seng-kia-pa-to-pa-mo

(Sri Narasimha Potavarman) proposed to the emperor in A.D. 720 to send elephants and cavalry to fight with the Arabs and the Tibetans. Narasimha Potavarman was the Pallava ruler of Kanchi. He sent two embassies to China, in A.D. 710 and 720, and the Chinese Emperor sent him an embassy in the latter year. The details of these embassies[19] show an intimate and cordial relation between the two.

It appears from the Chinese chronicles that China maintained diplomatic relations with Kapisa, Uddiyana, Gandhara, Magadha and Kashmir for more than a century since the first political mission was sent by Harsha-vardhana in A.D. 641. Many envoys were sent by China as well as by these kingdoms, but the details have not been preserved in all cases. Even so late as A.D. 787 we hear of the Chinese Emperor forming alliance with Indian princes against the Tibetans.

The increased intercourse with India naturally led to a further advancement of Buddhism in China and ushered in what may be called its most glorious period in that country. The rapid growth of this new foreign religion alarmed the orthodox section who carried on an active and vigorous campaign against it almost throughout the T'ang period. In a memorial submitted to the Emperor in A.D. 624, the leader of the campaign attributed to Buddhism almost all the ills the country was suffering from—even the foreign invasions, the tyranny of the government, and the treachery of the ministers. But there were more legitimate grievances too. Apart from the neglect of religious sacrifices, the memorialist drew pointed attention to the deterioration in civic life caused by Buddhism, as the following passage shows : "The result is that the monks and the nuns now count by tens of thousands. I request you to get them married so that the country may have a hundred thousand families. They will then bring up childrens to fill the ranks of your army".

The campaign had some success at first, and for time the T'ang Emperor withdrew his patronage of Buddhism. But whatever might have been his personal feelings, the issue was really decided by political considerations. All the important political powers and the petty states surrounding China—the Turks, the Tibetans and the various peoples of Central Asia—had adopted Buddhism, and the newly founded T'ang empire could hardly dare to oppose what was now a great international power in Asia. Accordingly the T'ang emperors, after a brief interval, again adopted a pro-Buddhist policy, and the triumph of the new religion was assured.

The close contact with India established by Hiuen Tsang must be regarded as another important factor in this change of policy, and the success of Buddhism in China was phenomenal. New monasteries were built in all the important cities, and increasingly larger numbers were attracted to Buddhism. Hiuen Tsang introduced a new era in the translation of Buddhist works. Numerous Buddhist texts were translated and, as we have seen above, regular boards were set up to organise and expedite the work of translation.[20] Owing to this work of translation, undertaken on a colossal scale, the voluminous body of Sanskrit Buddhist literature, now almost entirely lost in India has been preserved in Chinese translation. An idea of the bulk of this literature may be had from the various catalogues compiled in China from time to time. The oldest catalogue, compiled by a Chinese scholar in the sixth century A.D., mentions 2, 213 works and the official catalogue, prepared about the same time at the orders of the Emperor, gives a list of Buddhist texts numbering about 5,400 volumes. An authoritative catalogue of the Buddhist canon prepared in the T'ang period mentions in the first section 2,487 works in 8,476 *fasciculi,* and in the second, 799 works in 3,364 *fasciculi*. There were many other catalogues to which it is not necessary to refer in detail. The printing of these texts by wooden blocks began as early as A.D. 972.

Hiuen Tsang, to whom the Buddhist literature in China owes so much, was also instrumental in establishing two new schools of Buddhism, *viz.* Yogachara or the Vijnanavada and the Sarvastivada school. The former belonged to the Mahayana and the latter to the Hinayana sect, and this shows the syncretising spirit in China, referred to above. A disciple of Hiuen Tsang founded the Vinaya school. The mystic or Tantric school, introduced by Vajrabodhi in the eighth century,[21] paved the way for the decline of Buddhism as in India.

We need not pursue further the history of Buddhism in China but may conclude this review by a brief reference to the other aspects of Indian culture which Buddhism brought along with it. The most important of these was art, which exerted a great influence on the native traditions and produced a new school of art that may be called Sino-Indian. The Wei period saw a great development of this art. A number of rock-cut caves at Tunhwang, Yun-kang and Long-men, colossal images of Buddha, 60 to 70 ft. high, and fresco paintings on the walls of the caves illustrate this art. It was inspired not only by the images and pictures and the reports and models of sanctuaries carried from India by Buddhist monks (both Indian and Chinese), but also by the Indian artists who visited China. We know the names of at least three Indian painters—Sakyabuddha, Buddhakirti and Kumarabodhi—who worked in China in the Wei period. The different early schools of sculpture in India, such as the Gandhara, Mathura, and the Gupta, are all represented in the Chinese art. The best statues of the Wei period, which have justly received very high praise from modern European scholars, recall, and seem to have been inspired by, the elegant Buddha images of Ajanta and Sarnath.

A further development of this art is noticed in the T'ang period. The construction of cave-temples was continued at Tunhwang, and these are known collectively as "Grottos of the thousand Buddhas," as there were one thousand images of Buddha in them. The later caves here show the art of the T'ang period at its best and "a progressive Chinese adaptation of the Gandhara, Gupta, and Iranian models." Gradually the Chinese artists absorbed the Indian art tradition and gave it an increasingly Chinese character. Apart from sculptures, paintings, and rock-cut caves, the Indian influence is manifest in the peculiar type of temples with superimposed storeys whose origin may be traced to India. In fact the name 'Indian style' was given to a class of temples in China in the Song period. This style was very much in use in the province of Shan-si and found its way to Japan.

Among the fine arts, Indian music also seems to have exerted a great influence upon China. It was introduced by Indian musicians settled in Kuchi, and soon became very popular. A musical party went direct from India to China in A.D. 581. While the Emperor Kaotsu (581-595) vainly tried to proscribe it by an imperial decree, his successor encouraged it and got a number of new tunes composed. According to the traditions current in Japan in ancient times, two principal types of music called Bodhisatva and Bhairo were taken from China to Japan by an Indian Brahmana named Bodhi in the T'ang period.

Indian astronomy, mathematics, and medicine were also popular in China. Indian astronomers were appointed on the official boards set up to prepare the calendars. There were three Indian astronomical schools, known as Gautama, Kasyapa and Kumara, in the capital city in the seventh century. The Indian system of nine planets was adopted in China, and the translation of a Sanskrit astronomical work, *Navagraha-siddhanta,* is still to be found in the collection of the T'ang period. A number of Indian mathematical and astronomical works were translated at an earlier date, but they have been lost.

Indian medical treatises were also in great favour in China. A Chinese work, composed in A.D. 455, is either a translation of a Sanskrit text or a compilation from several Sanskrit texts. A number of medical texts are found in the Chinese Buddhist collection, and *Ravana-Kumara-charita,* a Sanskrit treatise on the method of treatment of children's diseases, was translated in the eleventh century.

The Chinese emperors and nobles were fond of Indian thaumaturges who professed to possess the secrets of longevity. On more than one occasion the emperors had them fetch from India in order to prolong their lives. Sometimes they sent an official to India in order to collect rare medicines.

The T'ang period also witnessed a great development of the seaborne trade between India and China. An account written about A.D. 749 refers to the numerous merchantmen belonging to the Polomen, *i.e.*, Brahmanas of India, and other countries, on the river of Canton. The same account refers to three Brahmana monasteries at Canton where Brahmanas were residing. It is evident that Hindu merchants sailed in large number to this Chinese port, and had built temples there for worship during their stay. According to *Harshacharita*, Chinese cuirasses were used by the chiefs of Harsha's army.[22] The discovery of coins of the T'ang Dynasty in South India may also be regarded as an interesting relic of the commercial relations between India and China during this period.[22]

The foreign ships in Canton are said to be 60 to 70 ft. deep. Another Chinese work says that the foreign ships visiting Canton "were very large, and so high out of the water that ladders, several tens of feet in length, had to be used to get abroad."

3. Central Asia

It will appear from what has been said above in regard to China that Central Asia continued to be a strong centre of Indian culture and influence, and could justly be regarded as Ser-India. As in the earlier period, we have remains of ancient *stupas,* temples, monasteries, images, and paintings, and also a large number of Sanskrit Buddhist texts and translations in different languages. Fortunately, we have no longer to depend upon mere archaeological finds in reconstructing the history and culture of this region, as the detailed accounts of the Chinese travellers to India, notably those of Fa-hien and Hiuen Tsang, have thrown a flood of light on this subject.

Shen-shen, the first kingdom visited by Fa-hien on leaving China, was situated near Lop Nor at the eastern extremity of Central Asia. The king was Buddhist and there were more than four thousand monks in the country. Nothing illustrates more forcibly the vitality of Indian culture at this period all over central Asia than the following observations made by Fa-hien in reference to Shen-shen :

"The common people of this and other kingdoms, as well as the *sramans* (monks), all practise the rules of India, only that the latter do so more exactly, and the former more loosely. So (the travellers) found it in all the kingdoms through which they went on their way from this to the west, only that each had its own peculiar barbarous speech. The monks, however, were all students of Indian books and the Indian language."

This general picture is fully borne out by the details given by Fa-hien of the two kingdoms through which he passed before reaching India. Hiuen Tsang supplies further particulars of Agni (Qara Shahr), Kuchi, Bharuka (Aqsu), Kashgar, Khotan, and one or two other localities which cannot be exactly identified. In all these places, Buddhism was in a flourishing condition, and Indian scripts and books were used. Buddhism was also flourishing in Turfan in the extreme eastern part of this region. There were several hundreds of monasteries in Kashgar. As in the earlier period, Khotan in the south and Kuchi in the north were two powerful centres of Indian culture in the Tarim basin.

Both Fa-hien and Hiuen Tsang refer in glowing terms to the flourishing condition of Buddhism in Khotan. In Fa-hien's time the monks amounted to tens of thousands, who strictly followed the rules of discipline and possessed a high sense of decorum. The royal family and people were all Buddhists, and each family had a small *stupa* in front of its door, the smallest of which was twenty cubits high. There were four great monasteries of which the most distinguished was the Gomati Vihara, containing three thousand monks. These took precedence in the big annual religious processions of images carried in lofty chariots (like Rathayatra processions of modern India) of which a detailed account is given.[24] These processions, attended by the king and queen, were continued for fourteen days, each monastery being allotted a separate day for the procession of its own chariots. Fa-hien gives the following description of another big monastery :

"The king's New Monastery, the construction of which took eighty years and extended over three reigns, in about 250 cubits in height; it is rich in elegant carving and inlaid work, and covered above with gold and silver. The Hall of Buddha is of the utmost magnificence and beauty, the beams, pillars, venetianed doors and windows being all overlaid with gold-leaf. The apartments for the monks are imposingly and elegantly decorated beyond the power of words to express." Fa-hien states that six kings of Eastern Turkestan gave all their valuables as offerings to this monastery keeping only a few things for their own use.

Hiuen Tsang also refers to the various sanctuaries and sacred sites in Khotan, and narrates the traditions connected with them.

Reference has been made above[25] to the Tibetan account of the royal family of Khotan up to the reign of Vijita-kirti. No information is available about the next ten or eleven generations during which Khotan was oppressed by foreigners. These probably refer to T'u-yu-hun (A.D. 445), the Juan-Juan (*c.* A.D. 470), the Hephthalities (A.D. 500-556), and the Western Turks (A.D. 565-631), who conquered Khotan.

We are next introduced to king Vijita-samgrama who evidently freed the country from the Turks. In A.D. 632 he sent an envoy, and three years later his son, to the Chinese court. The next king Vijita-Simha sent his son to China in A.D. 648 and later went there himself. He was probably ruling when Hiuen Tsang stayed at Khotan during his return journey. The dynasty continued to rule for at least another century, and the Tibetan annals mention Vijita-kirti, Vijita-samgrama, Vijita-vikrama, Vijita-dharma, Vijita-sambhava and Vijita-bohan. The last of them ruled in the second half of the eighth century A.D., and is probably to be identified with Visavaham, whose name occurs in two documents, found somewhere in Central Asia, which are written in Indian alphabet and Iranian language.

Like Khotan, Kuchi was also an important centre of Buddhism, as noted above.[26] The people of Kuchi spoke a language belonging to the Indo-European family (called by various names such as Kuchean, Tokharian, Arsi, etc.). The intimate intercourse between India and Kuchi as early as the fourth century A.D. will be evident from the story of Kumarajiva.[27] According to Chinese records, there were nearly 10,000 *stupas* and temples in this kingdom at the beginning of the fourth century A.D. The History of the First Tsin Dynasty gives a detailed account of Buddhism in Kuchi in the fourth and fifth centuries A.D. There were numerous monasteries and also several convents for nuns. Four of these monasteries and three convents were in charge of Buddhasvamin, the teacher of Kumarajiva. The nuns in these convents were mostly the daughters and wives of kings and princes. They received regular training and obeyed strict rules of discipline and decorum.

Kuchi was a flourishing seat of Buddhism in the days of Hiuen Tsang. It had one hundred monasteries housing more than five thousand monks. They followed Indian doctrines and rules of discipline, and studied the original Indian texts. Outside the capital city were two standing figures of Buddha, 90 ft. high, in front of which a religious assembly was held every five years for a period of ten days. These were observed as public holidays, and the king and all classes of people attended the assembly. There were also religious processions as in Khotan.

According to Hiuen Tsang the people of Kuchi excelled in their skill in playing on the lute and the pipe. We get more interesting information about it from other Chinese sources. There is no doubt that Kuchean skill in music was due to Indian influence. Not only did the Indian musical system spread to Kuchi, but Indian musicians actually went there and some even settled down in the country. The Chinese annals refer to a Brahmanical family called Ts'ao (Jha or Upadhyaya?) in Kuchi who were hereditary musicians. A member of that family visited China between A.D. 550 and 577. Another musician named Sujiva went from Kuchi to China about the same time. These Indo-Kuchean musicians were so skilled that they could reproduce a tune after hearing it only once. The Chinese accounts leave no doubt that the musical system followed in Kuchi was essentially Indian, and that it was long in favour in the Chinese court. Besides music, other arts and sciences of India flourished in this region. The famous Bower Manuscript, found near Kuchi, contains seven texts of which three are medical treatises. This manuscript is written in Gupta characters, and the language is Sanskrit mixed with many Prakritisms. These texts prove the study of Indian medical science in Kuchi. Reference may also be made to the caves of thousand Buddhas excavated on the southern slopes of the Tien Shan mountains. They were decorated with mural paintings belonging to the period from seventh to tenth century A.D., and some Sanskrit manuscripts were also found in them.

Regarding the influence of Indian culture in the region to the west of the Tarim basin, our knowledge is more limited. There is no doubt, however, that Buddhism was widely prevalent all over the hilly region between the Tarim basin and the valley of the Upper Sindhu. Fa-hien, who followed the short and direct route between Khotan and N.W. India, has given a graphic description of the dominance of Buddhism all over the region through which he passed. The condition was more or less the same even in Hiuen Tsang's time. From the valley of the Upper Oxus, almost all along the route to Hindu Kush and back, Hiuen Tsang found abundant traces of Buddhism. Balkh (old Bactriana), to the south of the Oxus, was a great centre of Buddhism. Its capital was called little Rajagariha, evidently after the famous city in ancient India. It had one hundred monasteries containing three thousand monks. Hiuen Tsang found here many relics of Buddha and old sanctuaries. The convent called Navasangharama was a renowned Buddhist institution.

We learn from Arab chronicles that Khalid, the Vizier of Caliph al-Mansur, was the son of a *Barmak, i.e.,* chief priest in Buddhist monastery in Balkh called Nawbahar. This is evidently the Arabic form of Navavihara, *i.e.*, Navashangarama. The Arab conqueror of Balkh captured Khalid's mother in A.D. 705. The son was converted to Islam and founded the famous Barmaki family. Khalid ibn-Barmak came to occupy the highest office under the Caliph, and his son and two grandsons practically ruled the Abbassid Empire from A.D. 786 to 803. They were instrumental in introducing Indian astronomy, mathematics, medicine, and other sciences into Arabia.

Among other localities where Buddhism flourished in the time of Hiuen Tsang may be named Tsau Kuta (Ghazni), Hwoh (Kunduz), and various places between Badakshan and Kashgar. Rulers of two of these localities are said to have been descended from the Sakyas of Kapilavastu. Brahmanical religion also flourished in some of these places and specially at An-ta-lo-po (Andarab).

There was, however, a considerable decline in the influence of Buddhism in the land between the Oxus and the Jaxartes. On his way to India, Hiuen Tsang passed through various localities in this region. He does not mention any trace of Buddhism in the large stretch of territory between Lake Issiq Kol (immediately beyond Tarim basin on the other side of the mountain passes) and the valley of the Oxus. The people were fire-worshippers and Buddhism had no hold on them. But the influence of Buddhism was not altogether absent. The Great Khan of the Western Turks, who lived west of Issiq Kol, had a high reverence for Buddhism. He received Hiuen Tsang hospitably and asked him to expound the religious teachings. At the conclusion of it, "the Khan raising his hands bowed and gladly believed and accepted the teaching." The Khan detained Hiuen Tsang and wanted to keep him permanently. But when he could not dissuade Hiuen Tsang from continuing his journey, he sent a reliable guide with the pilgrim to conduct him up to Afganistan. As stated already, the Indian monk Prabhakaramitra of Nalanda stayed with the Turkish chief and taught him Buddhism. This must have deeply impressed the latter and paved the way for the great welcome that Hiuen Tsang received at his hands. Thus Buddhism had begun to exercise its influence over the Western Turks who were the dominant power in this region. Some time before the middle of the eighth century A.D., a Turkish king visited India with his queen and son, and built two temples in Kashmir and two in Gandhara. Sanghavarman, an inhabitant of Samarkand, became an eminent Buddhist monk and visited the Mahabodhi temple at Gaya. I-tsing makes some incidental references to the influence of Buddhism in Turkestan and its contact with India. He refers to the temple 'which the people of Tukhara (*i.e.,* turks) formerly built in India for the monks of their own country.' "The temple is rich and opulent and surpasses others in respect of endowments and good management." We are further told that "when the monks of northern countries come to India they live in the temple of which they are considered Viharasvamin." I-tsing elsewhere informs us that the Viharasvamins formed the community proper in a monastery to whom belonged in command all its property.[28]

4. Afghanistan

The testimony of Fa-hien and Hiuen Tsang leaves no doubt that a considerable portion of Afghanistan was still regarded as a part of India. Referring to Udyana or the Valley of the Swat river, Fa-hien remarks : 'It is indeed (a part) of North India. The people all use the language of Central India. The food and clothes of the common people are the same as in that Central kingdom. The Law of Buddha is very flourishing.' Hiuen Tsang also includes Lamgan, Jelalabad, and the regions further east including the Swat valley within India proper.

Hiuen Tsang, however, notices that the people of Bamiyan and Kapisa were considerably influenced by the rude civilisation of the Turks. As regards the former we are told that 'their written language, their popular institutions, and their currency were like those of Tokhara, and they resembled the people of that country in appearance but differed from them in their spoken language. They had harsh rude ways, though they were honest. The written language of Kapisa was also very like that of Tokhara, but it differed in other respects. The people were rude and coarse. The change was undoubtedly due to the large influx of Huns and other Turkish hordes in this region in the fifth and sixth centuries A.D. Nevertheless, Buddhism was in a very flourishing condition in both these places.

The Bamiyan valley lay at the foot of the Hindu Kush mountains. It was surrounded by hills, and commanded one of the most important passes which connect the Kabul valley with Balkh (Bactria). It was an important halting place on the overland route from India to the west. According to local traditions the royal family had migrated from Kapilavastu. Whether this is true or not, Bamiyan was an important centre of Buddhism from very early times. Caves were hewn out of the surrounding hills for the residence of monks, and Buddhist texts, written in Kushana and Gupta alphabets, have been found in these caves.

In Hiuen Tsang's time, Buddhism was very powerful in Bamiyan. There were numerous monasteries with several thousands of monks, and many sacred relics. The king was a Buddhist and performed a quinquennial festival like Harsha-vardhana. Hiuen Tsang found here many caves and colossal figures of Buddha, carved on the hillsides, many of which exist even today.

Kapisa (Kafiristan) was a large and powerful kingdom exercising supremacy over ten neighbouring states extending as far as the Sindhu. The king was a Kshatriya by caste and was a devout Buddhist. There were 100 monasteries, with 6000 priests, and many sacred relics and sites associated with the early history of Buddhism. There were also some Brahmanical temples. I-tsing says that there was a 'Kapisa Temple' in Bodh-Gaya where priests from the north dwelt.

Recent archeological excavations have revealed the strong influence of Indian culture over the whole of Afghanistan, as far as and even beyond the Hindu Kush. The artistic remains unearthed by these expeditions show the existence of Indian art traditions, which had their full development in Khotan, Kuchi, Turfan, Tunh-wang and the other Indian Colonies in Central Asia. The site of Hadda, visited both by Fa-hien and Hiuen Tsang, has been explored. Ruins of 531 *stupas* have been excavated and about 500 sculptures, mostly stucco heads, have been found. These stucco figures display artistic skill of a very high order. The important site of Bamiyan has also been explored, and a number of valuable fresco paintings and Sanskrit manuscripts have been discovered. In addition to the colossal figures of Buddha and numerous caves, which were hitherto well known, some old caves, with decorative paintings, have come to light. These paintings show some Iranian influence. A Surya image and the remains of a temple of the Gupta style have been found at the hill of Khair Khaneh, north-west of Kabul. Begram, the site of Kapisi, has yielded a large number of ivories with designs recalling the Mathura art of the Kushana period. At another site, a little to the east, have been found a number of clay modellings and mural paintings of Indian type resembling those of the Gupta and Pala periods.

5. Tibet

According to the Tibetan chronicles of mediaeval ages the founder of the Tibetan royal dynasty was the son of an Indian king. The kings of Ladakh or Western Tibet also traced their descent form the Sakya family of India. While these traditions prove the strong influence of India on the history and culture of Tibet, they cannot be regarded as historical facts.

There is no definite information about any contacts between India and Tibet prior to the sixth century A.D. In the last two decades of that century one of the local chiefs, who were hitherto ruling in different parts of Tibet, subjugated the rest and set up a powerful kingdom. This king, named Gnam-ri-sron-btsan[29], is said to have led a victorious campaign to Central India.[30] This statement is very doubtful, but there is no doubt that his kingdom touched the frontier of India and he might have had some relations with a few border-states.

The son and successor of this king was the famous Sron-btsan-sgam-po who occupied the throne of Tibet during the first half of the seventh century A.D. He is said to have conquered Assam and Nepal and exercised suzerainty over half of Jambudvipa (*i.e.*, India). In spite of obvious exaggeration, there is no doubt that this Tibetan ruler exercised suzerainty over Nepal, and probably also over Assam and some other regions.[31]

With Sron-btsan-sgam-po begins the influence of Buddhism which was soon to transform the whole culture of Tibet. He married a daughter of king Amsuvarman of Nepal and also a Chinese princess. Both the queens were devout Buddhists, and the king, under their influence, adopted the religion. He had temples and monasteries built, and a number of Buddhist texts translated. Images and sacred relics were also brought from India and China.

But the most notable condition of the king to the cultural development of Tibet was the introduction of Sanskrit language and the system of writing from India. The following account of it is culled from Tibetan sources[32] :

"The king clearly saw that written language was most essential to the establishment of religion, and more particularly to the institution of laws for the good of the people. He therefore sent Sambhota, with sixteen companions, to study carefully the Sanskrit language and thereby obtain access to the sacred literature of Indian Buddhists. He also instructed them to devise means for the invention of a written language for Tibet by adapting the Sanskrit alphabet to the phonetic peculiarities of the Tibetan dialect. He furnished the members of the mission with a large quantity of gold to make presents to the Professors.

"Sambhota and his companions reached India and acquired a thorough knowledge of Sanskrit language, Buddhist scriptures, and Indian scripts. After returning to Tibet they framed the system of Tibetan characters and composed a grammatical work. The king ordered the intelligent class of people to be taught the art of reading and writing and many Sanskrit Buddhist books to be translated into Tibetan. He then required all his subjects by royal edicts to observe the ten virtues besides a code of sixteen moral virtues specified by him."

Whatever we might think of the details in the foregoing account, there is no doubt that the Tibetan alphabet is derived from the Indian Gupta script current from fifth to seventh century A.D. The grammar composed by Sambhota is practically the same which is in use in Tibetan schools even today.[33]

Thus the foundation of Buddhism was laid and Tibet started on her way of cultural evolution under the guidance of India. Sron-btsan-sgam-po, who initiated the new movement, naturally loomed large in the eyes of the people when, in a later age, Buddhism became the dominant force in Tibet. He was regarded as an incarnation of the Bodhisattva Avalokita; the Nepalese queen was considered the incarnation of Bhrikuti, and the Chinese queen, that Tara. No less than 900 monasteries, including the famous Ra-mo-che, are said to have been built by this king. He also invited to his court the Indian teacher Kumara, the Nepalese teacher Sila-manju, the Kashmiri teachers Tabuta and Ganuta, the Brahmana Li-byin and the Chinese teacher, Ha-san-Mahadheva.[34]

Sron-btsan-sgam-po died about A.D. 650. For the next half a century we do not hear much of the new religion or of Tibetan contact with India. Some time about A.D. 702 Nepal and the border states of Indian threw off the yoke of Tibet and the Tibetan king died in the course of a campaign against them (A.D. 704). The next king was Khri-lde-btsug-brtan, more commonly known by his surname Mes-'ag-tshoms(A.D. 705-55). In order to avenge the defeat of 704 he led frequent raids into India. The North Indian rulers Latita-ditya and Yasovarman, harassed by these frequent aggressions, even applied to China for help.[35]

The renewed contact with India promoted the cause of Buddhism in Tibet. The new king erected temples and monasteries, and arranged for the translation of sacred texts. But soon there was a reaction. During a pestilence in A.D. 740-41 all the foreign monks were expelled from the country in order to appease the irritated gods. Thus when king Mes'-ag-tshoms died in A.D. 755 the prospects of Buddhism were not very bright in Tibet.[36]

6. Other Countries in the Far East

Buddhism, and along with it Indian culture, spread from Central Asia, China, and Tibet to other parts of Northern and Eastern Asia. Mongolia, Korea, and Japan were the most important countries to be affected in this way. Korea and Japan were no doubt, greatly influenced by Chinese Buddhists, and in a later age, Tibet was an important centre for propagation of Buddhism, especially in Mongolia. But we have also evidence of direct intercourse between India and some of these countries.

As regards Korea, we know from I-tsing that five Korean monks visited India in the seventh century A.D. Two of these set out in A.D. 638, and lived and died at Nalanda. A third, Sarvajndeva, came through Tibet and Nepal in A.D. 650. The fourth monk Prajna-varman stayed for ten years in India. Another Korean monk died in India, and two more died on their way to India.

There was also direct intercourse between India and Japan. The Indian monk who is best known in this connection is Bodhisena whose history has been preserved in Japanese chronicles.[37] Bodhisena was a Brahmana of South India and his family name was Barachi (Bharadvaja gotra?). He set out for China by sea, and met on the way a ship-wrecked priest of Champa named Buttetsu. They arrived together in China in A.D. 733.

Boddhisena went to China to meet Manjusri, who was generally believed in India to have lived there. Bodhisena could not find him there, but was told that he had left for Japan. An imperial Japanese envoy at the court of China, who was just leaving for his country invited Boddhisena to accompany him. Both Bodhisena and Buttetsu joined him and reached Japan in A.D. 736. On their arrival at the port of Naniwa (Osaka) they were received with great honour by the imperial messenger, the chief priest accompanied by a hundred others, masters of ceremonies, musicians, and high dignitaries of the foreign office.

It appears that both Buddhism and Sanskrit were already well-known in Japan. For Bodhisena carried on conversation with the Japanese priest 'both in Sanskrit and Japanese' as if they were old friends. He was lodged in a Buddhist monastery, and the imperial court furnished him with clothes and other necessaries of life.

When in A.D. 749 a colossal image of Buddha Vairochana was installed, Bodhisena was asked to perform the consecration ceremony, and Buttetsu took charge of the musical arrangements.

In 750 Bodhisena was appointed the head of the Buddhist order in Japan and he came to be popularly known as the Baramon Sojo (Brahmana Bishop). He taught Sanskrit and the Mahayana doctrine of Gandavyuha in three different monasteries and died in 760 at the age of 57. A *stupa* was erected over his remains, and one of his disciples composed an inscription for it in A.D. 770.

The arrangement of Japanese syllabary in fifty phonetic sounds, closely following the Sanskrit alphabet and undoubtedly based upon it, is attributed by some Japanese scholars to Bodhisena, though others relegate it to a later period. The use of the Indian alphabet in Japan, however, dates probably from even an earlier period. It is interesting to note that fragments of palm-leaf manuscripts written in Indian alphabets of the fourth century A.D. have been found in some monasteries of Japan.[38] There is also good evidence to show that the palm-leaf manuscript at the Horiuzi monastery, which cannot be later than the sixth century A.D., was brought to Japan in A.D. 609.[39]

Buttetsu was not a scholar but was highly proficient in

music and dance. He spent a number of years in the famous Nara University of Japan and gave lessons and demonstrations in Indian music and dance. The Indian system of seven musical notes (Shadja, Rishabha, etc.) was highly admired and in great demand, both in religious assemblies and at the imperial court. Buttetsu taught Sanskrit and wrote a manual for teaching this language.

7. Western Countries[40]

(i) Trade and political intercourse

Although Indian trade with the Roman empire declined to a considerable extent after the third century A.D. there is no doubt that it continued for at least two or three hundred years more. This is clearly demonstrated by the finds of Roman coins in Southern India. At Madura, for example, were found a large quantity of copper coins of Arcadius, Emperor of the East (A.D. 395-408), and Honorius, Emperor of the West (A.D. 395-423), one gold coin of Constantius II (337-361), one of Theodosius II (408-450), one of Zeno (474-491), and one of Anastatius (491-518). Coins of Theodosius II, Marcian (450-457), Leo (457-474), Zeno Anastatius, and Justinus I (518-527) have been found in Travancore. Coins of Theodosius I (379-395), Valentinian (364-375) and Eudoxia (401-404) have been found in various places in South India. These coins as well as the Indian embassies to Roman Emperors mentioned above[41] prove the continuity of trade between India and Rome down to the beginning of the sixth century A.D. Another evidence of the flourishing nature of this trade is furnished by the fact that when Alaric 'spared Rome in A.D. 408, he demanded and obtained as part of the ransom three thousand pounds of pepper.'[42]

Trade relations with Western Asia were also flourishing throughout the period treated in this volume. We learn from Amianus Marcellinus[43] that Indian wares were sent to the great annual fair at the mart of Batne, not far from the bank of the Euphrates, about the second half of the fourth century A.D. Chinese Annals refer to a brisk trade between China and western countries like Arabia and Persia. This trade must have passed through India, and kept up the old trade relations between India and the western countries. The Arabs and Persians sent a large number of vessels to China and these passed through Indian ports. I-tsing left China for India in a Persian ship.[44] We learn from the account of Vajrabodhi's journey to China in A.D. 720[45] that when he reached a port in Ceylon he saw thirty-five Persian vessels there.

There was commercial intercourse between India and Arabia even in pre-Islamic days. The sword made of Indian steel is proverbial in Arabic literature.[46] Aden is mentioned as a centre of the perfumery industry which had markets in Sindh and Hind and all parts of the world. Indian spices were imported in large quantities into Arabia, and Arabic words like *quranful* are derived from Indian names (*Karan-phul*).

We learn from Arab literature that Daba was one of the two major ports of Arabia in pre-Islamic days. It was situated in Oman, in the south-eastern corner of Arabia. There was an annual fair at Daba to which traders came from Sindh, Hind, China, and Greece,—in short from all the countries of world.

An interesting evidence of a close contact between India and Persia has been preserved by Tabari (A.D. 838-923), the Persian historian, on the authority of a Pehlevi work written shortly after the death of Khusru II. We learn form his account that in the 36th year of the reign of Khusru (A.D. 590-628) a king of India sent to the Persian king ambassadors carrying a letter and presents for him and his sons. The letter to one of the princes was marked 'private' and contained the information—a sort of prophecy—that he would be crowned king two years hence. It has been held that the Indian king was Pulakesin II, and that one of the paintings in the ceiling of cave 1 at Ajanta portrays not only the Persian king Khusru II and his famous queen Shirin, but also the scene of a Persian embassy at the court of king Pulakesin. This interpretation of the picture, as well as the identification of the Indian king mentioned by Tabari with Pulakesin, has been questioned,[47] but there is no doubt that both the story and the painting prove an intimate connection between India and Persia. It may be also noted that according to Banabhatta's *Harsha-charita,* the stable of the emperor Harsha-vardhana was filled with horses from Persia. It appears from the same authority that Harsha's court was familiar with Persia and other kingdoms in the west. For among the boastful expressions, uttered by Harsha's military chiefs, occurs the following : "The land of the Turushkas is to the brave but a cubit; Persia is only a span; Sakasthana, but a rabbit's track."[48]

We learn from a Pehlevi work that half a century before Harsha and Pulakesin another Indian king, named Devsaram (Devasarman?), sent an embassy to the Persian king Khusru I with rich presents and a set of chessmen with board.[49]

The historian Tabari, mentioned above, has preserved a number of anecdotes which, whatever may be their historical value, indicate an intimate intercourse between Indian and western Asiatic countries. According to him Anushirvan despatched an expedition to India and conquered some provinces, but the truth of this story may be doubted.[50]

There is a long story describing in detail how an Indian king, with a huge army, including contingents from his vassal states in Turkey and Persia, attacked Palestine. Being defeated by divine intervention on behalf of the king of Palestine, the Indian king fled to the coast with a lakh of soldiers and tried to escape with the help of their boats. But the whole army perished in ship-wreck by a typhoon in the Mediterranean.

The Indian navy is referred to even in historical times. Ubulla, near Basra, was known in those days as the 'gateway of India,' and its governor is said to have "always had to fight against either the Arab Beduins on land or Indian navy on sea."

Many kings of the west are said to have visited India, and some of them conquered, or received tributes from, different kingdoms in this country.

(ii) Influence of India on the West

We have positive evidence that Indian literature and sciences exerted great influence upon Western countries during the period under review.

That Indian literature was highly valued in these countries and made a deep impression upon their people is proved by the history of a single book *Panchatantra*[51] which is a collection of fables containing wise maxims. It was translated in the sixth century A.D. from Sanskrit into Pehlevi, and then from Pehlevi into Arabic and Syrian.[52] The Arabic translation made the book well known all over the Western world, and it was rendered into Persian, Hebrew, Latin, Spanish, Italian and various other languages of Europe and Asia. As Max Muller has remarked, the triumphant progress of this work from India to the west is more wonderful and instructive than the stories contained in it. Other Indian folk-tales also found their way to Europe and can be traced in Mediaeval collections such as the *Gesta Romanorum,* and in the stories of Boccacio, Straparola, Chaucer, and La Fontaine. Jataka stories and the traditional account of Buddha were also current in Western countries. St. John of Damascus (eighth century A.D.) wrote *Barlaam and Josaphat* which contained numerous Buddhist legends and portrayed the life of Buddha as a pious Christian saint. As a result of this Gautama, the Bodhisattva, under the guise of Saint Josaphat, was included in the Martyrology of Gregory XIII (1582).[53]

Like Hindu literature, the Hindu sciences, notably Medical Science and Arithmetic, were highly prized in the West. Many scholars hold that the later Greek physicians were acquainted with the medical works of the Hindus. Nearer home Iran also was largely indebted to India for her knowledge of medicine and other sciences. It is on record that Barzouhyeh, a subject of the Sassanid king Anushirvan (Khusru I, A.D. 531-579), visited India to acquire proficiency in Indian medicine and other sciences.

It is thus evident that Indian literature and sciences made their influence felt and that the cultural relation with the west was continued throughout the period. The religious influence was also not altogether absent. Hiuen Tsang notes that Lang-kie-lo, a country to the west of India and subject to Persia, had more than 100 monasteries and 6,000 monks, and several hundred Deva (*i.e.* Brahmanical) temples, mostly of the Pasupata Sect. Even in Persia itself, according to the same Chinese authority, there were two or three Buddhist monasteries and numerous Deva temples.

Reference may be made in this connection to a picture found at Dandanuliq in the Chinese Turkestan. It presents a four-armed Buddhist saint or Bodhisattva in the guise of a Persian, with black beard and whiskers, holding a thunderbolt in his left hand. The picture shows distinct Indian features, but it is the product of a type of Buddhist art which developed in Iran and thence travelled towards the east. It may be referred to the eighth century A.D., and proves that even up to the sixth or seventh century Buddhism was a living force in Iran and had cultural contact with Indian and other centres of Buddhism in Asia. The introduction of Persian figures in Ajanta, mentioned above, considered along with this picture, establishes, in the opinion of some scholars, a close relationship between the arts of India, Persia and Central Asia in the seventh century A.D.[54]

REFERENCES

1. Vol. II, Ch. XXV.
2. The dates pu: within brackets refer to the known period of residence in China. The account of the Indian and Chinese missionaries and the progress of Buddhism in China, unless otherwise stated, is based on Dr. P.C. Bagchi's *India and China* and his articles in *Sino-Indian Studies,* Vol. I, pp. 1-17, 65-84.
3. See Vol. II, p. 6.
4. According to Anesaki Buddhabhadra arrived in China in A.D. 398, *i.e.,* two years before Fa-hien entered India (*JRAS,* 1903, p. 368).
5. According to Dr. P.C. Bagchi Vinitaruchi was a Buddhist monk of Uddiyana (*India and China,* p. 228), but cf. *BEFEO,*

XXXII 235, which also gives an account of his activity in Tonkin. For an account of some other missionaries, specially those from Ceylon, who visited China, cf. *JRAS*, 1903, pp. 368-70.

6. Cf. Bagchi, *Sino-Indian Studies*, II. 42; L. Petech, *Northern India according to the Shui-Ching-Chu* (Rome, 1950), pp. 63 ff. The list of embassies during the Wei period is given on p. 74 of this work.
7. Sastri, *Foreign Notices*, 83.
8. See p. 580f.
9. See pp. 118f, 139f.
10. See p. 280f.
11. For a different version, cf. Sastri, *op. cit.*, p. 17.
12. See pp. 120f, 124ff.
13. According to Bagchi, the Brahmana thaumaturge accompanied Wang-hiuen-tse to China in A.D. 648. He "failed to give long life to the Emperor who died in A.D. 649." Hence the new Emperor sent him back to India (*Sino-Indian Studies*, I. 69).
14. See pp. 130, 132ff.
15. This summary is based upon Chavannes, *Documents Sur les Tou-kiue (Turcs) Occidentaux* (Notes Additionelles). Cf. also Dr. P.C. Bagchi's account (*Sino-Indian Studies*, I. 70).
16. JA, 1895, p. 376.
17. See p. 617.
18. According to Ma-twan-lin, "the Five Indians (or five kingdoms of India) sent ambassadors to the court of the Emperor" in A.D. 667. (Sastri, *op. cit.*, p. 117). Probably Ma-twan-lin refers to the same embassies as are mentioned in the text above, and confused the date. Otherwise, we have to presume that the five Indian kings also sent embassies earlier, in A.D. 667.
19. Sastri, *op. cit.*, 116-7.
20. For a detailed account, cf. *B.C. Law Volume*, I. 66ff.
21. See p. 621.
22. *HC.*, p. 202.

23. *Sino-Indian Studies*, I. 60.
24. See p. 376.
25. Vol. II, p. 640.
26. Vol. II, p. 641.
27. See pp. 608f.
28. *JBRS*, XXXVIII, p. 411.
29. The Tibetan names are written in different ways by different authorities. The system of spelling, adopted by Francke (*Antiquities of Indian Tibet*), has been followed here.
30. According to the Chinese sources relied on by Levi (*Nepal* II, 147). But the *Chronicles of Ladakh* says that 'some kings who dwelt in the west of India were subdued' (Francke, *op. cit.*, p. 82) Cf. also Petech, *op. cit.*, pp. 35-6.
31. See above, pp. 86, 141.
32. *JASB*, 1881, pp. 218-19.
33. Francke, *op. cit.*, p. 84.
34. Thomas, *op. cit.*, pp. 62, 83, 84.
35. Sastri, *Foreign Notices*, p. 117; also see above, pp. 130, 134.
36. According to some version of the *Chronicles of Ladakh* the reaction against Buddhism commenced in the next region. (Francke, *op. cit.*, p. 86).
37. *BEFEO*, XXVIII 24-26.
38. *IA.*, 1885, pp. 228-9.
39. *Anecdota Oxoniensia*—Aryan Series Vol. I, Part III, p. 64.
40. The following may be cited as general references for this section :
    - *(a)* Rawlinson : *Intercourse between India and the Western World.*
    - *(b)* M. Hamidulla : Ancient India from Arabic Sources (*PIHC.*, V. 246-48).
    - *(c)* P.K. Hitti : *History of the Arabs.*
41. Vol. II, p. 625.
42. *JRAS.*, 1904, pp. 307 ff.
43. XIV. 3. 33.
44. *IRT.*, p. XXVIII.

45. See above, p. 610.
46. Schoff, *Periplus*, 70-71.
47. The question has been fully discussed with references to different views by Sastri (*Foreign Notices*, p. 9) and B. Ghose (JBRS., XXX, 1 ff.) Cf. also the author's article "Pulakesi and Khusru II" in *JIH.*, Vol. IV. Part II.
48. HC., 210.
49. The Persian poet Firdausi says in the *Shahnama* that ambassadors from the sovereign of Hind came to Khusru I (Anushirvan) with a chess-board and men asking him to solve the secrets of the game. Other Persian and Arbian writers state that Shatranj (*i.e.*, chess, from Sanskrit *Chaturanga*) came into Persia from India and there appears to be a consensus of opinion that may be considered to settle the question. Thus we have the game passing from the Hindus to the Persian and thence to the Arabians (the seventh century) and from them, directly or indirectly to various parts of Europe, at a time which cannot be definitely fixed, but either in or before the tenth century [cf. *Encycl. Britannica*—under chess; also H.J.R. Murray : *A History of Chess* (1913)].
50. Sir Percy Sykes : *History of Persia*. p. 456.
51. See above, p. 314.
52. Winternitz : *GIL.*, III. 294 ff. According to Hitti (*op. cit.*, 404), the basis of the famous *Thousand and one nights* was a Persian work containing several stories of Indian origin.
53. Rawlinson : *op. cit.*, 142, 180.
54. FAS. 310.

Index

N

U